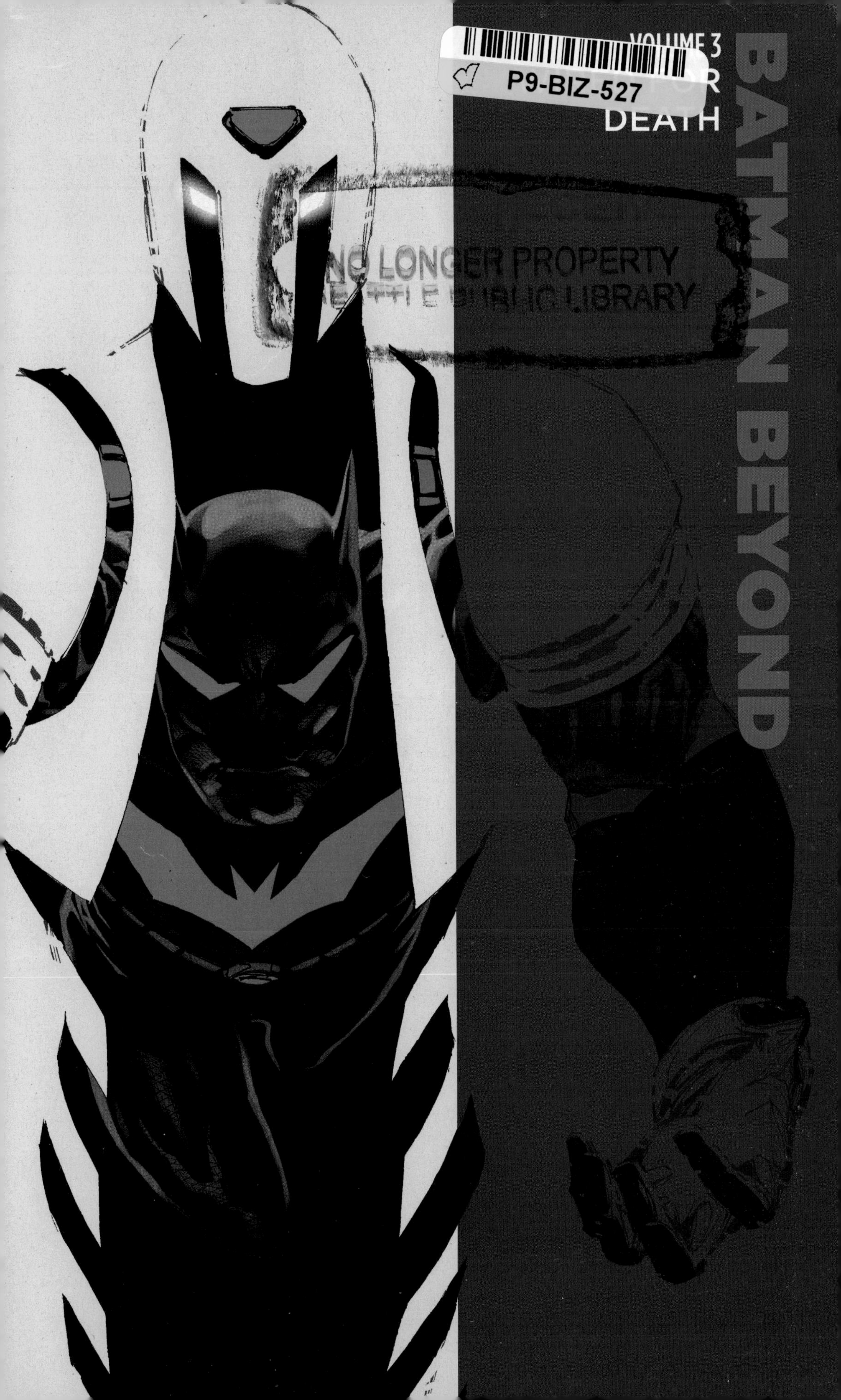

VOLUME 3
DEATH
BATMAN BEYOND

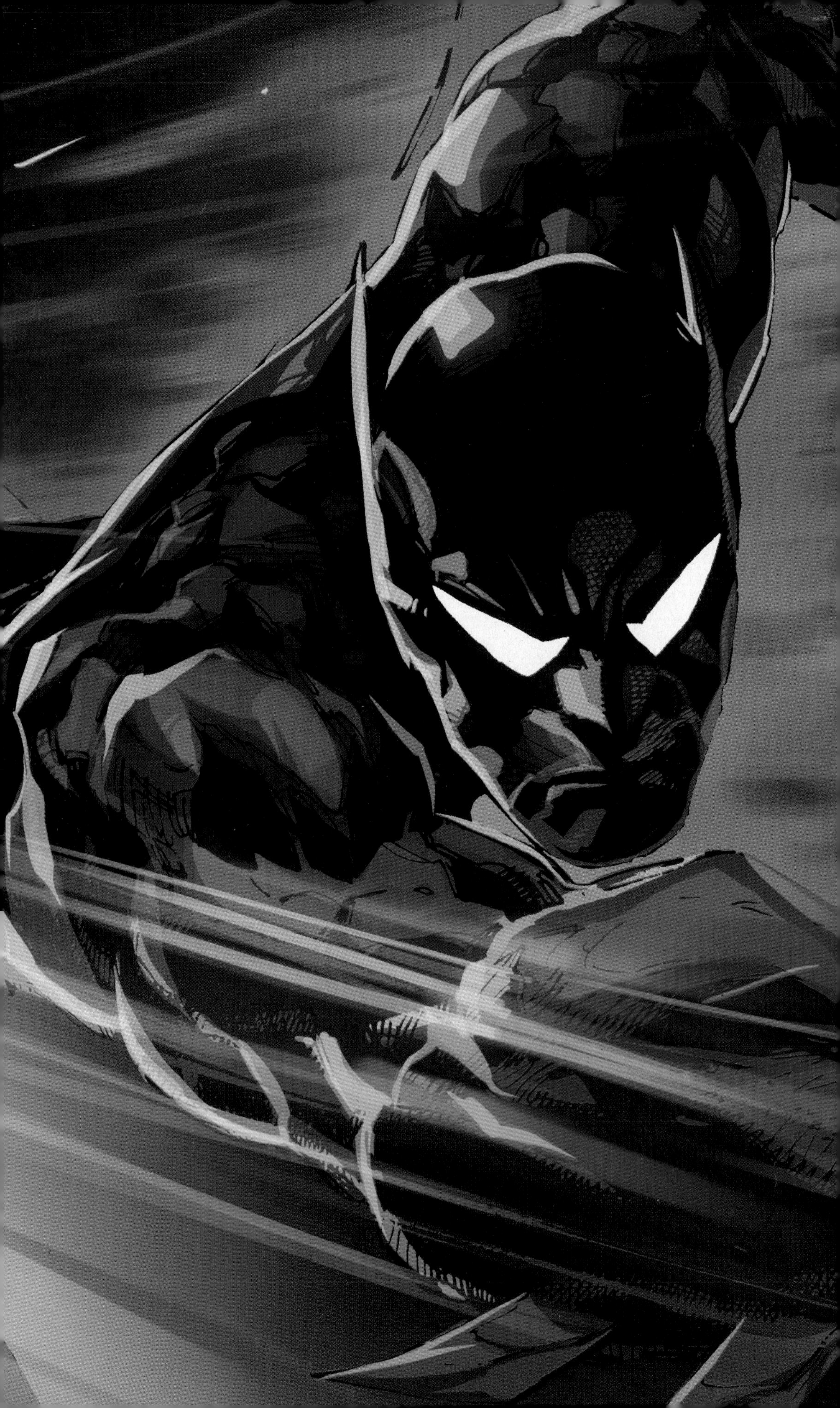

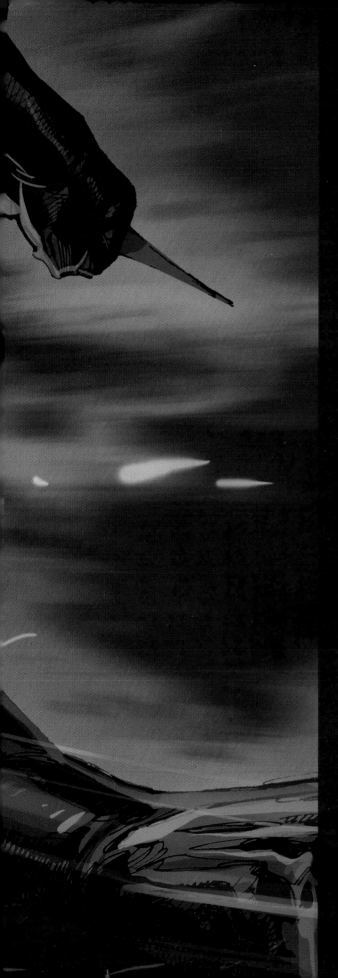

VOLUME 3
WIRED FOR DEATH

BATMAN BEYOND

WRITTEN BY
DAN JURGENS

ART BY
BERNARD CHANG
PHILIP TAN
STEPHEN THOMPSON
JAY LEISTEN

COLOR BY
MARCELO MAIOLO
ELMER SANTOS
LISA JACKSON

LETTERS BY
DAVE SHARPE

SERIES &
COLLECTION COVER ARTISTS
PHILIP TAN &
ELMER SANTOS

BATMAN CREATED BY
BOB KANE WITH
BILL FINGER

JIM CHADWICK Editor – Original Series
JEB WOODARD Group Editor – Collected Editions
STEVE COOK Design Director – Books
DAMIAN RYLAND Publication Design

BOB HARRAS Senior VP – Editor-in-Chief, DC Comics

DIANE NELSON President
DAN DIDIO Publisher
JIM LEE Publisher
GEOFF JOHNS President & Chief Creative Officer
AMIT DESAI Executive VP – Business & Marketing Strategy, Direct to Consumer & Global Franchise Management
SAM ADES Senior VP – Direct to Consumer
BOBBIE CHASE VP – Talent Development
MARK CHIARELLO Senior VP – Art, Design & Collected Editions
JOHN CUNNINGHAM Senior VP – Sales & Trade Marketing
ANNE DEPIES Senior VP – Business Strategy, Finance & Administration
DON FALLETTI VP – Manufacturing Operations
LAWRENCE GANEM VP – Editorial Administration & Talent Relations
ALISON GILL Senior VP – Manufacturing & Operations
HANK KANALZ Senior VP – Editorial Strategy & Administration
JAY KOGAN VP – Legal Affairs
THOMAS LOFTUS VP – Business Affairs
JACK MAHAN VP – Business Affairs
NICK J. NAPOLITANO VP – Manufacturing Administration
EDDIE SCANNELL VP – Consumer Marketing
COURTNEY SIMMONS Senior VP – Publicity & Communications
JIM (SKI) SOKOLOWSKI VP – Comic Book Specialty Sales & Trade Marketing
NANCY SPEARS VP – Mass, Book, Digital Sales & Trade Marketing

BATMAN BEYOND VOLUME 3: WIRED FOR DEATH

Published by DC Comics. Compilation and all new material Copyright © 2017 DC Comics. All Rights Reserved. Originally published in single magazine form in BATMAN BEYOND 12-16, BATMAN BEYOND: REBIRTH 1. Copyright © 2016 DC Comics. All Rights Reserved. All characters, their distinctive likenesses and related elements featured in this publication are trademarks of DC Comics. The stories, characters and incidents featured in this publication are entirely fictional. DC Comics does not read or accept unsolicited submissions of ideas, stories or artwork.

DC Comics, 2900 West Alameda Ave., Burbank, CA 91505
Printed by Vanguard Graphics, LLC, Ithaca, NY, USA. 1/20/17. First Printing.
ISBN: 978-1-4012-7039-1

Library of Congress Cataloging-in-Publication Data is available.

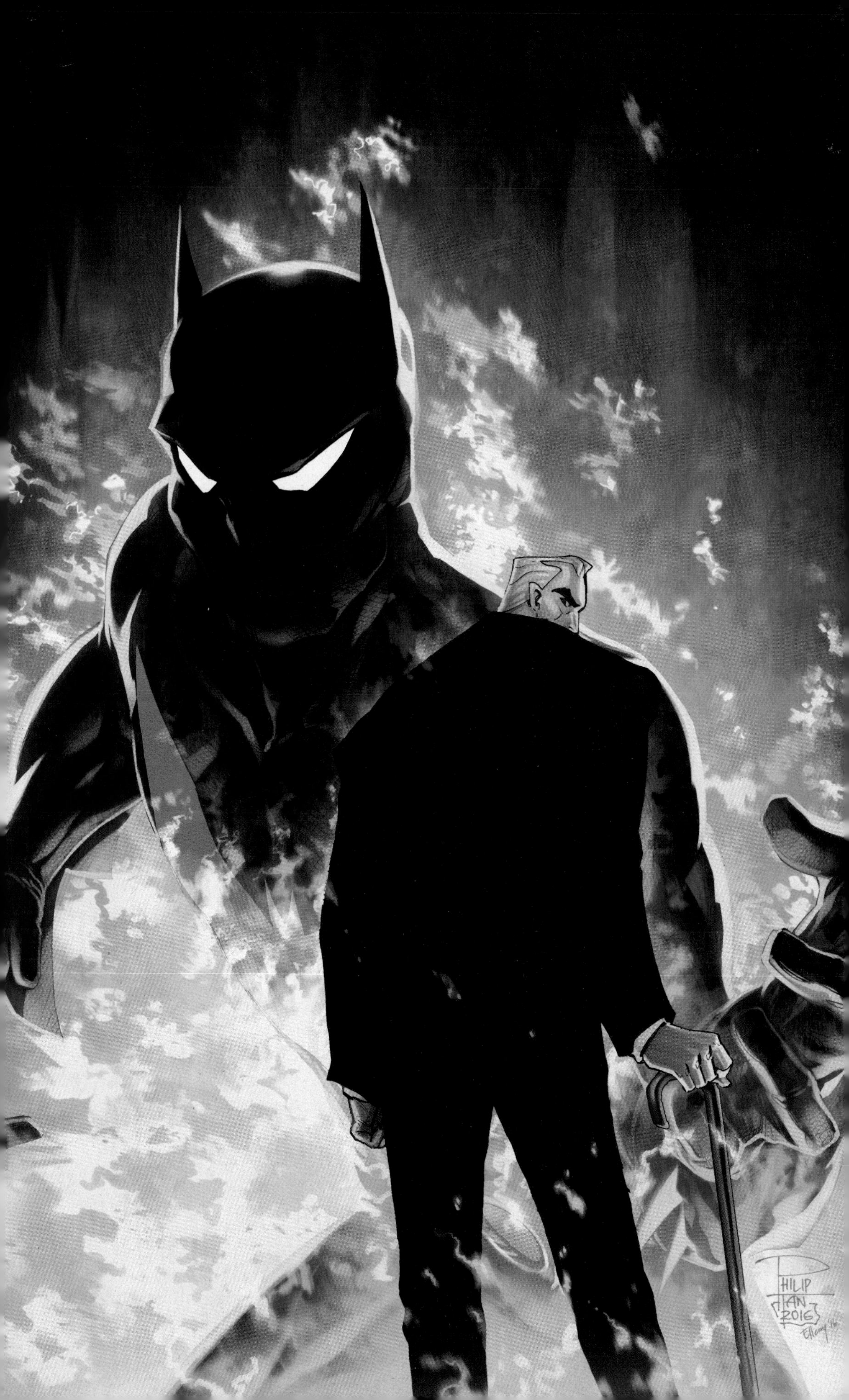
PHILIP TAN 2016

PHILIP TAN artist JAY LEISTEN inker ELMER SANTOS colorist PHILIP TAN & ELMER SANTOS cover

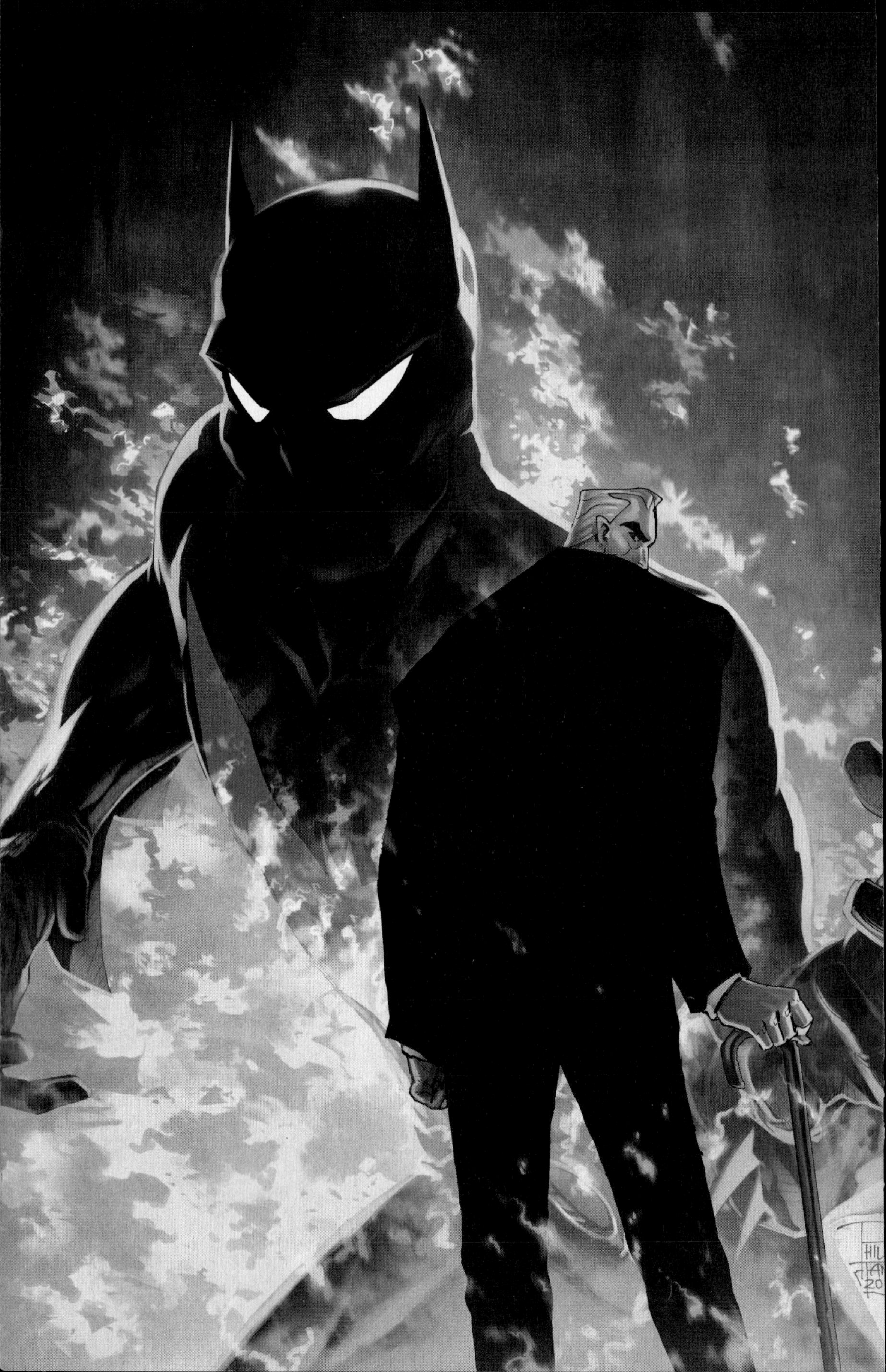

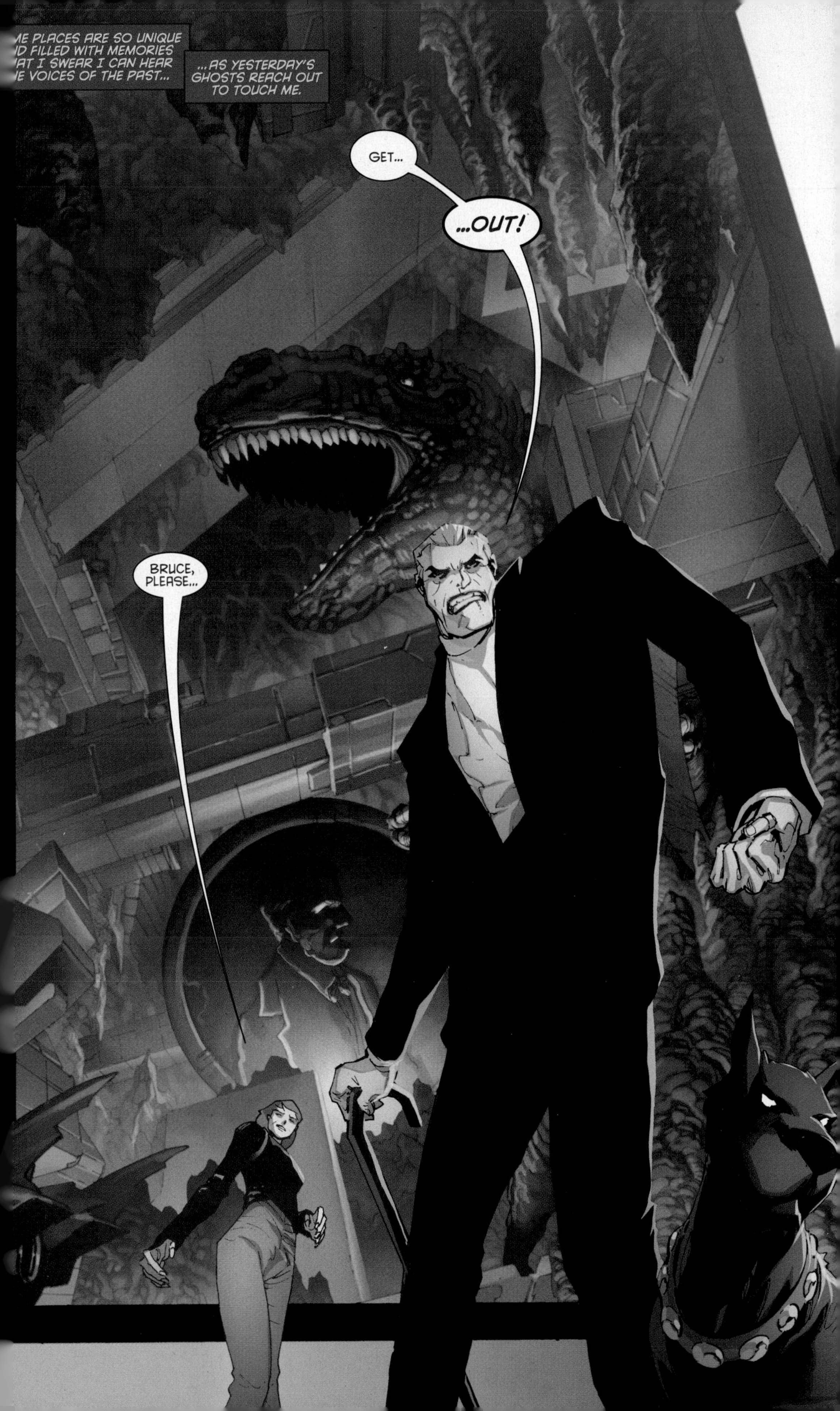
ME PLACES ARE SO UNIQUE ND FILLED WITH MEMORIES AT I SWEAR I CAN HEAR E VOICES OF THE PAST...
...AS YESTERDAY'S GHOSTS REACH OUT TO TOUCH ME.
GET...
...OUT!
BRUCE, PLEASE...

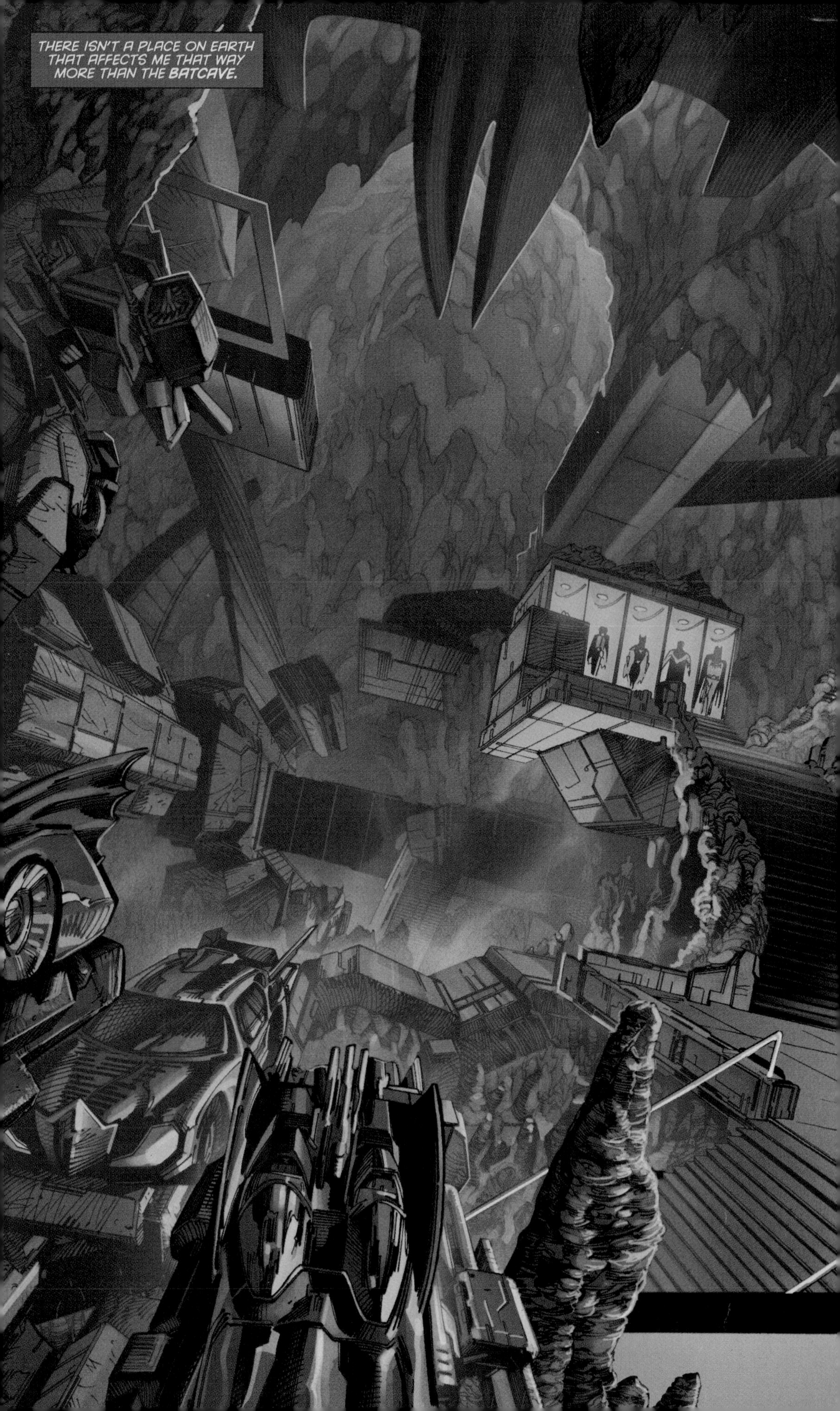
THERE ISN'T A PLACE ON EARTH THAT AFFECTS ME THAT WAY MORE THAN THE BATCAVE.

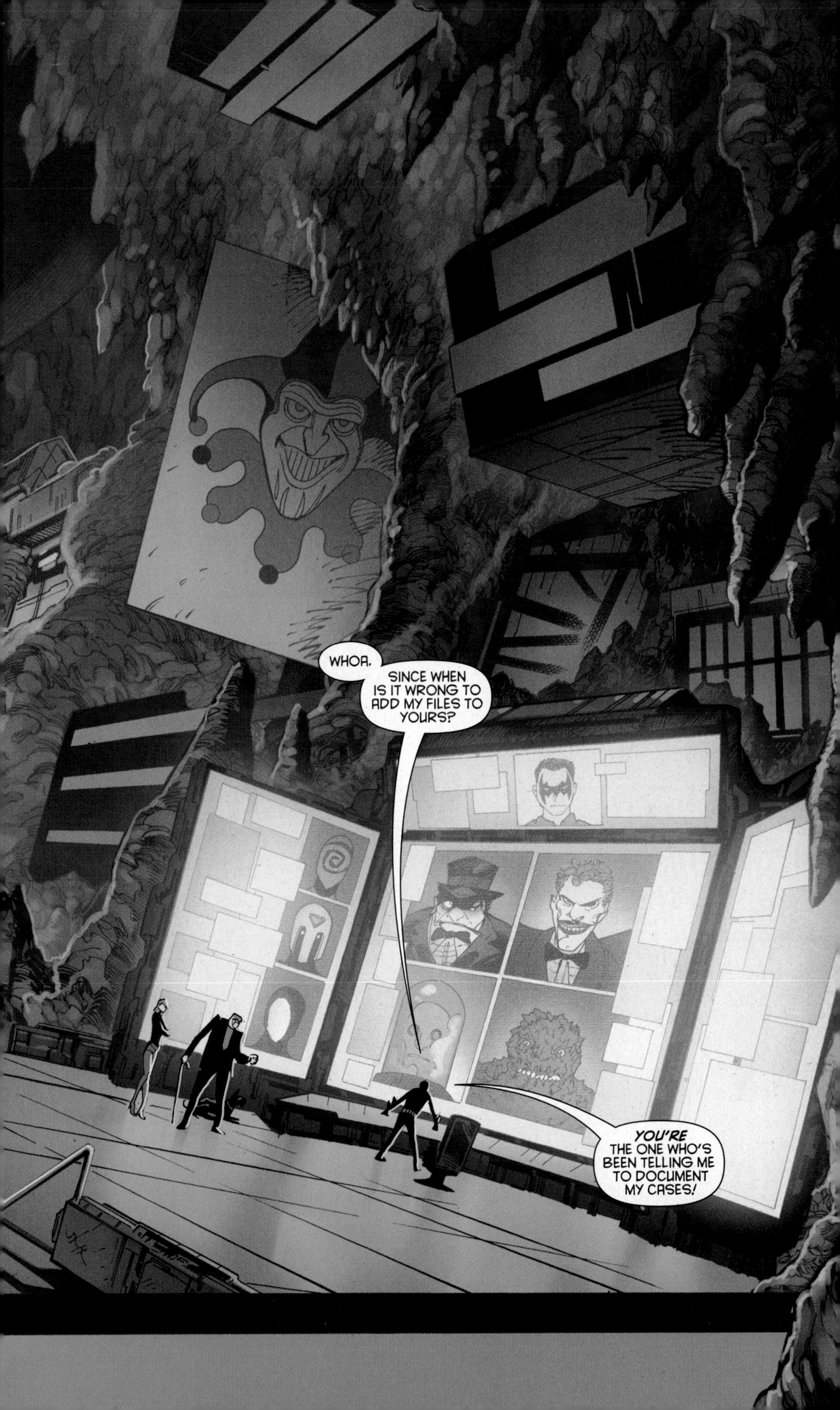
WHOA.
SINCE WHEN IS IT WRONG TO ADD MY FILES TO YOURS?
YOU'RE THE ONE WHO'S BEEN TELLING ME TO DOCUMENT MY CASES!

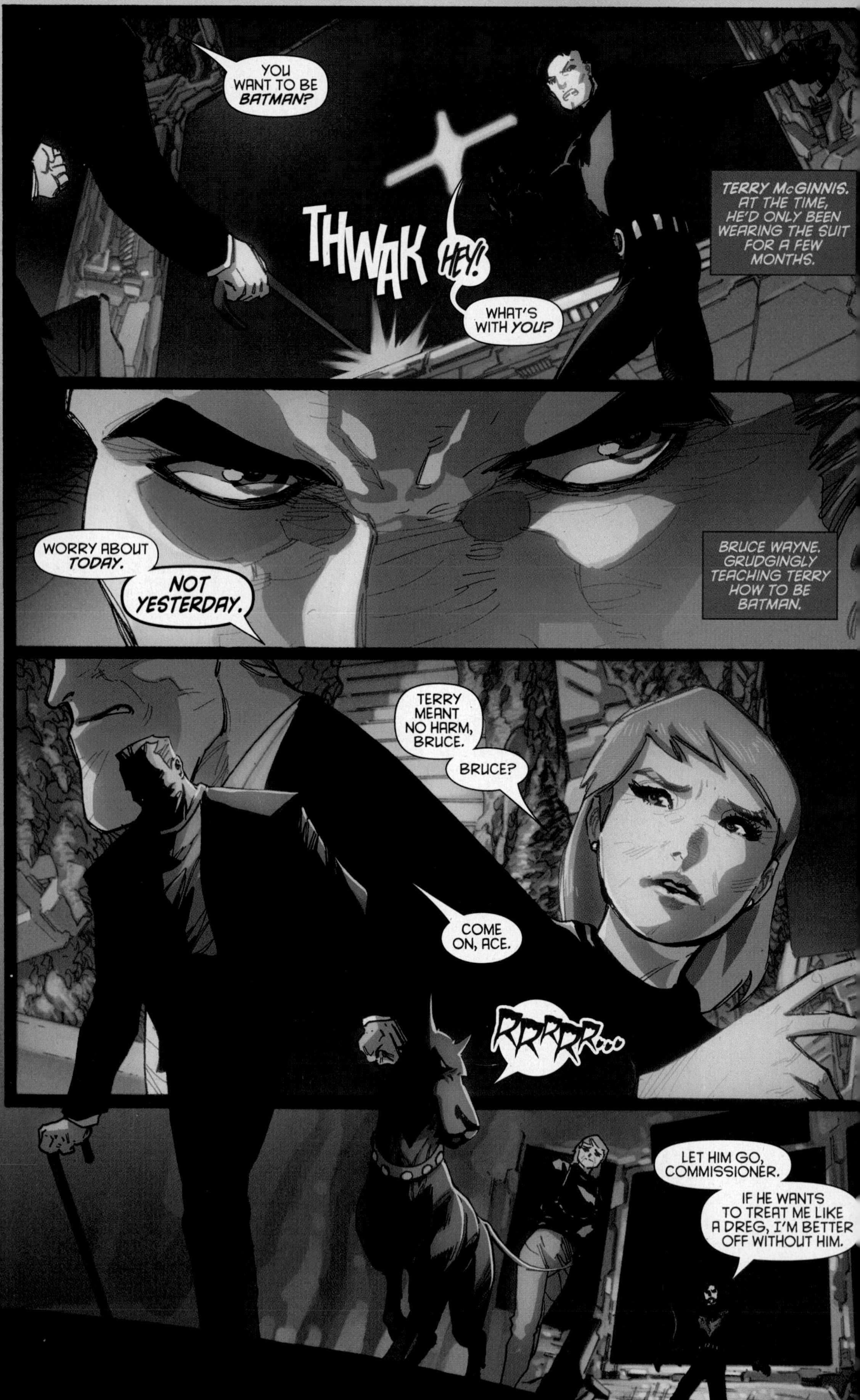
YOU WANT TO BE BATMAN?
THWAK
HEY!
WHAT'S WITH YOU?
TERRY McGINNIS. AT THE TIME, HE'D ONLY BEEN WEARING THE SUIT FOR A FEW MONTHS.
WORRY ABOUT TODAY.
NOT YESTERDAY.
BRUCE WAYNE. GRUDGINGLY TEACHING TERRY HOW TO BE BATMAN.
TERRY MEANT NO HARM, BRUCE.
BRUCE?
COME ON, ACE.
RRRRR...
LET HIM GO, COMMISSIONER.
IF HE WANTS TO TREAT ME LIKE A DREG, I'M BETTER OFF WITHOUT HIM.

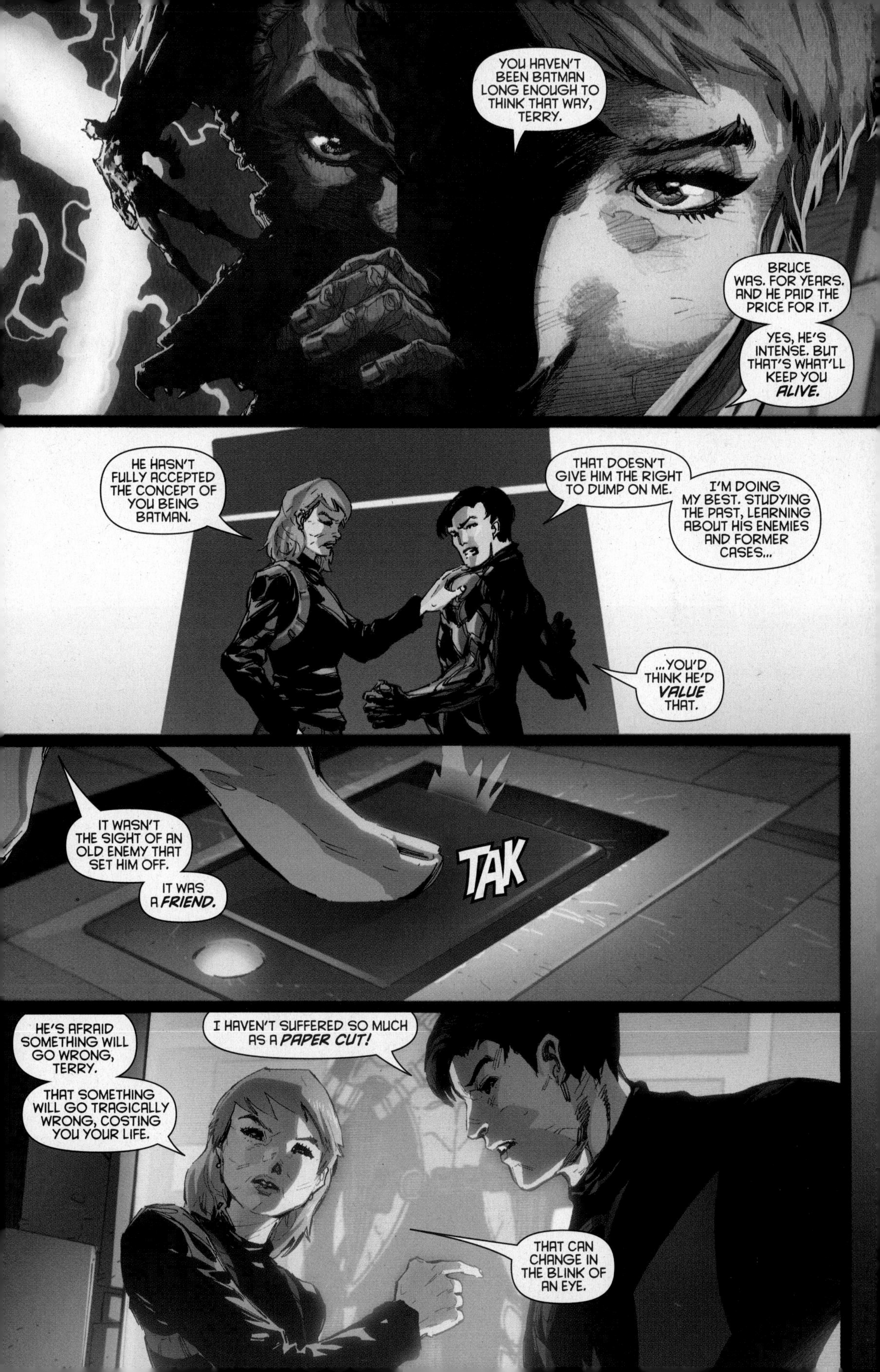

YOU HAVEN'T BEEN BATMAN LONG ENOUGH TO THINK THAT WAY, TERRY.
BRUCE WAS. FOR YEARS. AND HE PAID THE PRICE FOR IT.
YES, HE'S INTENSE. BUT THAT'S WHAT'LL KEEP YOU ALIVE.
HE HASN'T FULLY ACCEPTED THE CONCEPT OF YOU BEING BATMAN.
THAT DOESN'T GIVE HIM THE RIGHT TO DUMP ON ME.
I'M DOING MY BEST. STUDYING THE PAST, LEARNING ABOUT HIS ENEMIES AND FORMER CASES...
...YOU'D THINK HE'D VALUE THAT.
IT WASN'T THE SIGHT OF AN OLD ENEMY THAT SET HIM OFF.
IT WAS A FRIEND.
TAK
HE'S AFRAID SOMETHING WILL GO WRONG, TERRY.
THAT SOMETHING WILL GO TRAGICALLY WRONG, COSTING YOU YOUR LIFE.
I HAVEN'T SUFFERED SO MUCH AS A PAPER CUT!
THAT CAN CHANGE IN THE BLINK OF AN EYE.

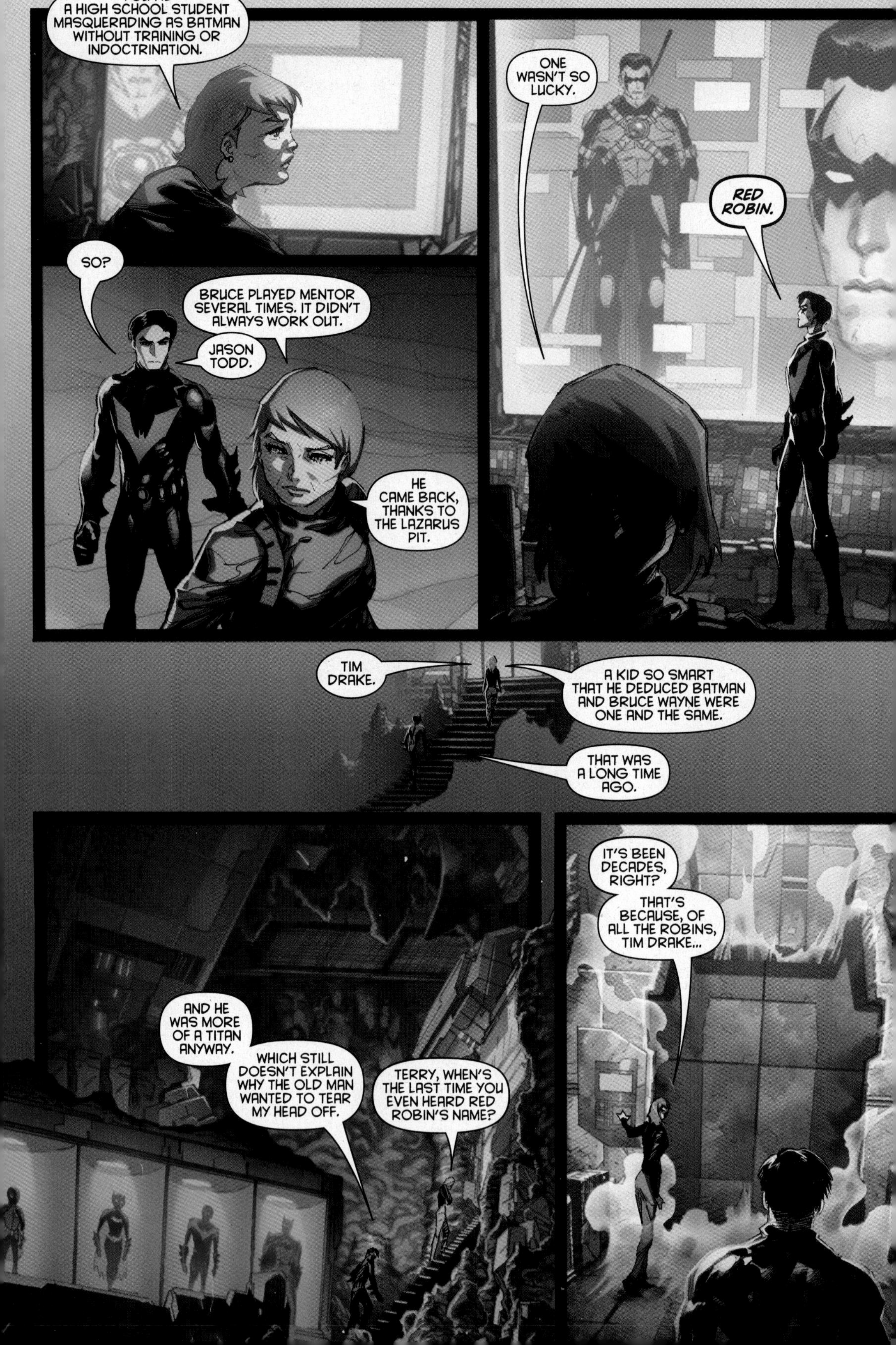
YOU'RE A HIGH SCHOOL STUDENT MASQUERADING AS BATMAN WITHOUT TRAINING OR INDOCTRINATION.
SO?
BRUCE PLAYED MENTOR SEVERAL TIMES. IT DIDN'T ALWAYS WORK OUT.
JASON TODD.
HE CAME BACK, THANKS TO THE LAZARUS PIT.
ONE WASN'T SO LUCKY.
RED ROBIN.
TIM DRAKE.
A KID SO SMART THAT HE DEDUCED BATMAN AND BRUCE WAYNE WERE ONE AND THE SAME.
THAT WAS A LONG TIME AGO.
AND HE WAS MORE OF A TITAN ANYWAY.
WHICH STILL DOESN'T EXPLAIN WHY THE OLD MAN WANTED TO TEAR MY HEAD OFF.
TERRY, WHEN'S THE LAST TIME YOU EVEN HEARD RED ROBIN'S NAME?
IT'S BEEN DECADES, RIGHT?
THAT'S BECAUSE, OF ALL THE ROBINS, TIM DRAKE...

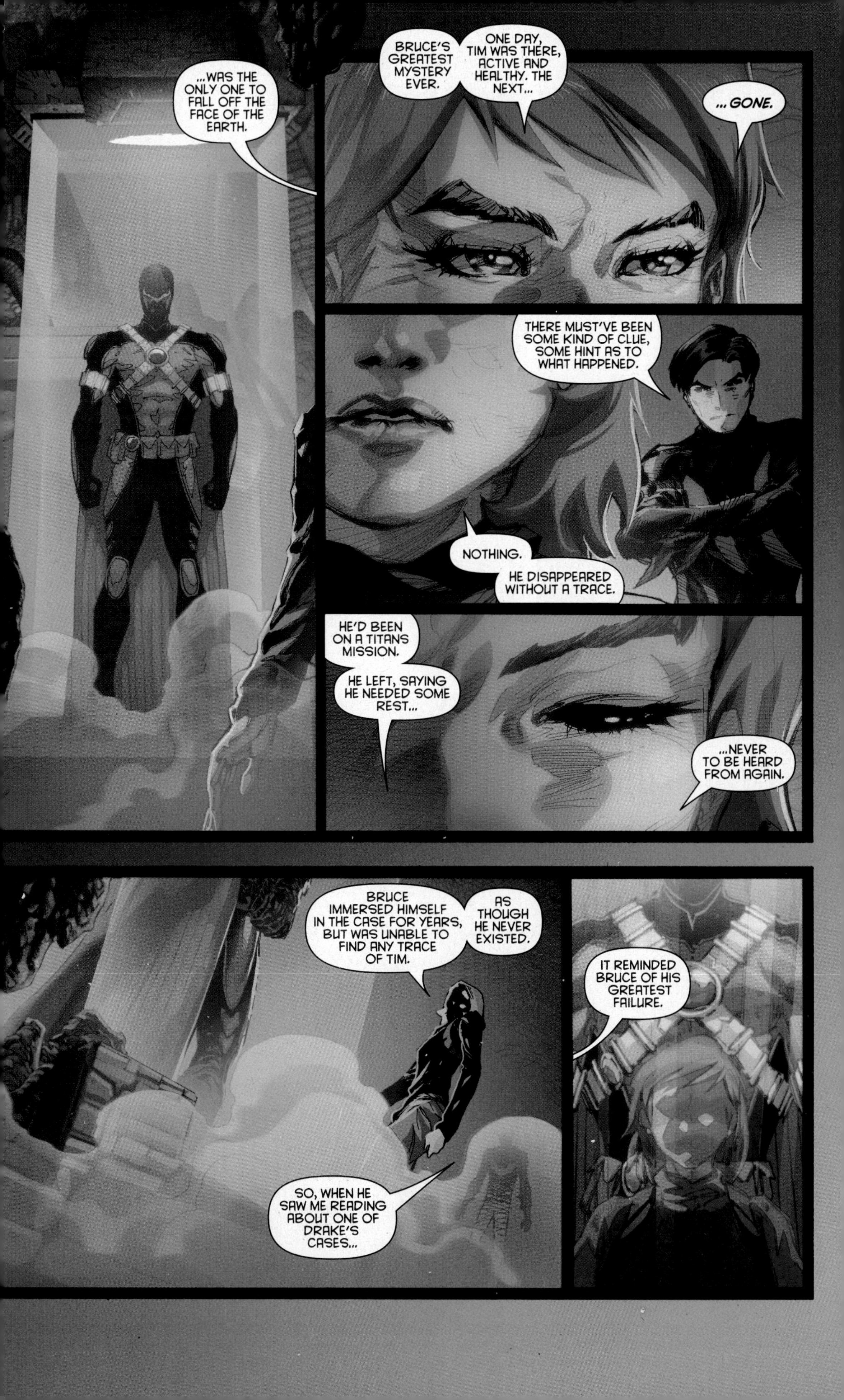
...WAS THE ONLY ONE TO FALL OFF THE FACE OF THE EARTH.
BRUCE'S GREATEST MYSTERY EVER.
ONE DAY, TIM WAS THERE, ACTIVE AND HEALTHY. THE NEXT...
...GONE.
THERE MUST'VE BEEN SOME KIND OF CLUE, SOME HINT AS TO WHAT HAPPENED.
NOTHING.
HE DISAPPEARED WITHOUT A TRACE.
HE'D BEEN ON A TITANS MISSION.
HE LEFT, SAYING HE NEEDED SOME REST...
...NEVER TO BE HEARD FROM AGAIN.
BRUCE IMMERSED HIMSELF IN THE CASE FOR YEARS, BUT WAS UNABLE TO FIND ANY TRACE OF TIM.
AS THOUGH HE NEVER EXISTED.
SO, WHEN HE SAW ME READING ABOUT ONE OF DRAKE'S CASES...
IT REMINDED BRUCE OF HIS GREATEST FAILURE.

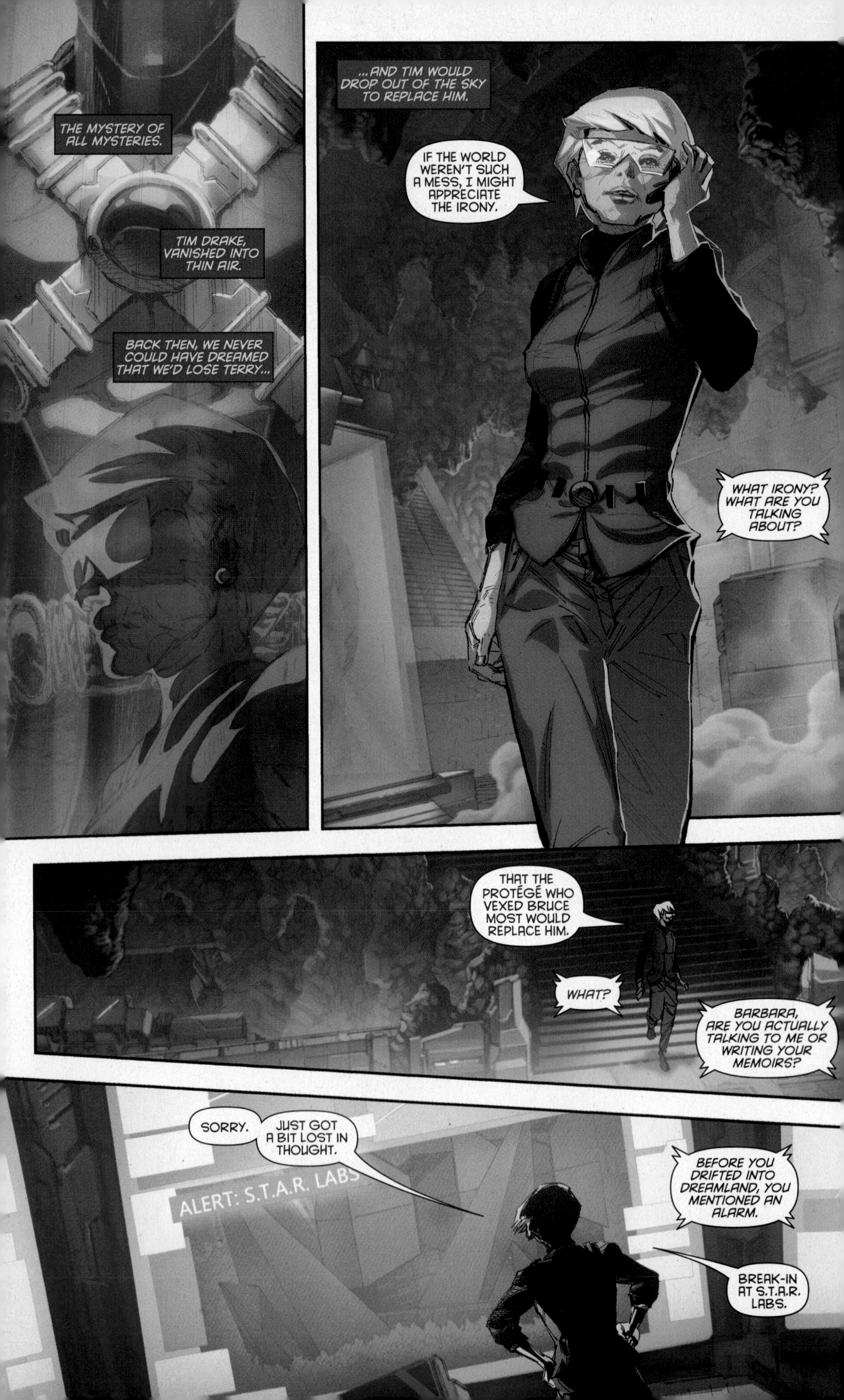
THE MYSTERY OF ALL MYSTERIES.
TIM DRAKE, VANISHED INTO THIN AIR.
BACK THEN, WE NEVER COULD HAVE DREAMED THAT WE'D LOSE TERRY...
...AND TIM WOULD DROP OUT OF THE SKY TO REPLACE HIM.
IF THE WORLD WEREN'T SUCH A MESS, I MIGHT APPRECIATE THE IRONY.
WHAT IRONY? WHAT ARE YOU TALKING ABOUT?
THAT THE PROTÉGÉ WHO VEXED BRUCE MOST WOULD REPLACE HIM.
WHAT?
BARBARA, ARE YOU ACTUALLY TALKING TO ME OR WRITING YOUR MEMOIRS?
SORRY.
JUST GOT A BIT LOST IN THOUGHT.
ALERT: S.T.A.R. LABS
BEFORE YOU DRIFTED INTO DREAMLAND, YOU MENTIONED AN ALARM.
BREAK-IN AT S.T.A.R. LABS.

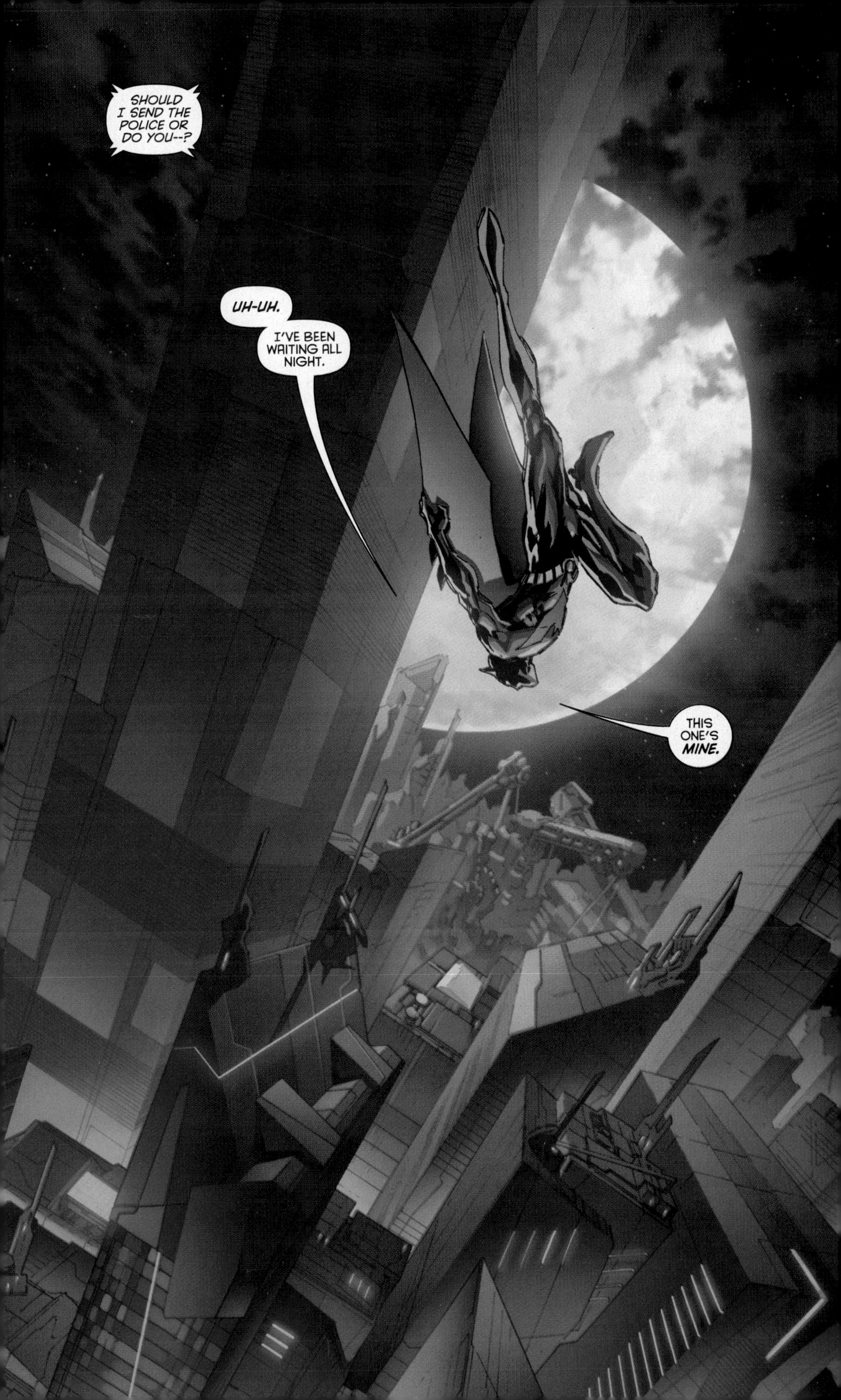
SHOULD I SEND THE POLICE OR DO YOU--?
UH-UH.
I'VE BEEN WAITING ALL NIGHT.
THIS ONE'S MINE.

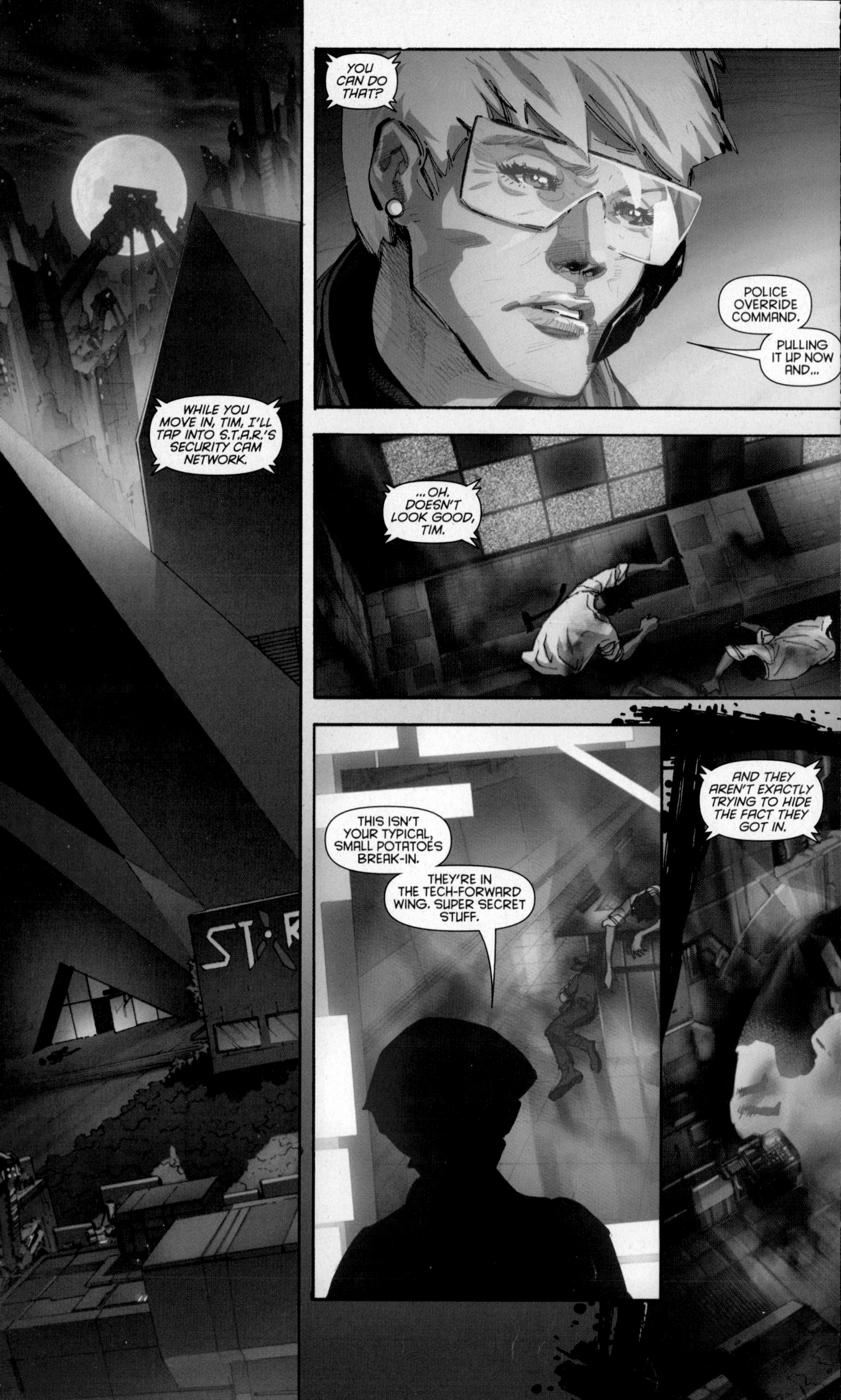
WHILE YOU MOVE IN, TIM, I'LL TAP INTO S.T.A.R.'S SECURITY CAM NETWORK.
YOU CAN DO THAT?
POLICE OVERRIDE COMMAND.
PULLING IT UP NOW AND...
...OH. DOESN'T LOOK GOOD, TIM.
THIS ISN'T YOUR TYPICAL, SMALL POTATOES BREAK-IN.
THEY'RE IN THE TECH-FORWARD WING. SUPER SECRET STUFF.
AND THEY AREN'T EXACTLY TRYING TO HIDE THE FACT THEY GOT IN.
ST•R

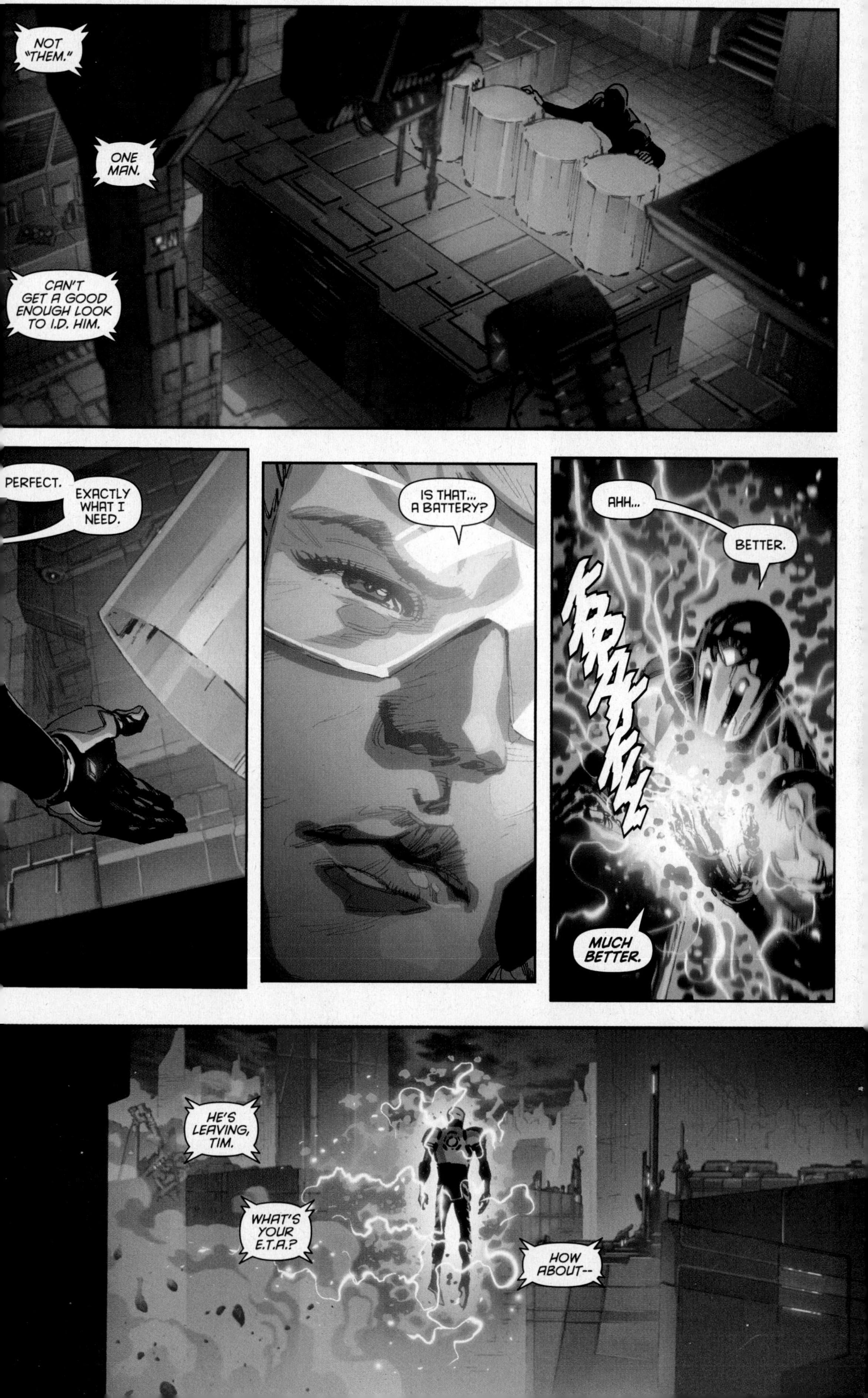
NOT "THEM."
ONE MAN.
CAN'T GET A GOOD ENOUGH LOOK TO I.D. HIM.
PERFECT.
EXACTLY WHAT I NEED.
IS THAT... A BATTERY?
AHH...
BETTER.
MUCH BETTER.
HE'S LEAVING, TIM.
WHAT'S YOUR E.T.A.?
HOW ABOUT--

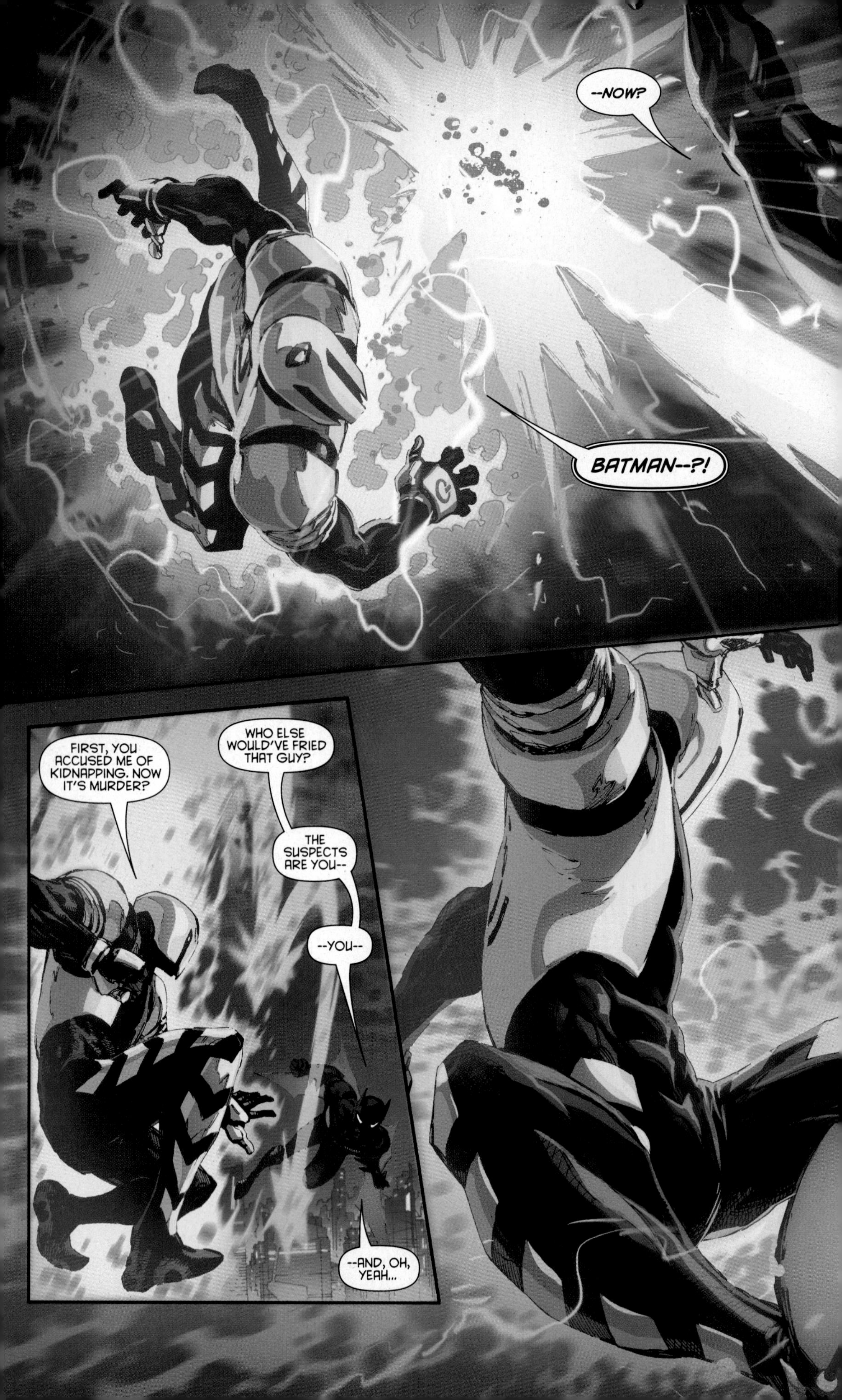

--NOW?
BATMAN--?!
FIRST, YOU ACCUSED ME OF KIDNAPPING. NOW IT'S MURDER?
WHO ELSE WOULD'VE FRIED THAT GUY?
THE SUSPECTS ARE YOU--
--YOU--
--AND, OH, YEAH...

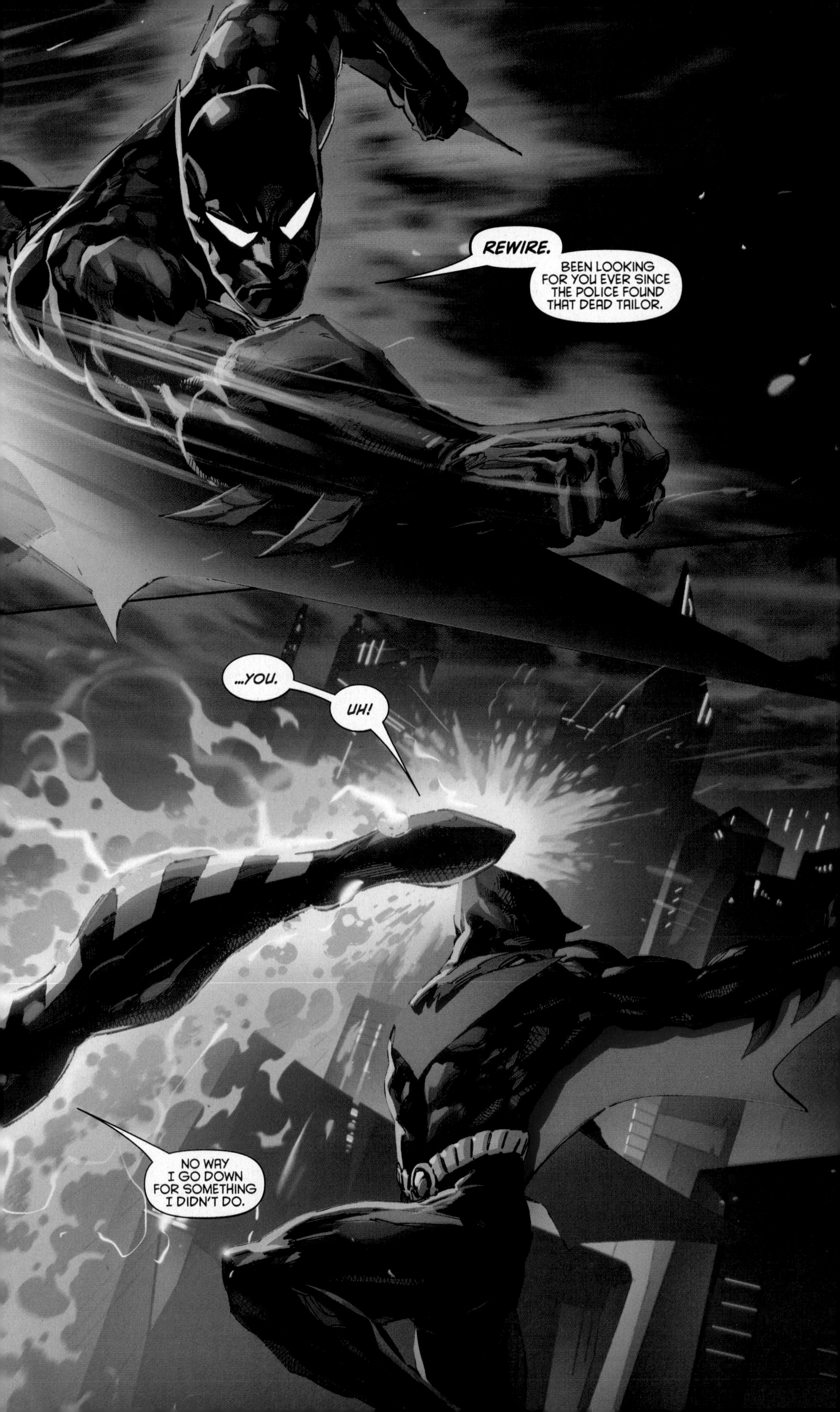
REWIRE.
BEEN LOOKING FOR YOU EVER SINCE THE POLICE FOUND THAT DEAD TAILOR.
...YOU.
UH!
NO WAY I GO DOWN FOR SOMETHING I DIDN'T DO.

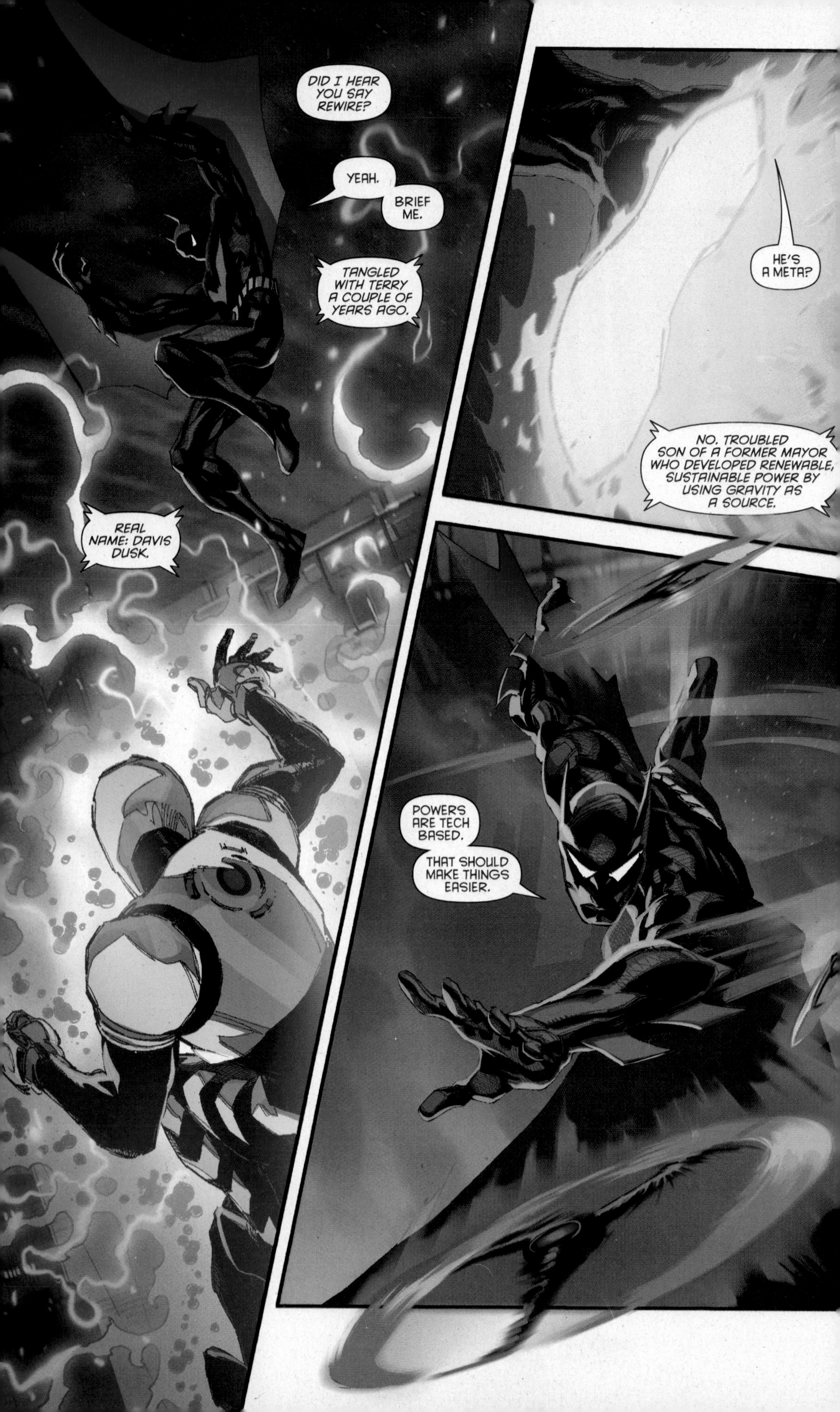
DID I HEAR YOU SAY REWIRE?
YEAH.
BRIEF ME.
TANGLED WITH TERRY A COUPLE OF YEARS AGO.
REAL NAME: DAVIS DUSK.
HE'S A META?
NO. TROUBLED SON OF A FORMER MAYOR WHO DEVELOPED RENEWABLE, SUSTAINABLE POWER BY USING GRAVITY AS A SOURCE.
POWERS ARE TECH BASED.
THAT SHOULD MAKE THINGS EASIER.

WITH TOTAL CONTROL OVER ELECTRICITY? DON'T BE SO SURE.
YOU CAN'T HURT ME.
THAT TAILOR-- KRINSKY?
HE WAS DIRTY.
ZAKK
ZAKT
AND ALIVE WHEN I LEFT HIM.
TALK IS CHEAP.
IF YOU'RE INNOCENT...
...LET'S GO VISIT COMMISSIONER GORDON AND CONVINCE *HER.*
SKAZZ
SKAZZ
FOR A ONE-WAY TICKET TO *BLACKGATE?*
THAT'S A *NEG.*

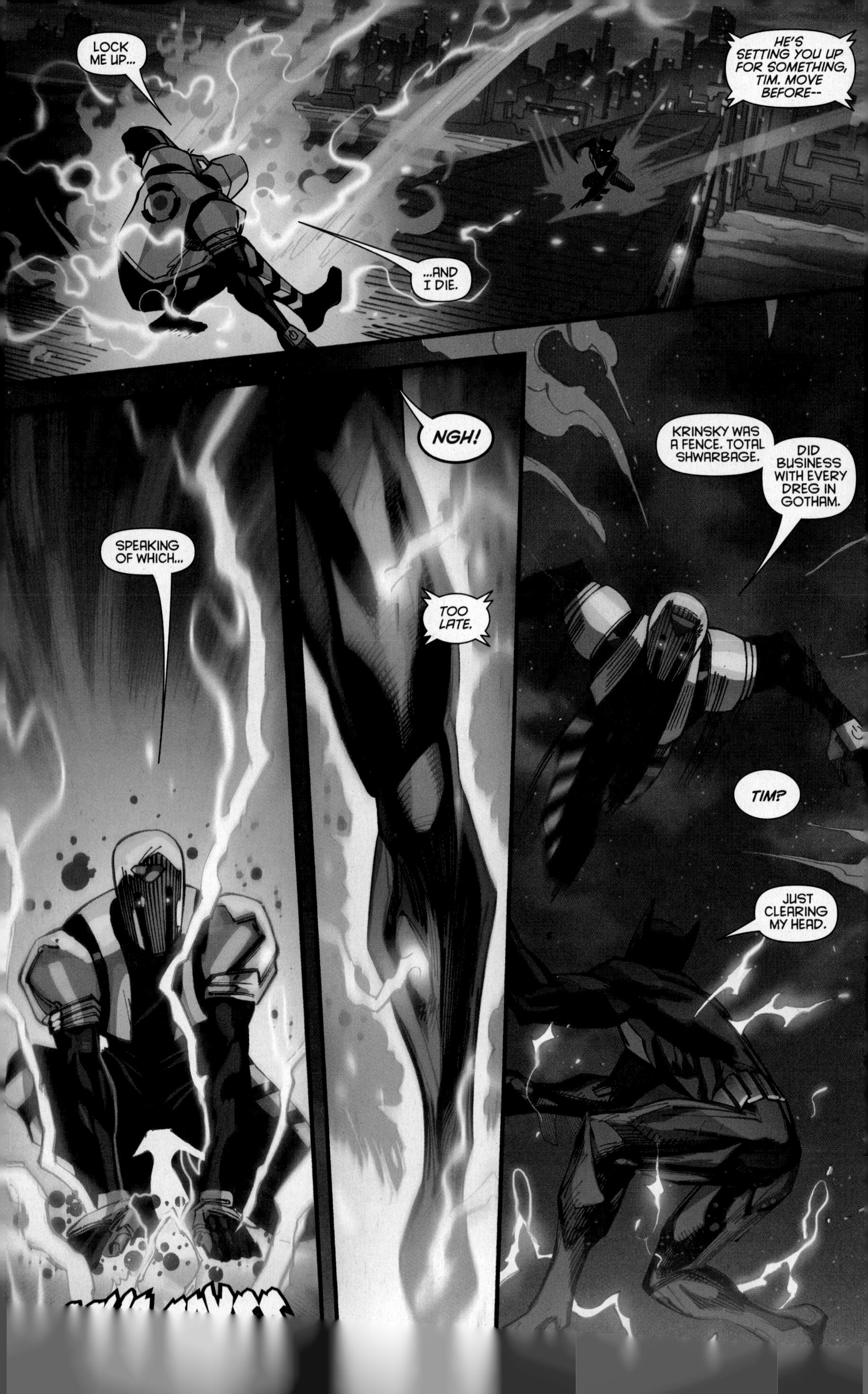
LOCK ME UP...
HE'S SETTING YOU UP FOR SOMETHING, TIM. MOVE BEFORE--
...AND I DIE.
SPEAKING OF WHICH...
NGH!
TOO LATE.
KRINSKY WAS A FENCE. TOTAL SHWARBAGE.
DID BUSINESS WITH EVERY DREG IN GOTHAM.
TIM?
JUST CLEARING MY HEAD.

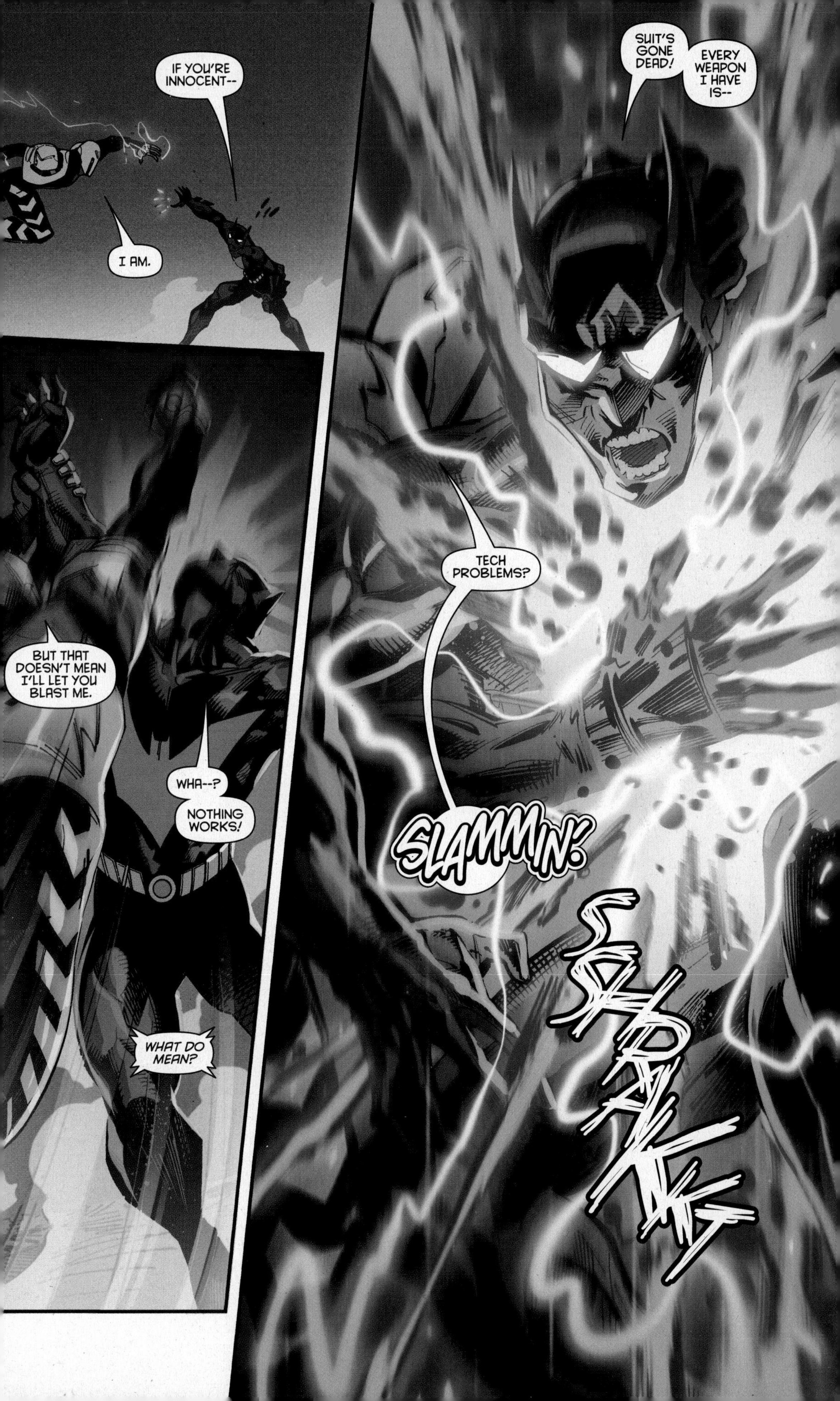
IF YOU'RE INNOCENT--
I AM.
BUT THAT DOESN'T MEAN I'LL LET YOU BLAST ME.
WHA--?
NOTHING WORKS!
WHAT DO MEAN?
SUIT'S GONE DEAD!
EVERY WEAPON I HAVE IS--
TECH PROBLEMS?
SLAMMIN'!
SHRAKKK

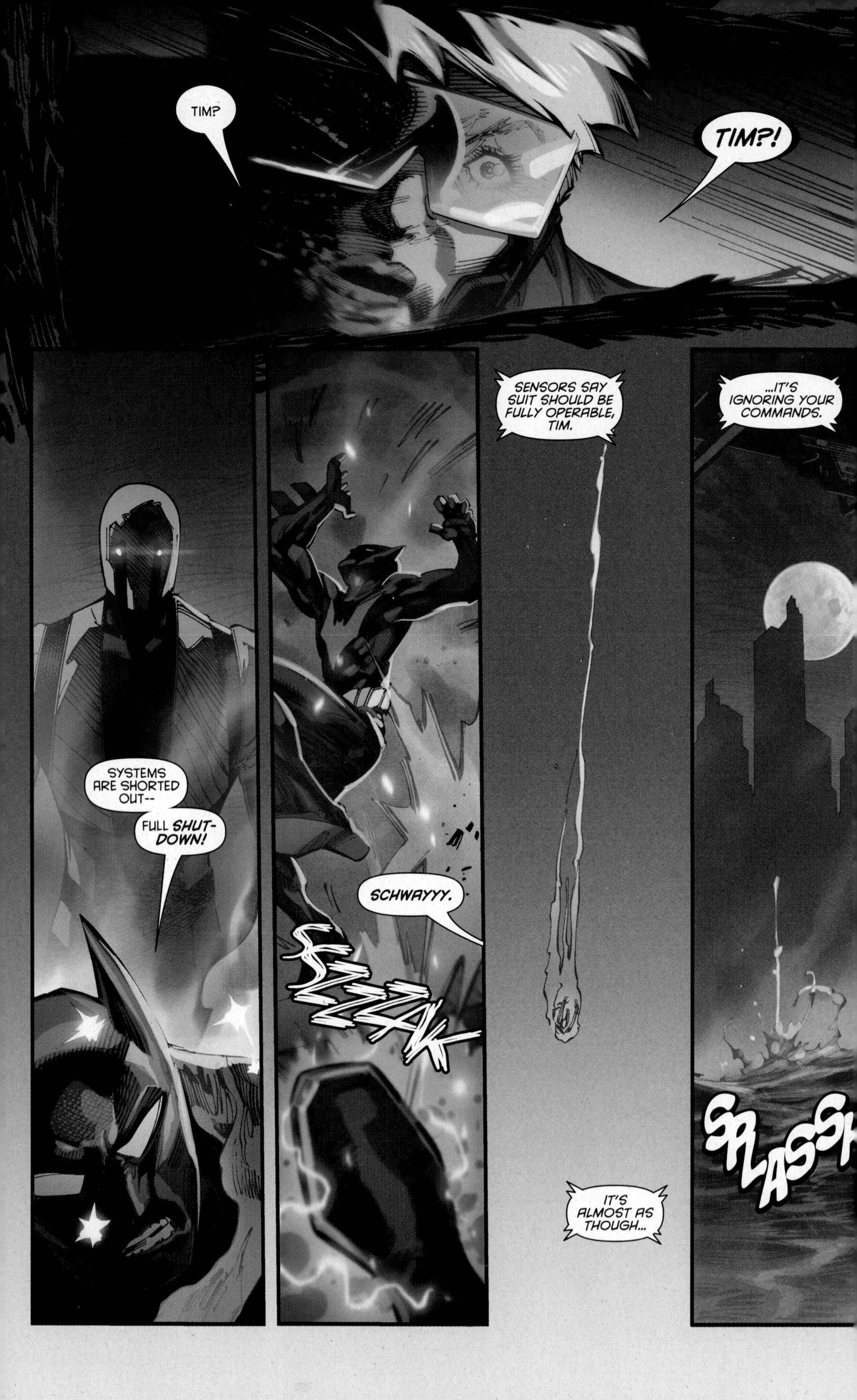
TIM?
TIM?!
SYSTEMS ARE SHORTED OUT--
FULL SHUT-DOWN!
SCHWAYYY.
SZZZAK
SENSORS SAY SUIT SHOULD BE FULLY OPERABLE, TIM.
IT'S ALMOST AS THOUGH...
...IT'S IGNORING YOUR COMMANDS.
SPLASSH

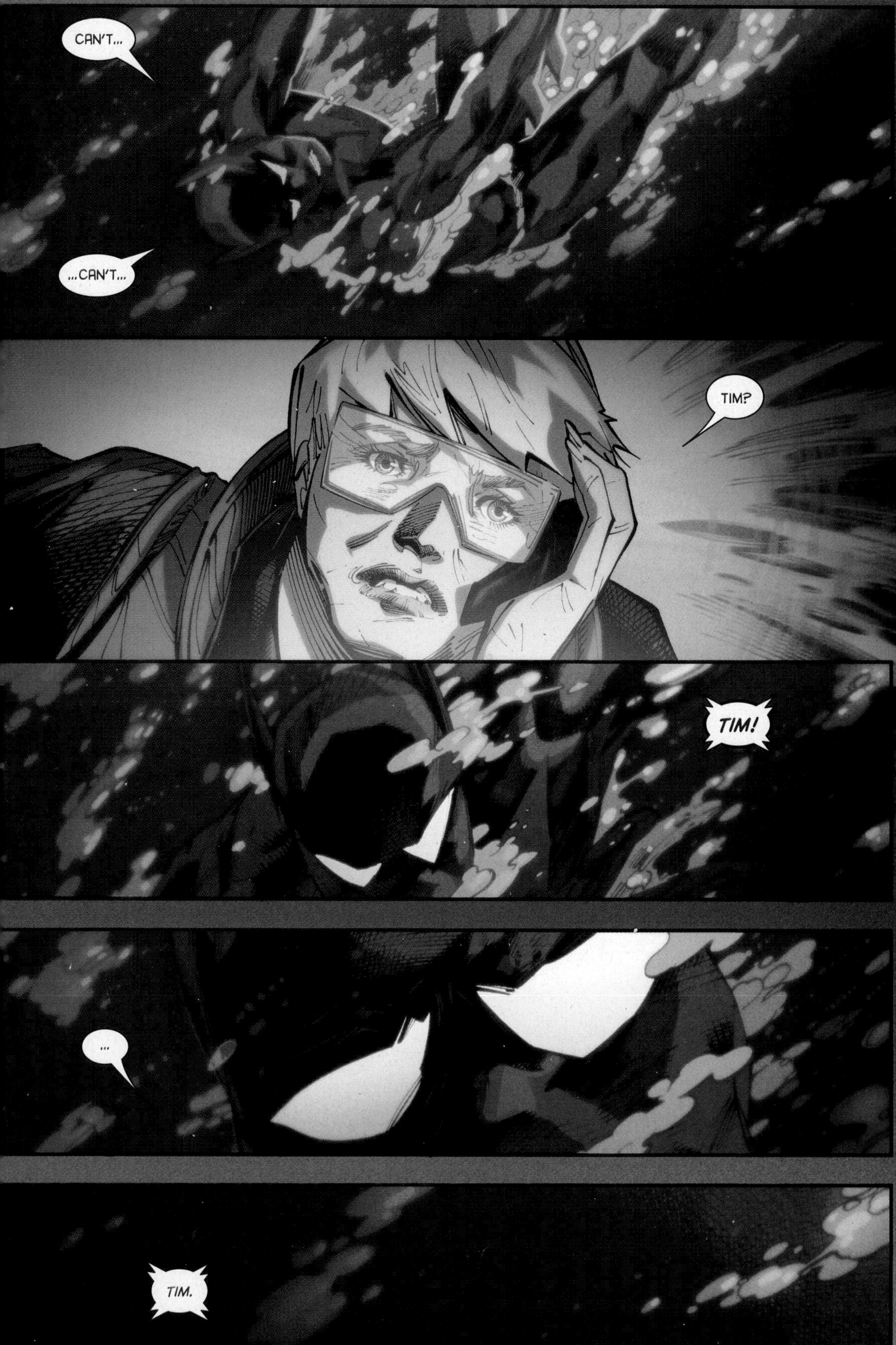
CAN'T...
...CAN'T...
TIM?
TIM!
...
TIM.

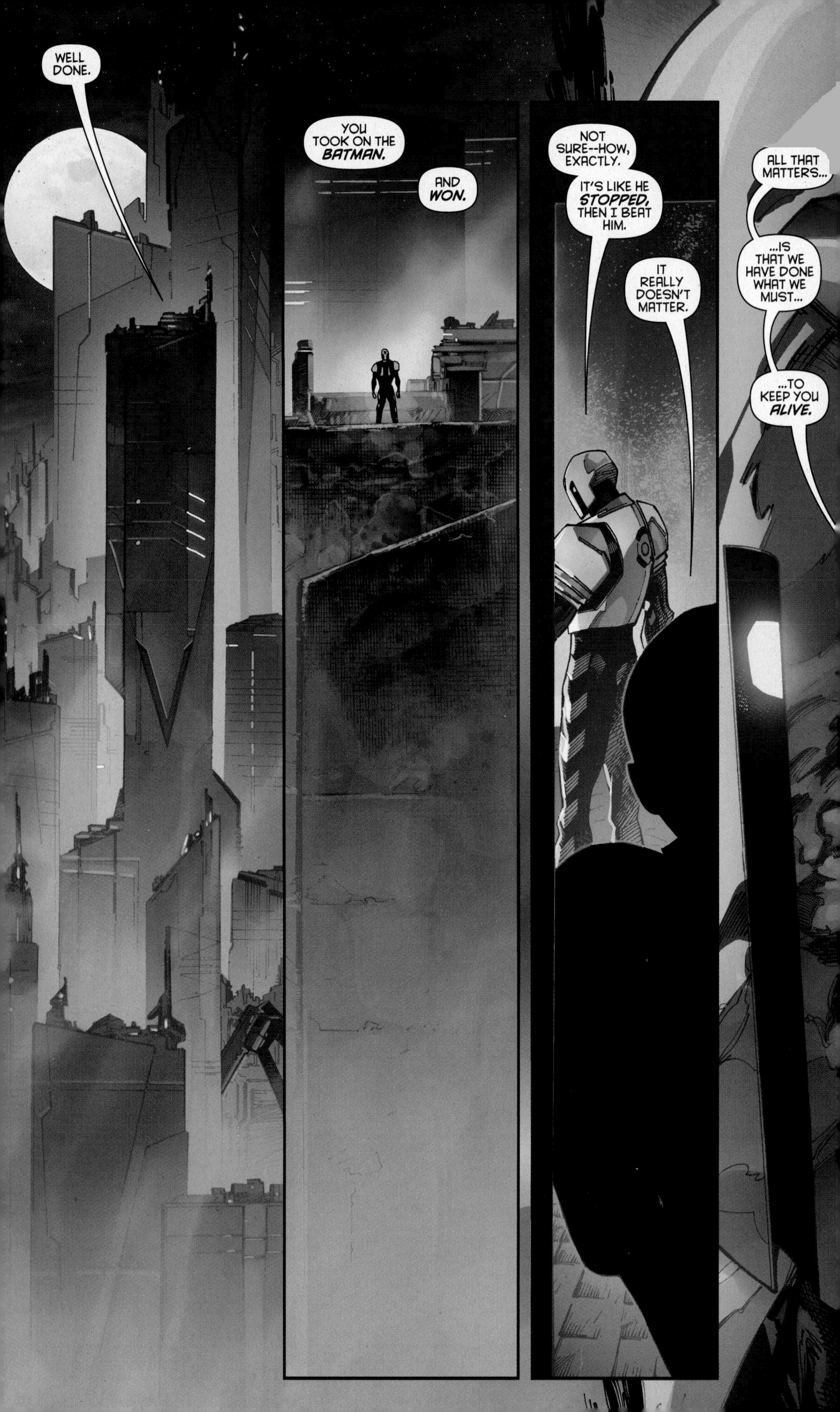
WELL DONE.
YOU TOOK ON THE BATMAN.
AND WON.
NOT SURE--HOW, EXACTLY.
IT'S LIKE HE STOPPED, THEN I BEAT HIM.
IT REALLY DOESN'T MATTER.
ALL THAT MATTERS...
...IS THAT WE HAVE DONE WHAT WE MUST...
...TO KEEP YOU ALIVE.

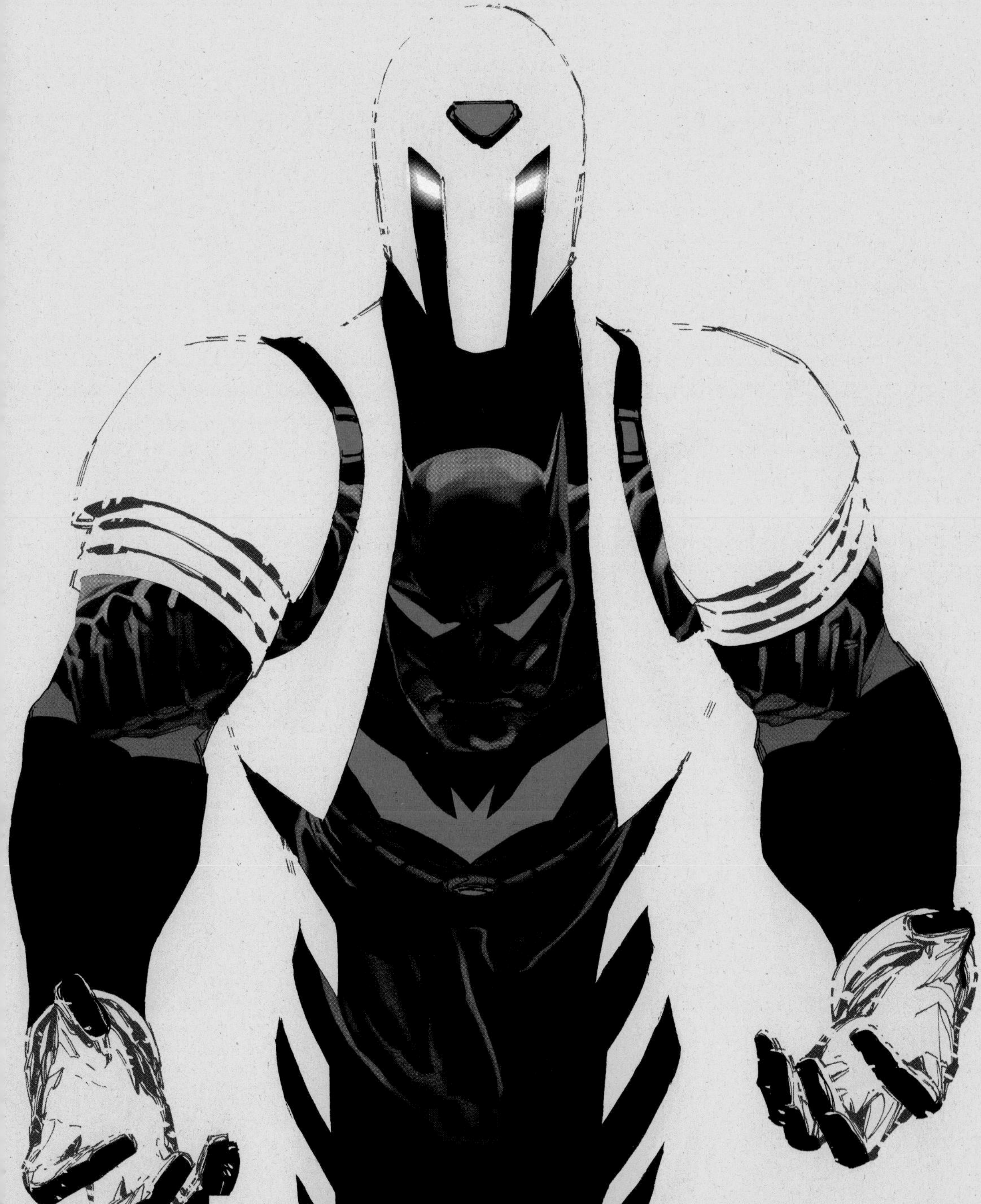

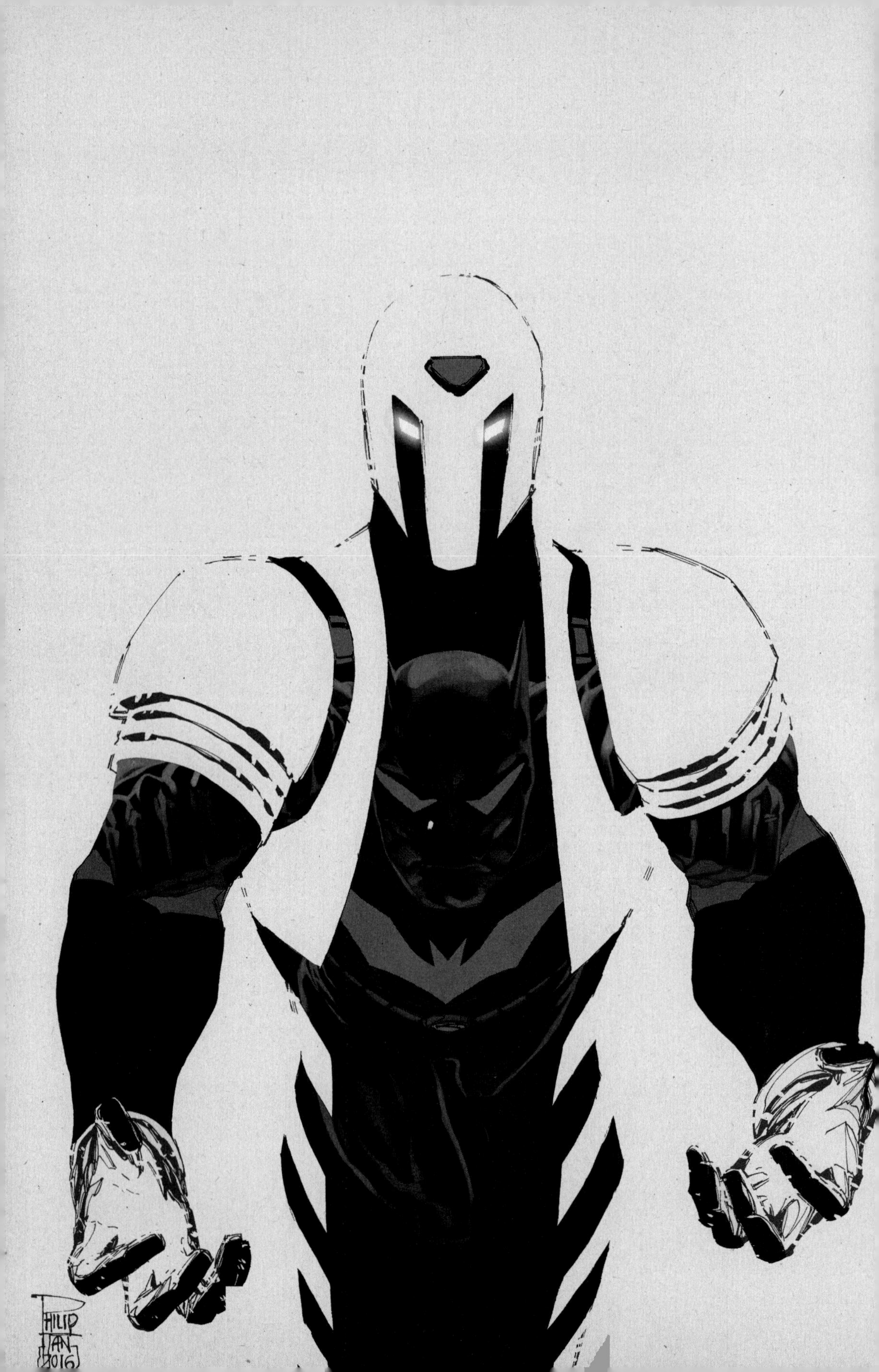
PHILIP TAN 2016

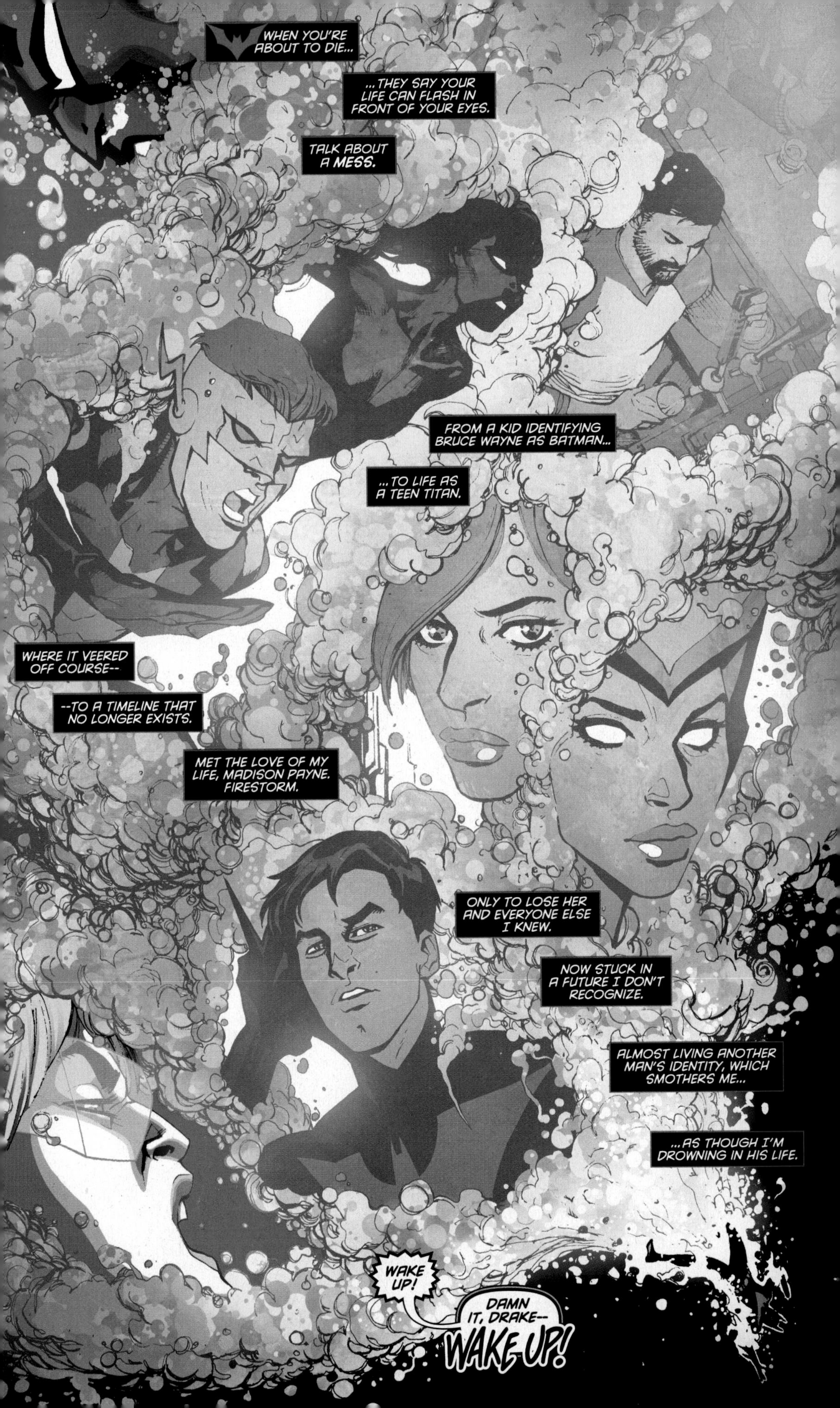
WHEN YOU'RE ABOUT TO DIE...
...THEY SAY YOUR LIFE CAN FLASH IN FRONT OF YOUR EYES.
TALK ABOUT A MESS.
FROM A KID IDENTIFYING BRUCE WAYNE AS BATMAN...
...TO LIFE AS A TEEN TITAN.
WHERE IT VEERED OFF COURSE--
--TO A TIMELINE THAT NO LONGER EXISTS.
MET THE LOVE OF MY LIFE, MADISON PAYNE. FIRESTORM.
ONLY TO LOSE HER AND EVERYONE ELSE I KNEW.
NOW STUCK IN A FUTURE I DON'T RECOGNIZE.
ALMOST LIVING ANOTHER MAN'S IDENTITY, WHICH SMOTHERS ME...
...AS THOUGH I'M DROWNING IN HIS LIFE.
WAKE UP!
DAMN IT, DRAKE-- WAKE UP!

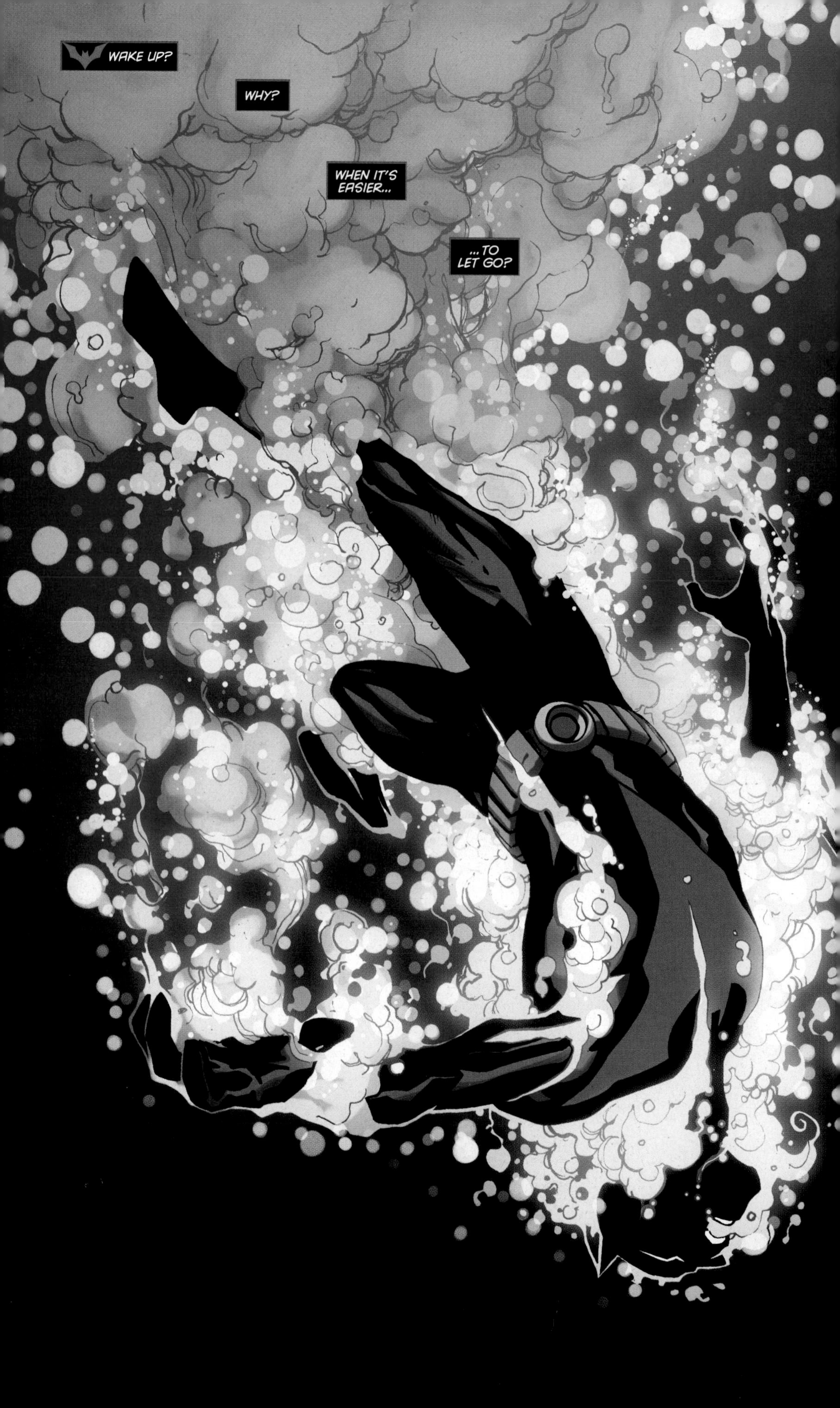
WAKE UP?
WHY?
WHEN IT'S EASIER...
...TO LET GO?

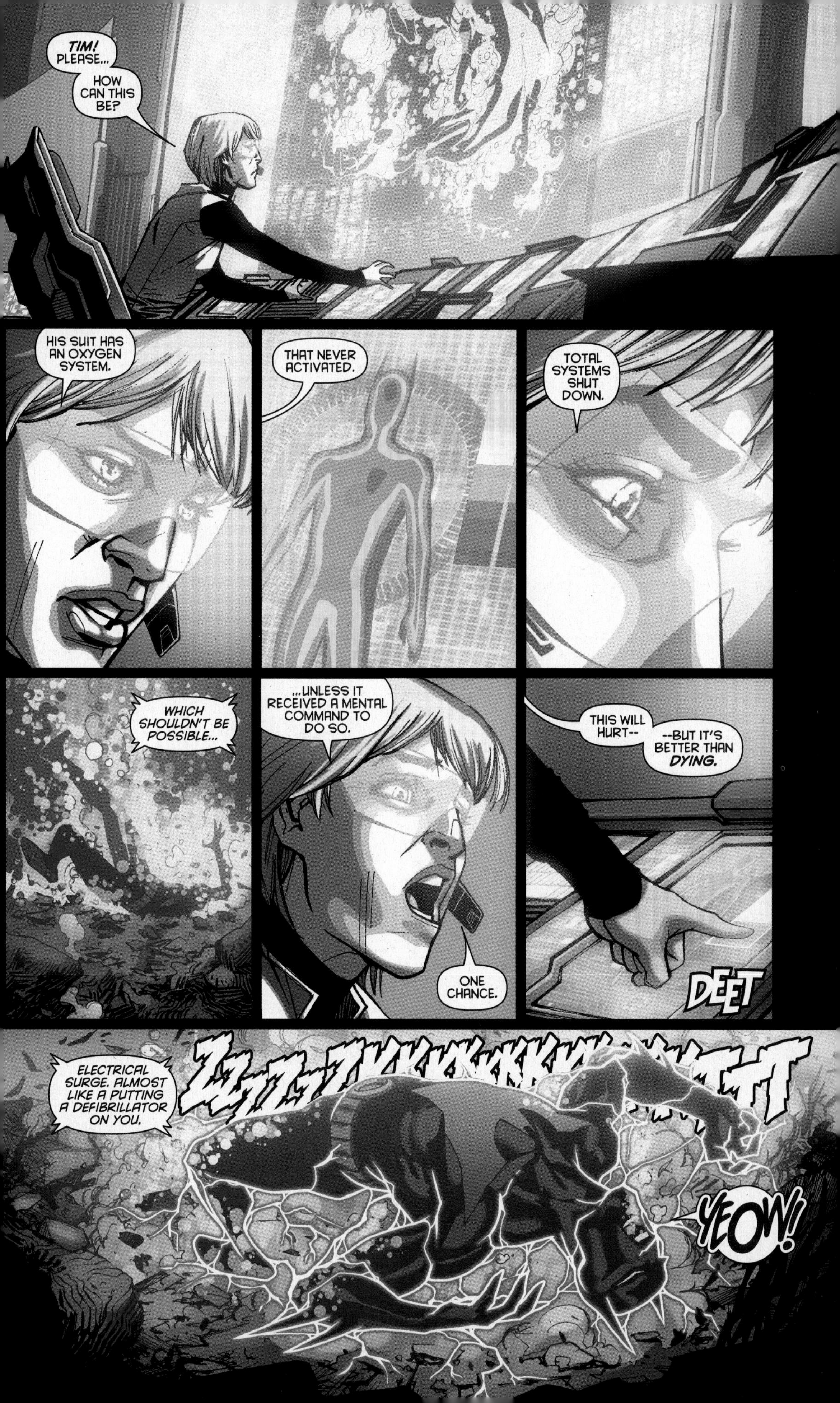

TIM! PLEASE...
HOW CAN THIS BE?
HIS SUIT HAS AN OXYGEN SYSTEM.
THAT NEVER ACTIVATED.
TOTAL SYSTEMS SHUT DOWN.
WHICH SHOULDN'T BE POSSIBLE...
...UNLESS IT RECEIVED A MENTAL COMMAND TO DO SO.
ONE CHANCE.
THIS WILL HURT--
--BUT IT'S BETTER THAN DYING.
DEET
ELECTRICAL SURGE. ALMOST LIKE A PUTTING A DEFIBRILLATOR ON YOU.
YEOW!

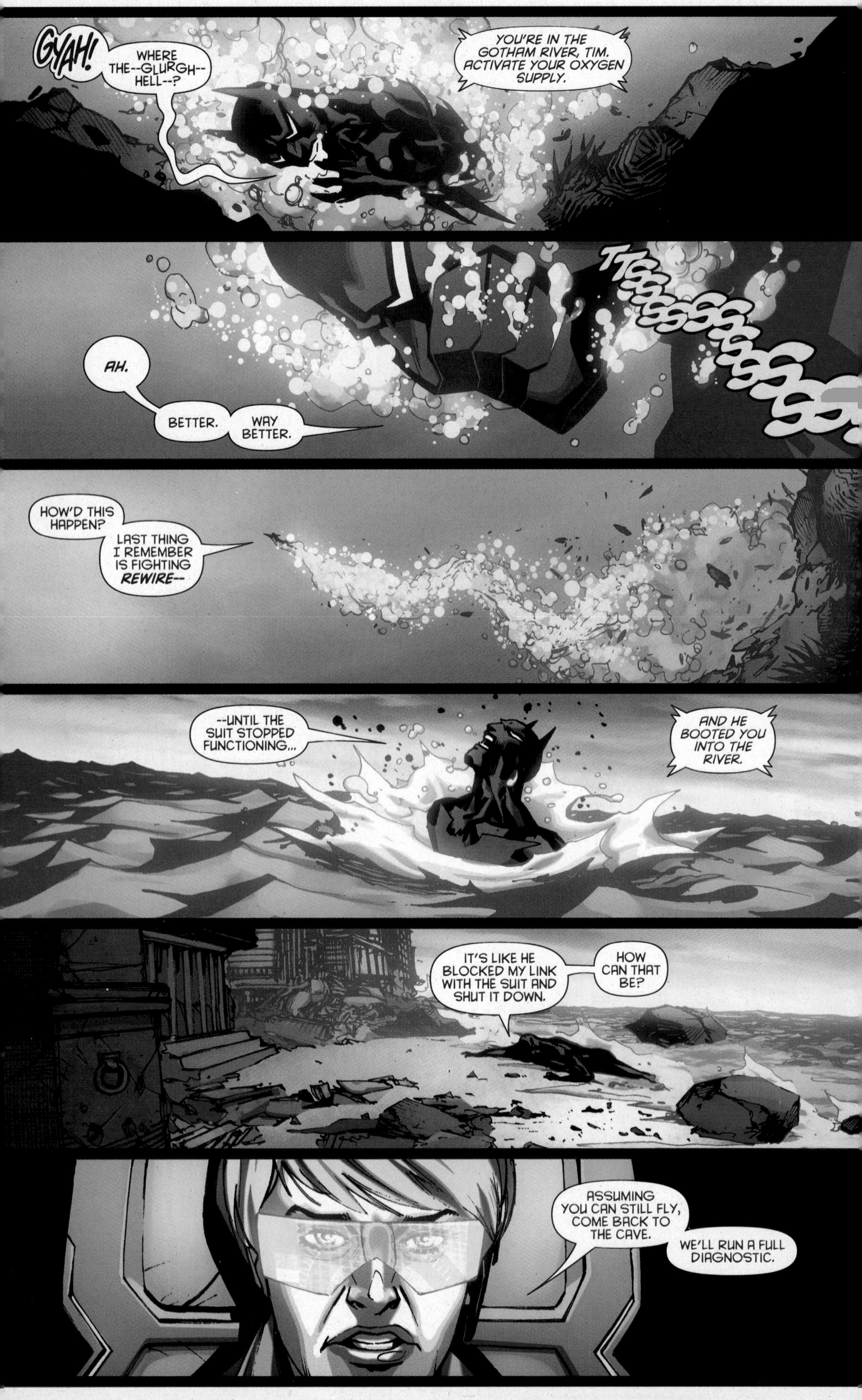
GYAH!
WHERE THE--GLURGH-- HELL--?
YOU'RE IN THE GOTHAM RIVER, TIM. ACTIVATE YOUR OXYGEN SUPPLY.
TTSSSSSSSSSSSSSS
AH.
BETTER.
WAY BETTER.
HOW'D THIS HAPPEN?
LAST THING I REMEMBER IS FIGHTING REWIRE--
--UNTIL THE SUIT STOPPED FUNCTIONING...
AND HE BOOTED YOU INTO THE RIVER.
IT'S LIKE HE BLOCKED MY LINK WITH THE SUIT AND SHUT IT DOWN.
HOW CAN THAT BE?
ASSUMING YOU CAN STILL FLY, COME BACK TO THE CAVE.
WE'LL RUN A FULL DIAGNOSTIC.

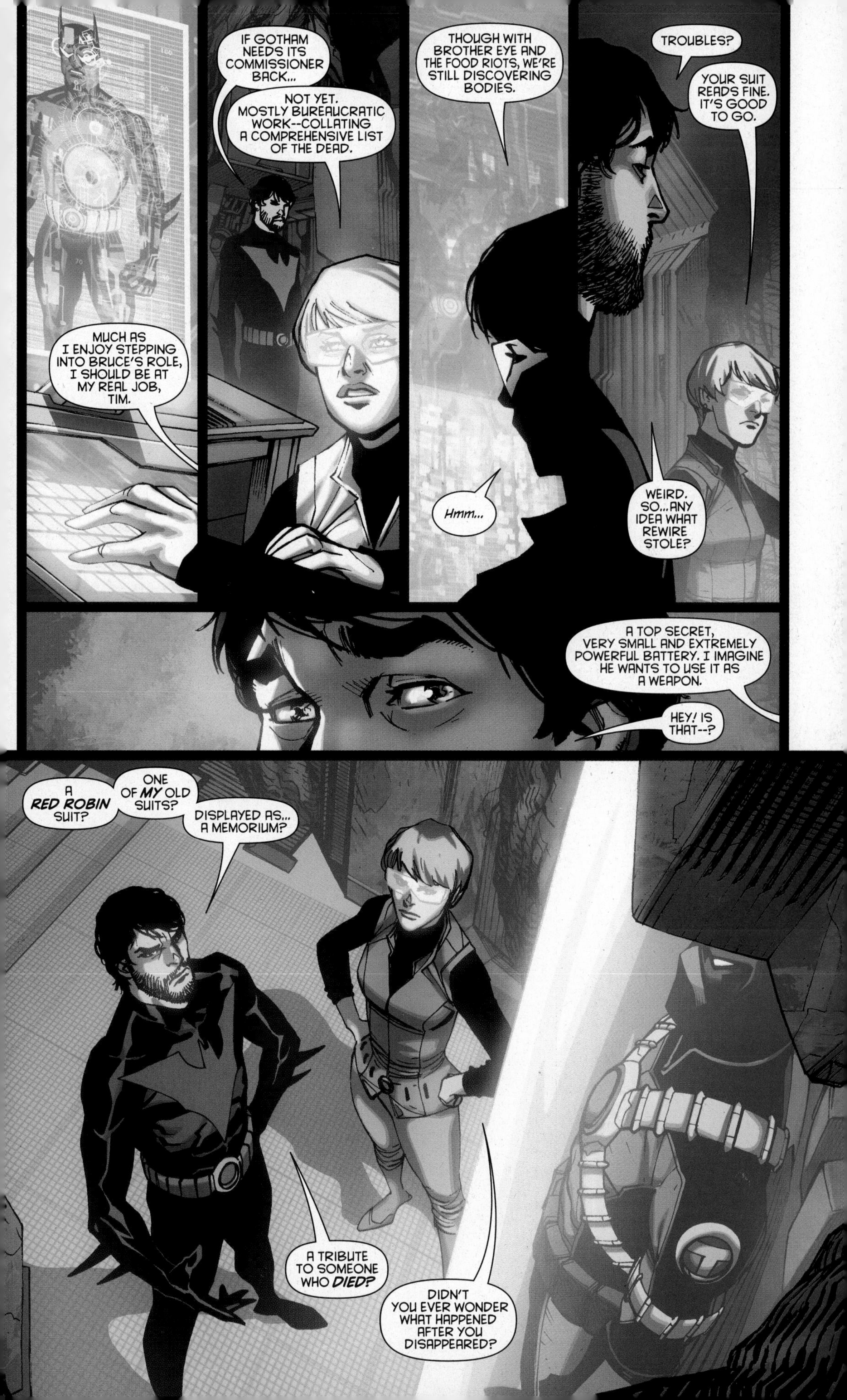
MUCH AS I ENJOY STEPPING INTO BRUCE'S ROLE, I SHOULD BE AT MY REAL JOB, TIM.
IF GOTHAM NEEDS ITS COMMISSIONER BACK...
NOT YET. MOSTLY BUREAUCRATIC WORK--COLLATING A COMPREHENSIVE LIST OF THE DEAD.
THOUGH WITH BROTHER EYE AND THE FOOD RIOTS, WE'RE STILL DISCOVERING BODIES.
Hmm...
TROUBLES?
YOUR SUIT READS FINE. IT'S GOOD TO GO.
WEIRD. SO...ANY IDEA WHAT REWIRE STOLE?
A TOP SECRET, VERY SMALL AND EXTREMELY POWERFUL BATTERY. I IMAGINE HE WANTS TO USE IT AS A WEAPON.
HEY! IS THAT--?
A RED ROBIN SUIT?
ONE OF MY OLD SUITS?
DISPLAYED AS... A MEMORIUM?
A TRIBUTE TO SOMEONE WHO DIED?
DIDN'T YOU EVER WONDER WHAT HAPPENED AFTER YOU DISAPPEARED?

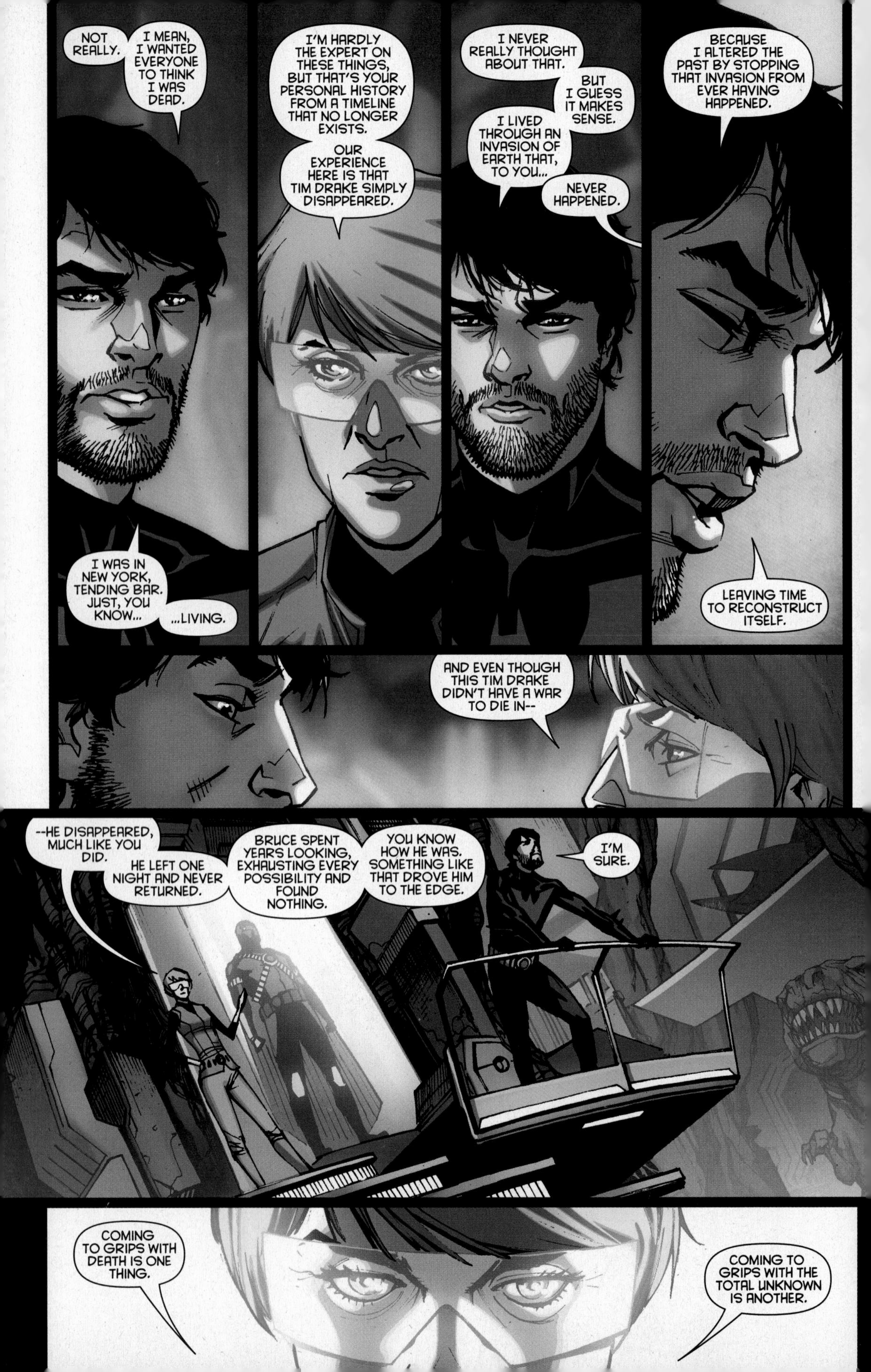
NOT REALLY.
I MEAN, I WANTED EVERYONE TO THINK I WAS DEAD.
I WAS IN NEW YORK, TENDING BAR. JUST, YOU KNOW...
...LIVING.
I'M HARDLY THE EXPERT ON THESE THINGS, BUT THAT'S YOUR PERSONAL HISTORY FROM A TIMELINE THAT NO LONGER EXISTS.
OUR EXPERIENCE HERE IS THAT TIM DRAKE SIMPLY DISAPPEARED.
I NEVER REALLY THOUGHT ABOUT THAT.
BUT I GUESS IT MAKES SENSE.
I LIVED THROUGH AN INVASION OF EARTH THAT, TO YOU...
NEVER HAPPENED.
BECAUSE I ALTERED THE PAST BY STOPPING THAT INVASION FROM EVER HAVING HAPPENED.
LEAVING TIME TO RECONSTRUCT ITSELF.
AND EVEN THOUGH THIS TIM DRAKE DIDN'T HAVE A WAR TO DIE IN--
--HE DISAPPEARED, MUCH LIKE YOU DID.
HE LEFT ONE NIGHT AND NEVER RETURNED.
BRUCE SPENT YEARS LOOKING, EXHAUSTING EVERY POSSIBILITY AND FOUND NOTHING.
YOU KNOW HOW HE WAS. SOMETHING LIKE THAT DROVE HIM TO THE EDGE.
I'M SURE.
COMING TO GRIPS WITH DEATH IS ONE THING.
COMING TO GRIPS WITH THE TOTAL UNKNOWN IS ANOTHER.

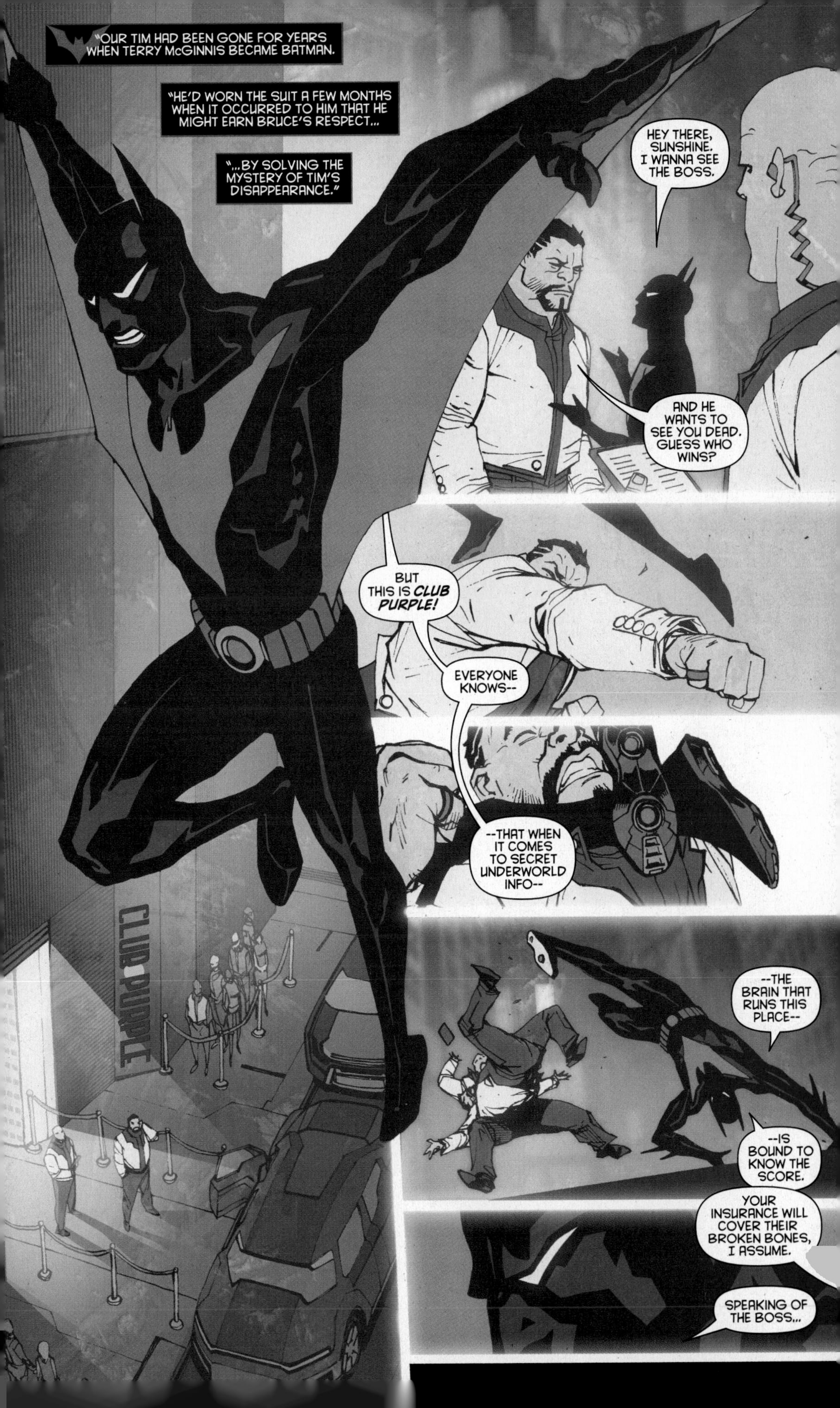
"OUR TIM HAD BEEN GONE FOR YEARS WHEN TERRY McGINNIS BECAME BATMAN.
"HE'D WORN THE SUIT A FEW MONTHS WHEN IT OCCURRED TO HIM THAT HE MIGHT EARN BRUCE'S RESPECT...
"...BY SOLVING THE MYSTERY OF TIM'S DISAPPEARANCE."
HEY THERE, SUNSHINE. I WANNA SEE THE BOSS.
AND HE WANTS TO SEE YOU DEAD. GUESS WHO WINS?
BUT THIS IS *CLUB PURPLE!*
EVERYONE KNOWS--
--THAT WHEN IT COMES TO SECRET UNDERWORLD INFO--
--THE BRAIN THAT RUNS THIS PLACE--
--IS BOUND TO KNOW THE SCORE.
YOUR INSURANCE WILL COVER THEIR BROKEN BONES, I ASSUME.
SPEAKING OF THE BOSS...
CLUB PURPLE

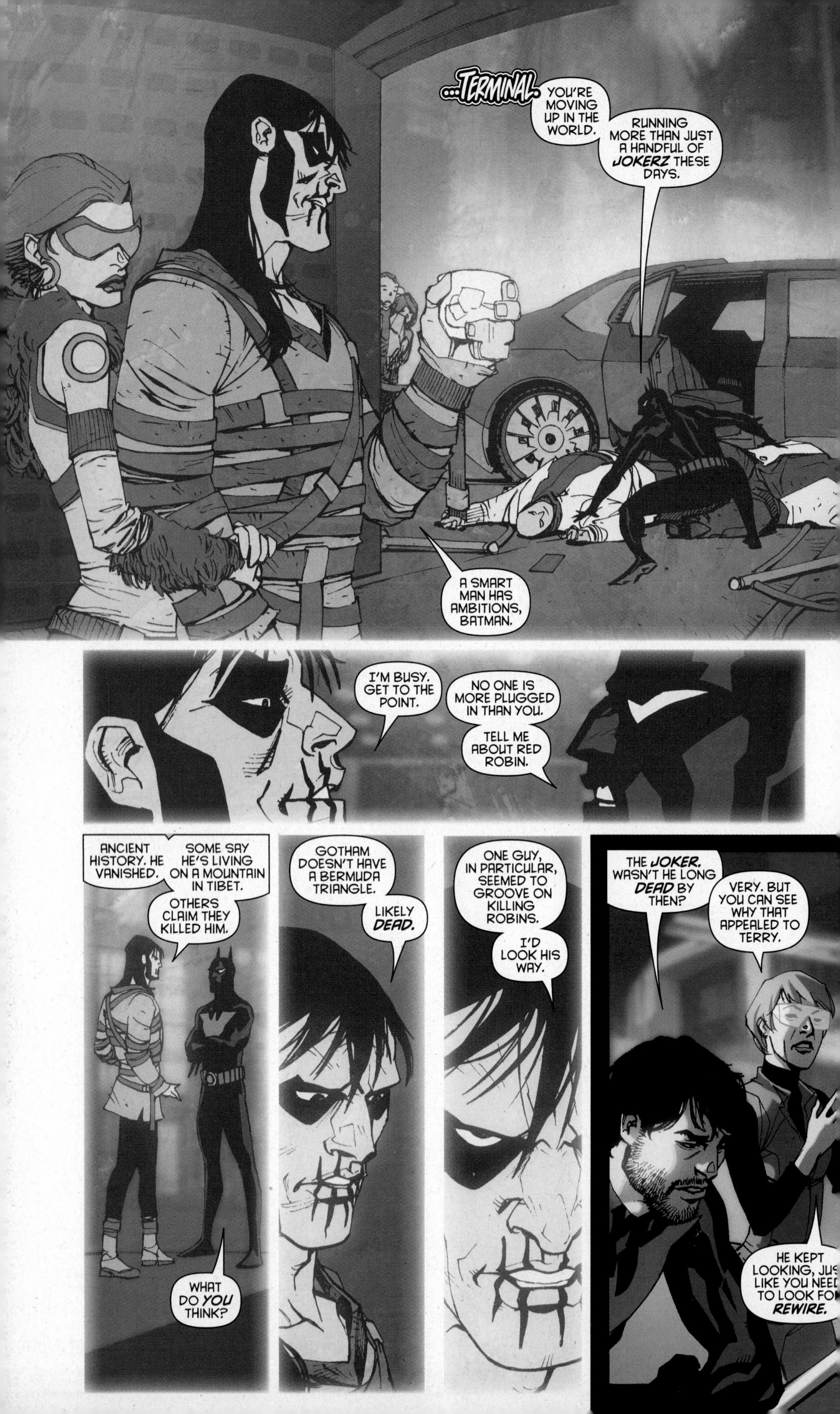

...TERMINAL.
YOU'RE MOVING UP IN THE WORLD.
RUNNING MORE THAN JUST A HANDFUL OF JOKERZ THESE DAYS.
A SMART MAN HAS AMBITIONS, BATMAN.
I'M BUSY. GET TO THE POINT.
NO ONE IS MORE PLUGGED IN THAN YOU.
TELL ME ABOUT RED ROBIN.
ANCIENT HISTORY. HE VANISHED.
SOME SAY HE'S LIVING ON A MOUNTAIN IN TIBET.
OTHERS CLAIM THEY KILLED HIM.
WHAT DO YOU THINK?
GOTHAM DOESN'T HAVE A BERMUDA TRIANGLE.
LIKELY DEAD.
ONE GUY, IN PARTICULAR, SEEMED TO GROOVE ON KILLING ROBINS.
I'D LOOK HIS WAY.
THE JOKER. WASN'T HE LONG DEAD BY THEN?
VERY. BUT YOU CAN SEE WHY THAT APPEALED TO TERRY.
HE KEPT LOOKING, JUS LIKE YOU NEED TO LOOK FO REWIRE.

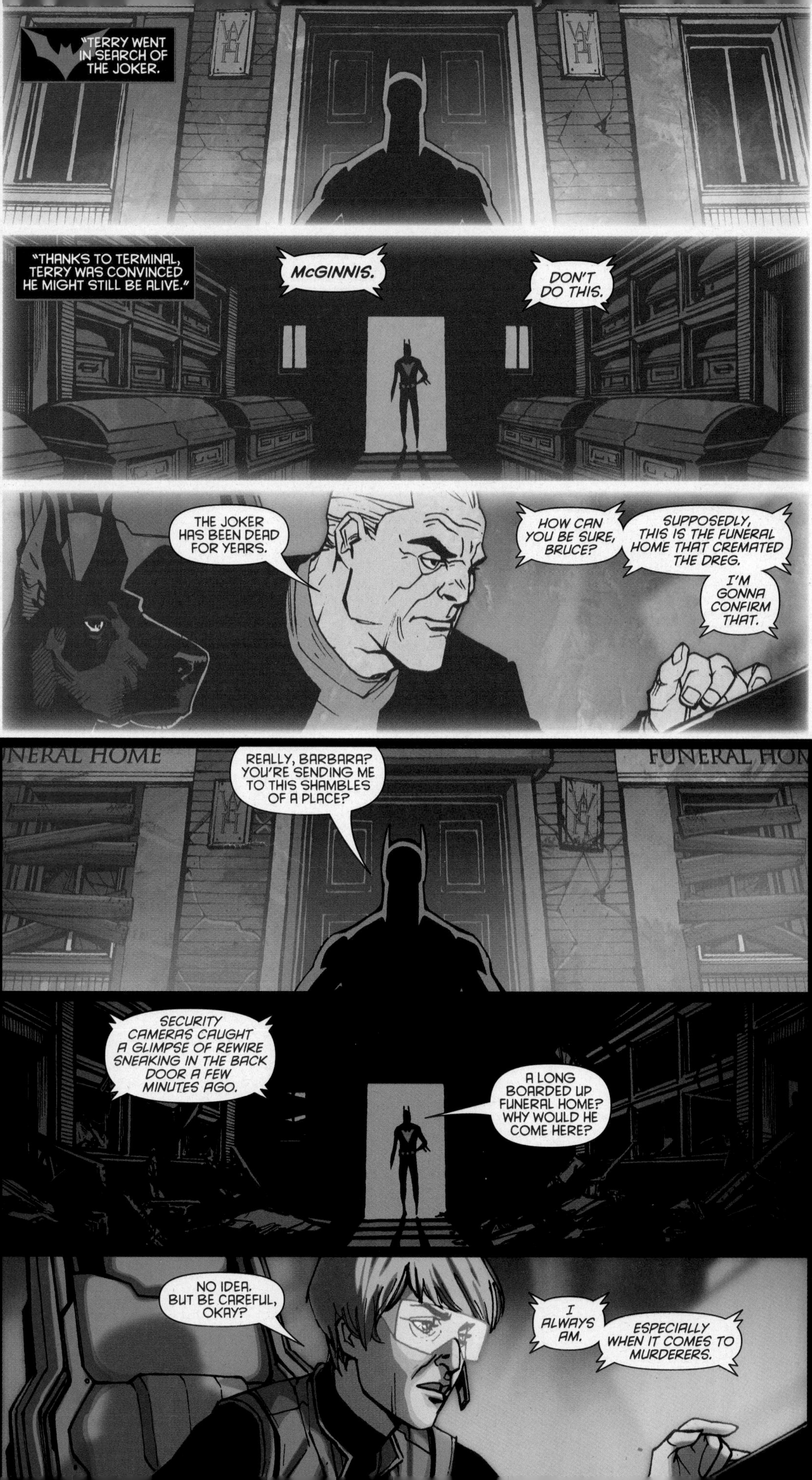
"TERRY WENT IN SEARCH OF THE JOKER.
"THANKS TO TERMINAL, TERRY WAS CONVINCED HE MIGHT STILL BE ALIVE."
McGINNIS.
DON'T DO THIS.
THE JOKER HAS BEEN DEAD FOR YEARS.
HOW CAN YOU BE SURE, BRUCE?
SUPPOSEDLY, THIS IS THE FUNERAL HOME THAT CREMATED THE DREG.
I'M GONNA CONFIRM THAT.
FUNERAL HOME
REALLY, BARBARA? YOU'RE SENDING ME TO THIS SHAMBLES OF A PLACE?
FUNERAL HOM
SECURITY CAMERAS CAUGHT A GLIMPSE OF REWIRE SNEAKING IN THE BACK DOOR A FEW MINUTES AGO.
A LONG BOARDED UP FUNERAL HOME? WHY WOULD HE COME HERE?
NO IDEA. BUT BE CAREFUL, OKAY?
I ALWAYS AM.
ESPECIALLY WHEN IT COMES TO MURDERERS.

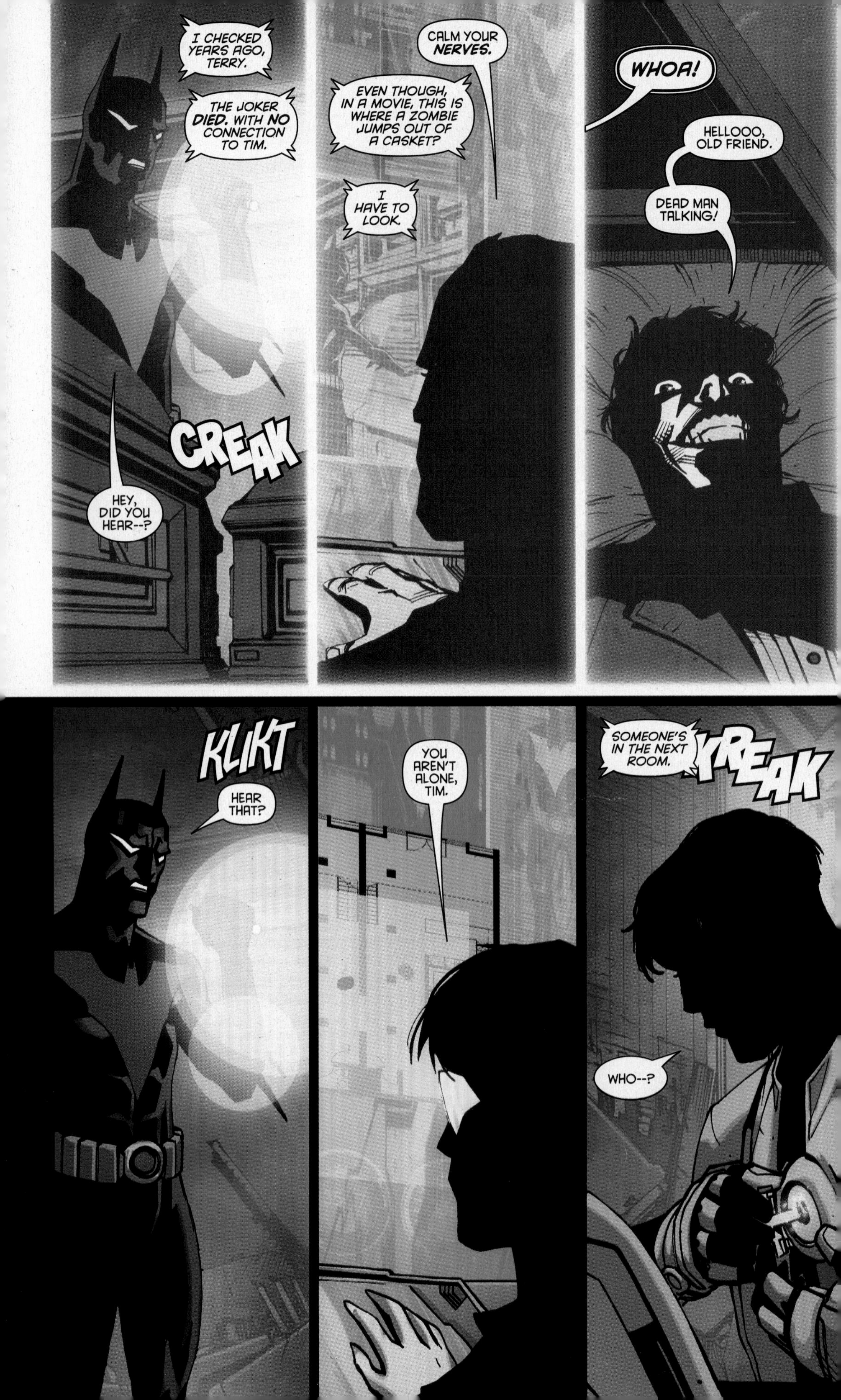
I CHECKED YEARS AGO, TERRY.
THE JOKER DIED. WITH NO CONNECTION TO TIM.
HEY, DID YOU HEAR--?
CREAK
CALM YOUR NERVES.
EVEN THOUGH, IN A MOVIE, THIS IS WHERE A ZOMBIE JUMPS OUT OF A CASKET?
I HAVE TO LOOK.
WHOA!
HELLOOO, OLD FRIEND.
DEAD MAN TALKING!
KLIKT
HEAR THAT?
YOU AREN'T ALONE, TIM.
SOMEONE'S IN THE NEXT ROOM.
KREAK
WHO--?

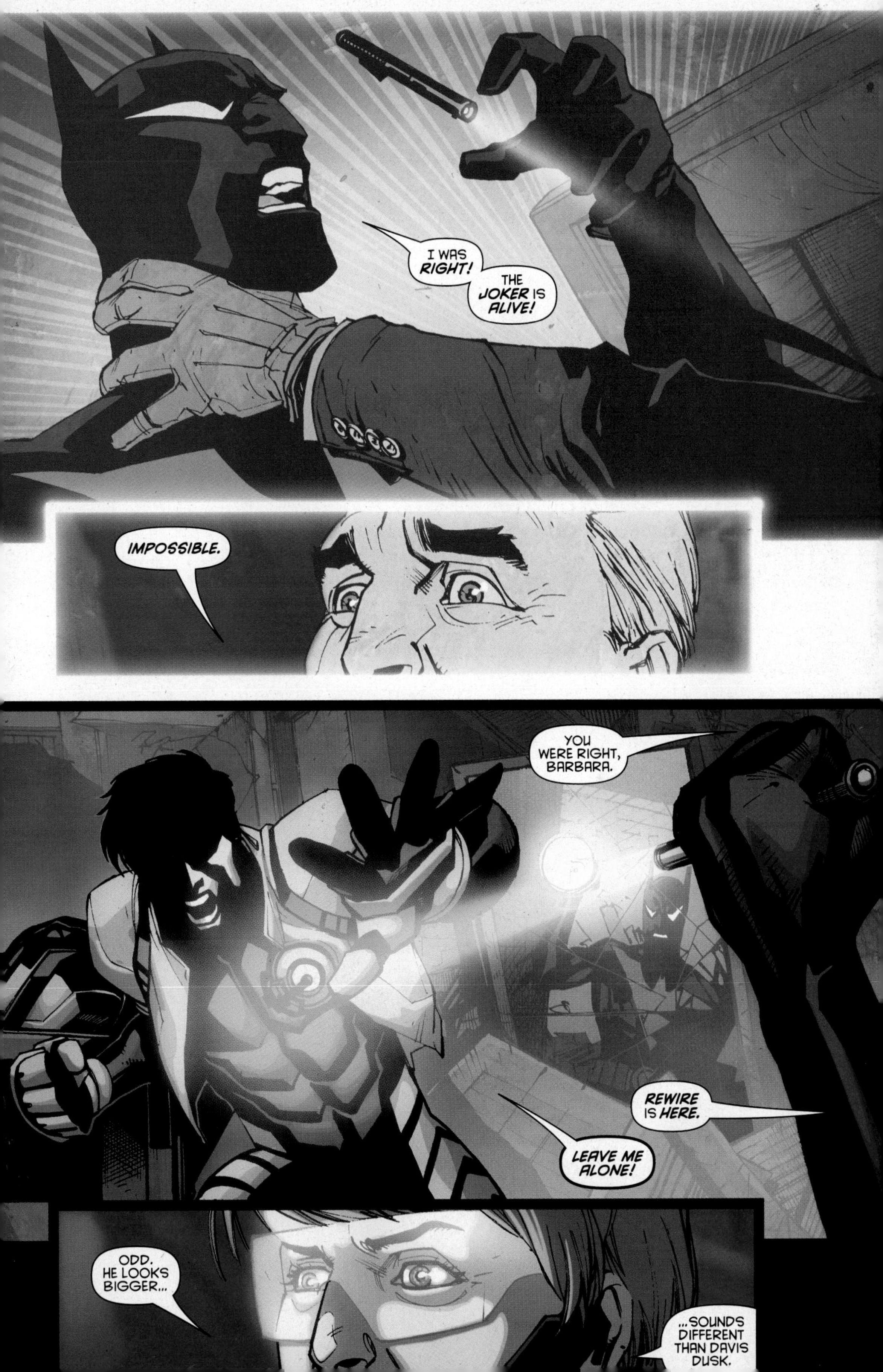
I WAS RIGHT!
THE JOKER IS ALIVE!
IMPOSSIBLE.
YOU WERE RIGHT, BARBARA.
REWIRE IS HERE.
LEAVE ME ALONE!
ODD. HE LOOKS BIGGER...
...SOUNDS DIFFERENT THAN DAVIS DUSK.

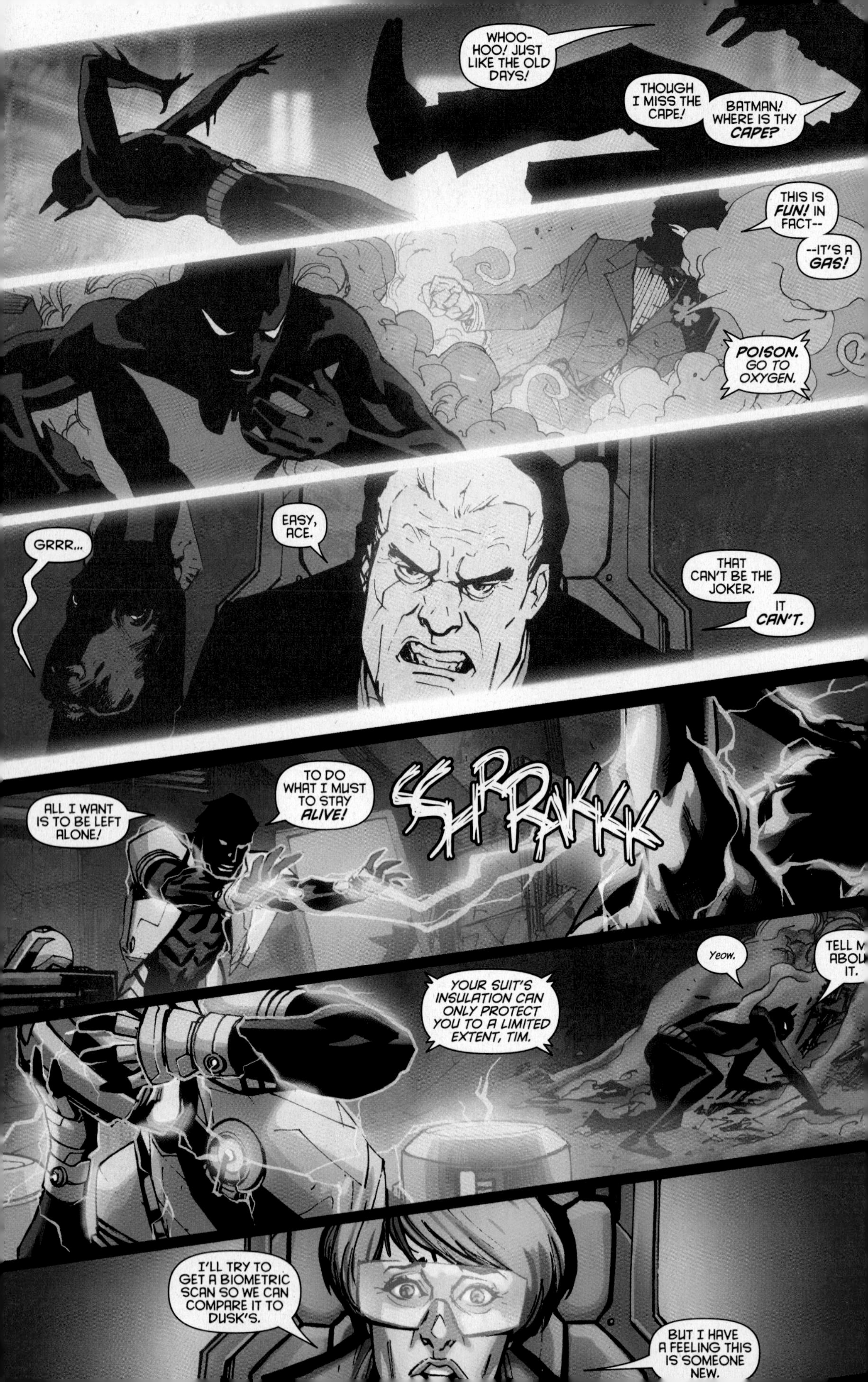
WHOO-HOO! JUST LIKE THE OLD DAYS!
THOUGH I MISS THE CAPE!
BATMAN! WHERE IS THY CAPE?
THIS IS FUN! IN FACT--
--IT'S A GAS!
POISON. GO TO OXYGEN.
GRRR...
EASY, ACE.
THAT CAN'T BE THE JOKER.
IT CAN'T.
ALL I WANT IS TO BE LEFT ALONE!
TO DO WHAT I MUST TO STAY ALIVE!
SHRAKKK
Yeow.
TELL M ABOU IT.
YOUR SUIT'S INSULATION CAN ONLY PROTECT YOU TO A LIMITED EXTENT, TIM.
I'LL TRY TO GET A BIOMETRIC SCAN SO WE CAN COMPARE IT TO DUSK'S.
BUT I HAVE A FEELING THIS IS SOMEONE NEW.

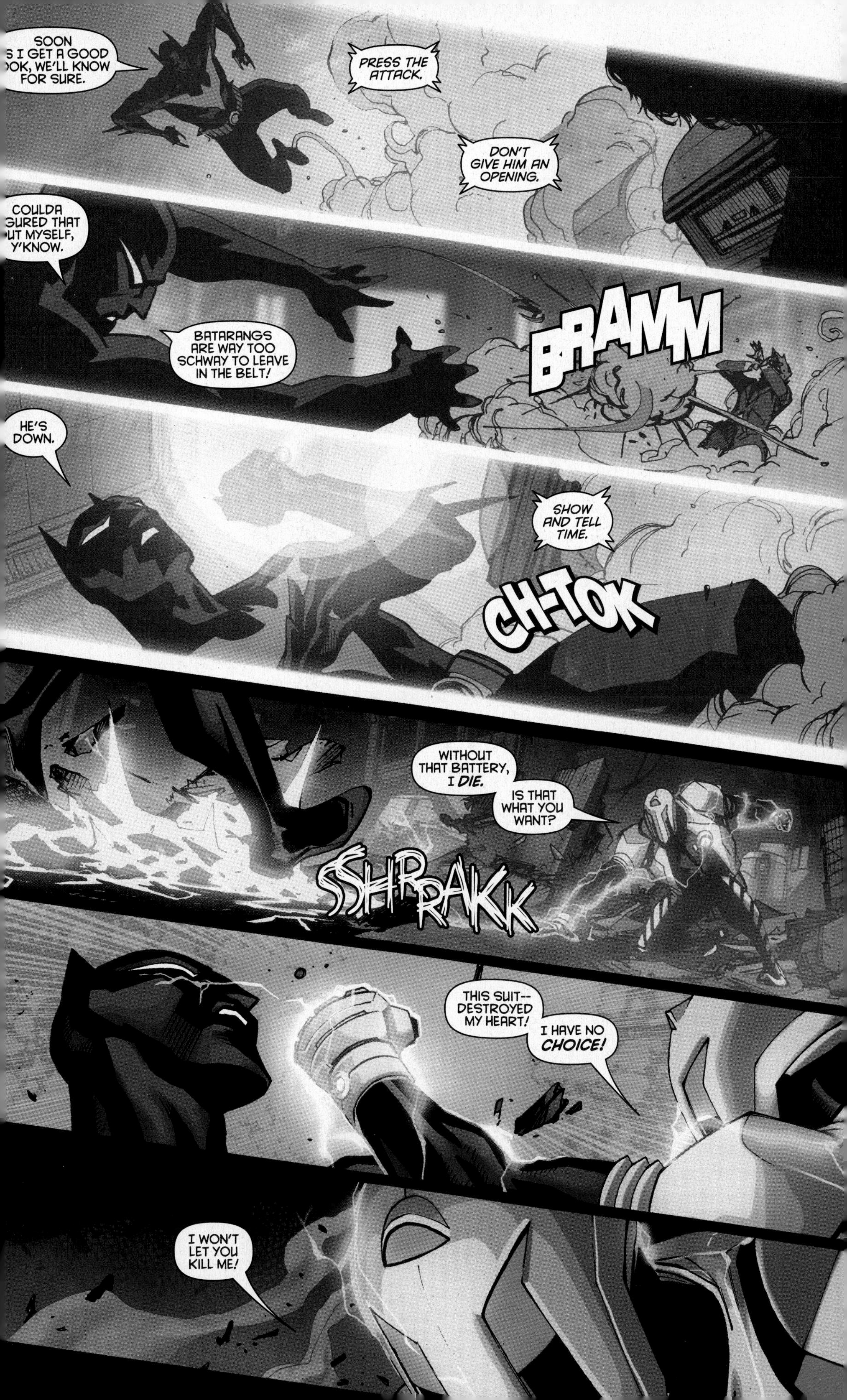

SOON
S I GET A GOOD
OK, WE'LL KNOW
FOR SURE.
PRESS THE ATTACK.
DON'T GIVE HIM AN OPENING.
COULDA
GURED THAT
UT MYSELF,
Y'KNOW.
BATARANGS ARE WAY TOO SCHWAY TO LEAVE IN THE BELT!
BRAMM
HE'S DOWN.
SHOW AND TELL TIME.
CH-TOK
WITHOUT THAT BATTERY, I DIE.
IS THAT WHAT YOU WANT?
SSHRRAKK
THIS SUIT-- DESTROYED MY HEART!
I HAVE NO CHOICE!
I WON'T LET YOU KILL ME!

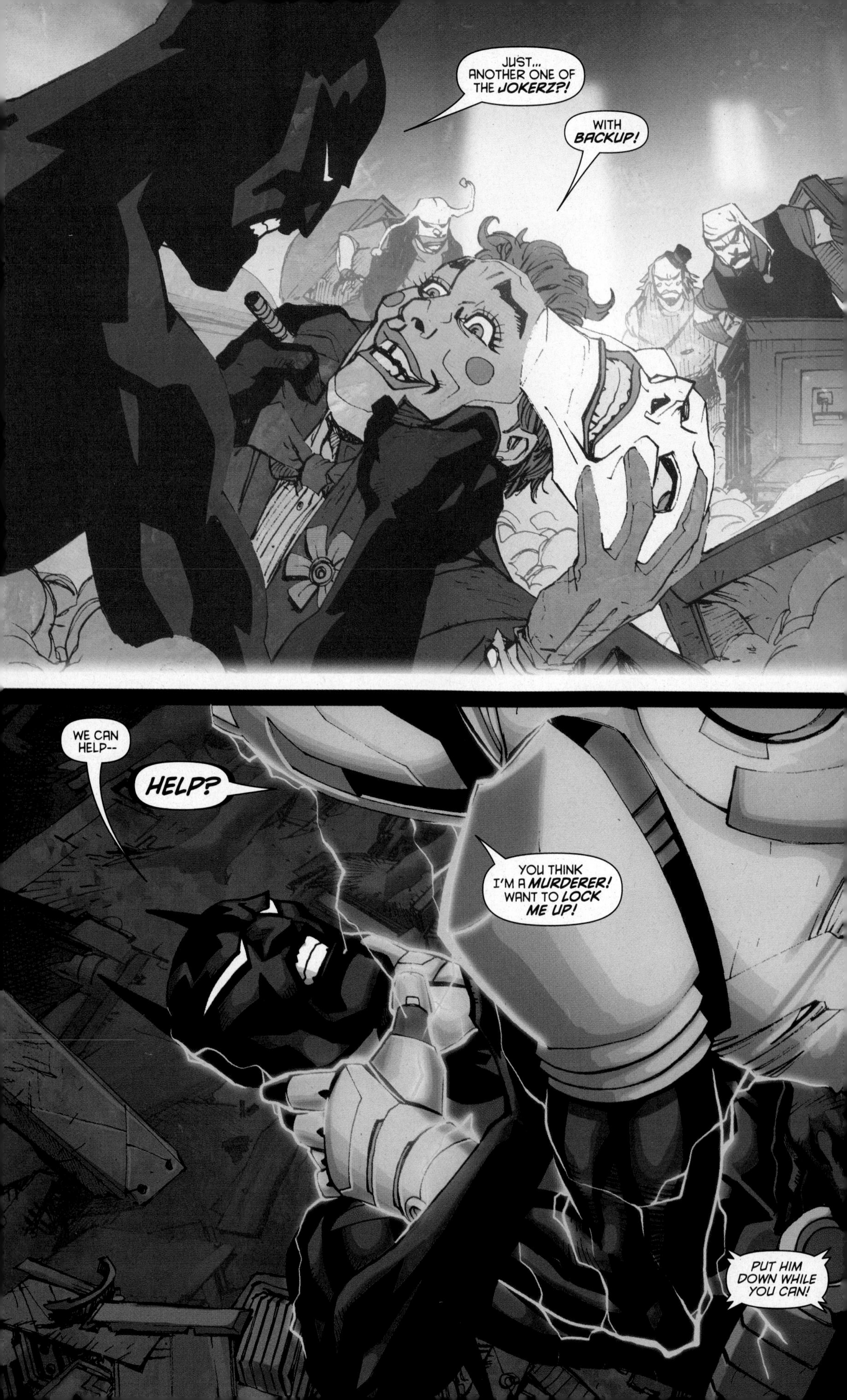
JUST... ANOTHER ONE OF THE JOKERZ?!
WITH BACKUP!
WE CAN HELP--
HELP?
YOU THINK I'M A MURDERER! WANT TO LOCK ME UP!
PUT HIM DOWN WHILE YOU CAN!

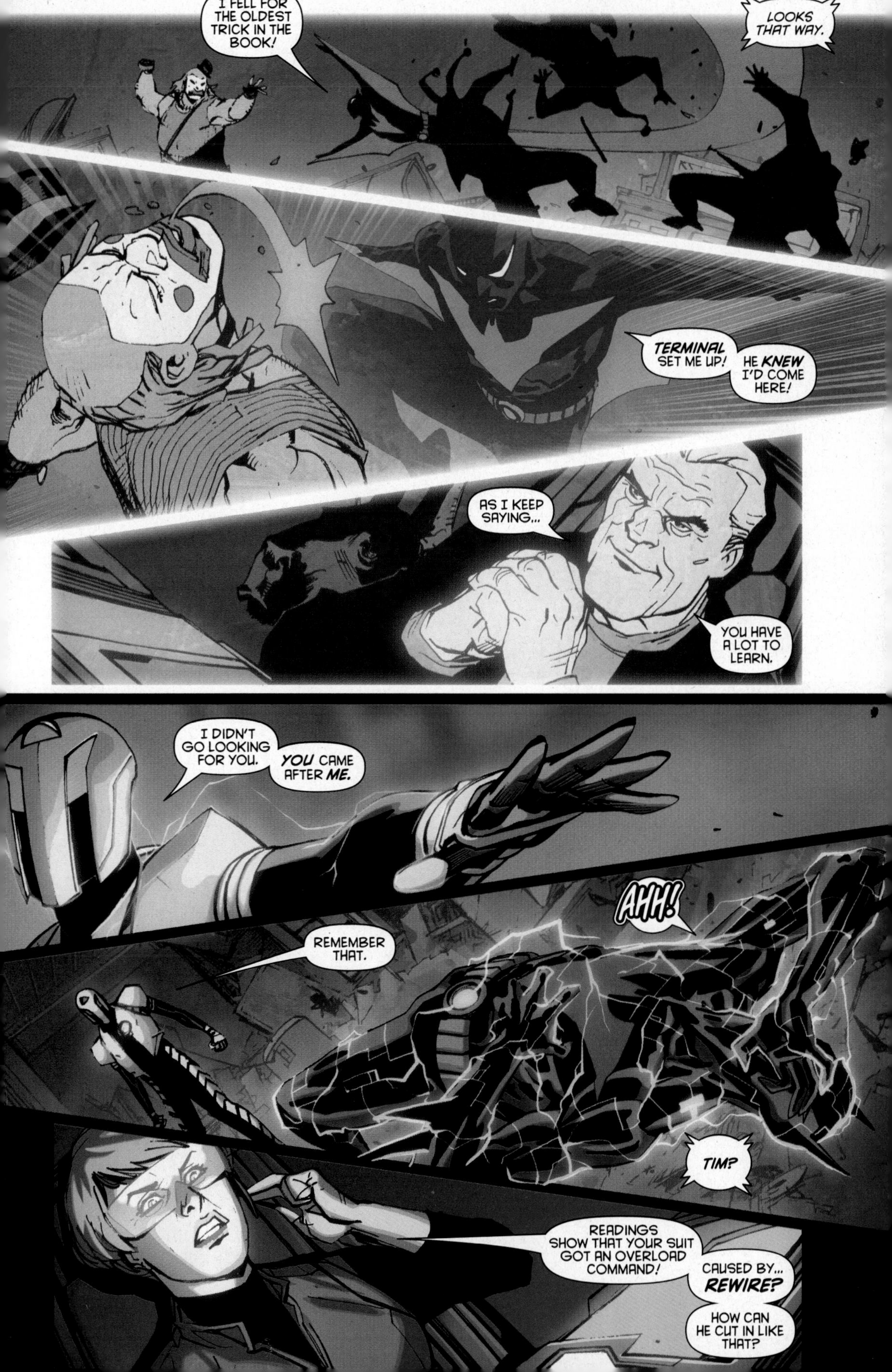
I FELL FOR THE OLDEST TRICK IN THE BOOK!
LOOKS THAT WAY.
TERMINAL SET ME UP!
HE KNEW I'D COME HERE!
AS I KEEP SAYING...
YOU HAVE A LOT TO LEARN.
I DIDN'T GO LOOKING FOR YOU. YOU CAME AFTER ME.
AHH!
REMEMBER THAT.
TIM?
READINGS SHOW THAT YOUR SUIT GOT AN OVERLOAD COMMAND!
CAUSED BY... REWIRE?
HOW CAN HE CUT IN LIKE THAT?

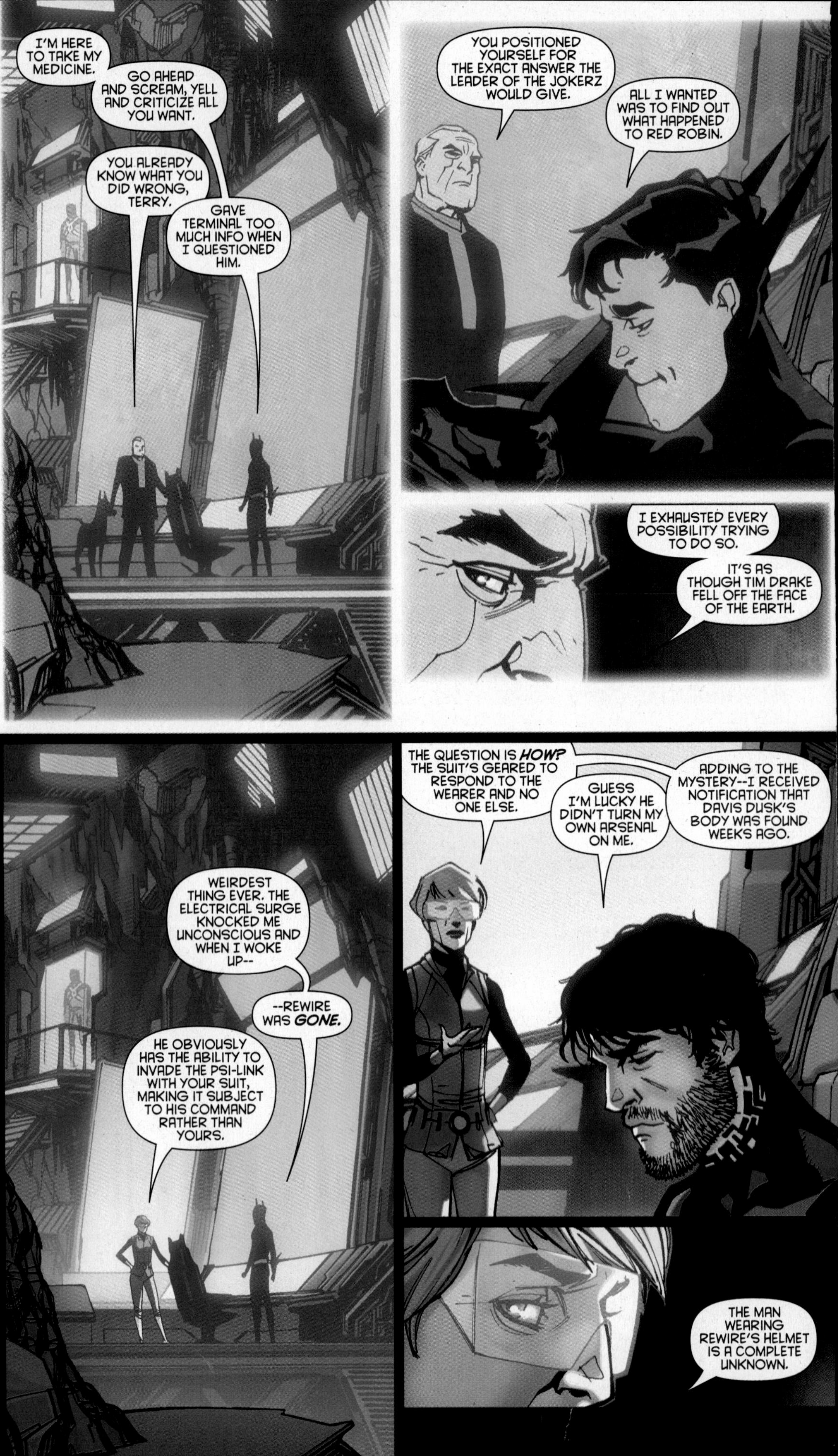
I'M HERE TO TAKE MY MEDICINE.
GO AHEAD AND SCREAM, YELL AND CRITICIZE ALL YOU WANT.
YOU ALREADY KNOW WHAT YOU DID WRONG, TERRY.
GAVE TERMINAL TOO MUCH INFO WHEN I QUESTIONED HIM.
YOU POSITIONED YOURSELF FOR THE EXACT ANSWER THE LEADER OF THE JOKERZ WOULD GIVE.
ALL I WANTED WAS TO FIND OUT WHAT HAPPENED TO RED ROBIN.
I EXHAUSTED EVERY POSSIBILITY TRYING TO DO SO.
IT'S AS THOUGH TIM DRAKE FELL OFF THE FACE OF THE EARTH.
WEIRDEST THING EVER. THE ELECTRICAL SURGE KNOCKED ME UNCONSCIOUS AND WHEN I WOKE UP--
--REWIRE WAS **GONE.**
HE OBVIOUSLY HAS THE ABILITY TO INVADE THE PSI-LINK WITH YOUR SUIT, MAKING IT SUBJECT TO HIS COMMAND RATHER THAN YOURS.
THE QUESTION IS ***HOW?*** THE SUIT'S GEARED TO RESPOND TO THE WEARER AND NO ONE ELSE.
GUESS I'M LUCKY HE DIDN'T TURN MY OWN ARSENAL ON ME.
ADDING TO THE MYSTERY--I RECEIVED NOTIFICATION THAT DAVIS DUSK'S BODY WAS FOUND WEEKS AGO.
THE MAN WEARING REWIRE'S HELMET IS A COMPLETE UNKNOWN.

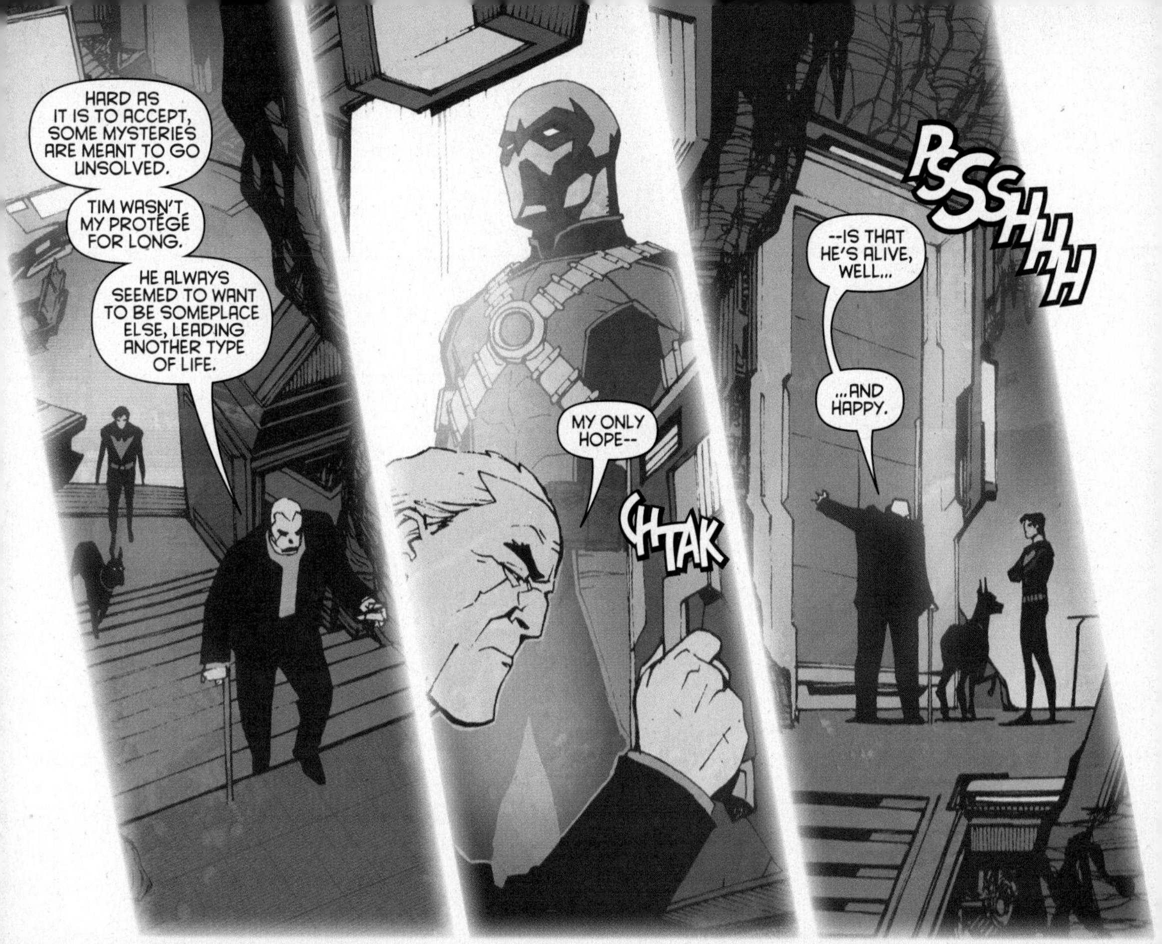
HARD AS IT IS TO ACCEPT, SOME MYSTERIES ARE MEANT TO GO UNSOLVED.
TIM WASN'T MY PROTÉGÉ FOR LONG.
HE ALWAYS SEEMED TO WANT TO BE SOMEPLACE ELSE, LEADING ANOTHER TYPE OF LIFE.
MY ONLY HOPE--
CHTAK
PSSSHHHH
--IS THAT HE'S ALIVE, WELL...
...AND HAPPY.

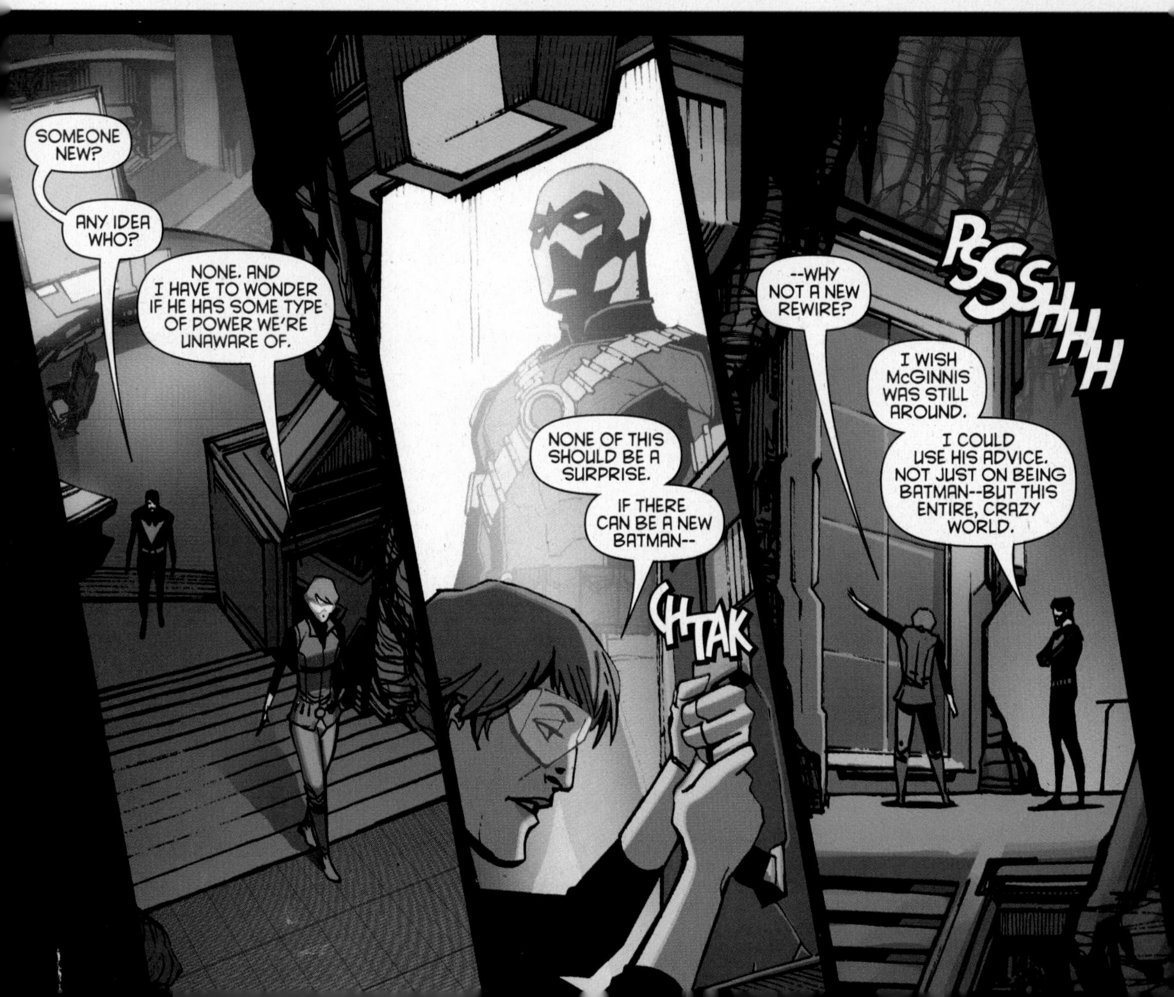
SOMEONE NEW?
ANY IDEA WHO?
NONE. AND I HAVE TO WONDER IF HE HAS SOME TYPE OF POWER WE'RE UNAWARE OF.
NONE OF THIS SHOULD BE A SURPRISE.
IF THERE CAN BE A NEW BATMAN--
CHTAK
PSSSHHHH
--WHY NOT A NEW REWIRE?
I WISH McGINNIS WAS STILL AROUND.
I COULD USE HIS ADVICE. NOT JUST ON BEING BATMAN--BUT THIS ENTIRE, CRAZY WORLD.

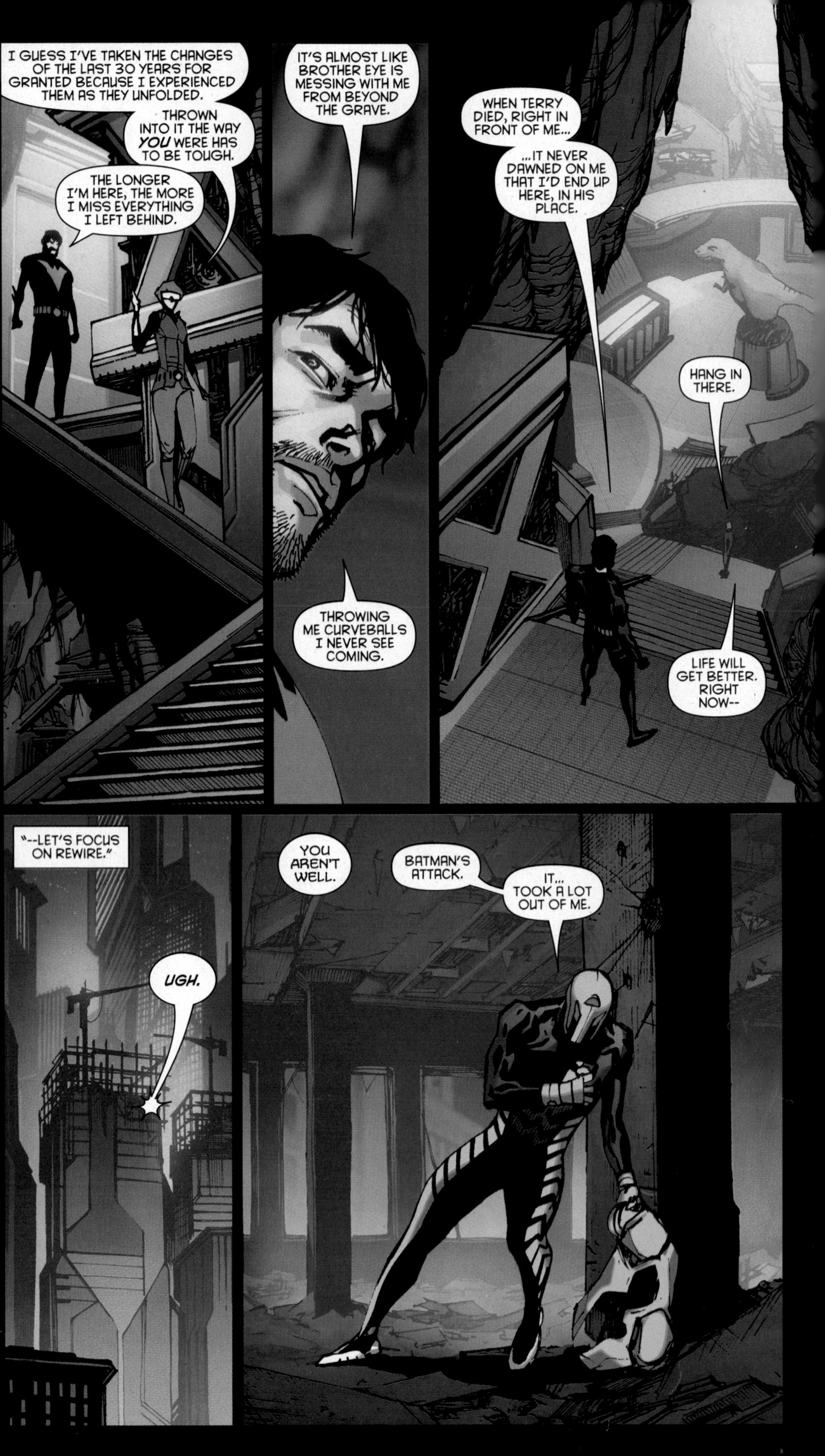
I GUESS I'VE TAKEN THE CHANGES OF THE LAST 30 YEARS FOR GRANTED BECAUSE I EXPERIENCED THEM AS THEY UNFOLDED.
THROWN INTO IT THE WAY *YOU* WERE HAS TO BE TOUGH.
THE LONGER I'M HERE, THE MORE I MISS EVERYTHING I LEFT BEHIND.
IT'S ALMOST LIKE BROTHER EYE IS MESSING WITH ME FROM BEYOND THE GRAVE.
THROWING ME CURVEBALLS I NEVER SEE COMING.
WHEN TERRY DIED, RIGHT IN FRONT OF ME...
...IT NEVER DAWNED ON ME THAT I'D END UP HERE, IN HIS PLACE.
HANG IN THERE.
LIFE WILL GET BETTER. RIGHT NOW--
"--LET'S FOCUS ON REWIRE."
UGH.
YOU AREN'T WELL.
BATMAN'S ATTACK.
IT... TOOK A LOT OUT OF ME.

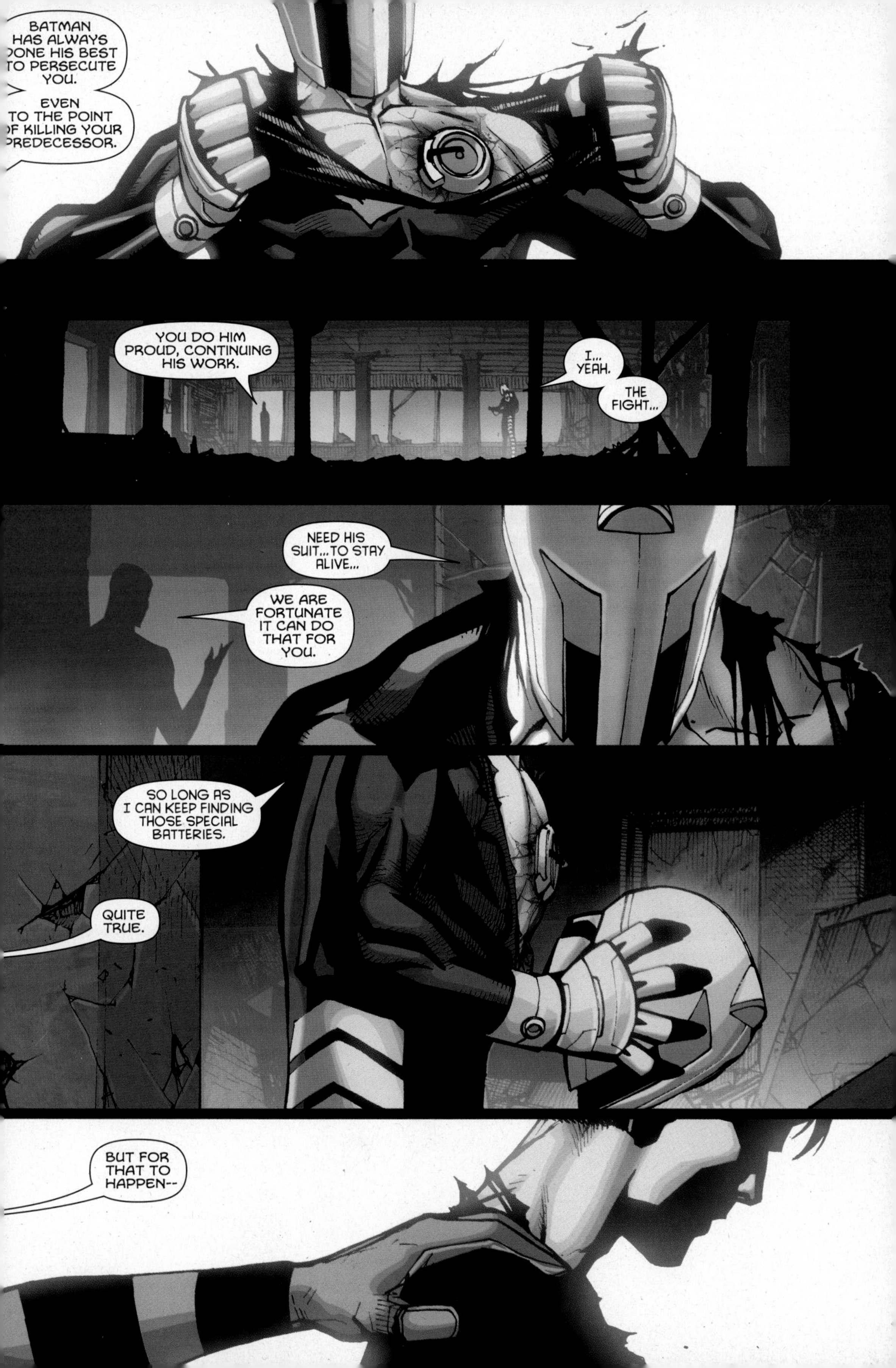
BATMAN HAS ALWAYS DONE HIS BEST TO PERSECUTE YOU.
EVEN TO THE POINT OF KILLING YOUR PREDECESSOR.
YOU DO HIM PROUD, CONTINUING HIS WORK.
I... YEAH.
THE FIGHT...
NEED HIS SUIT...TO STAY ALIVE...
WE ARE FORTUNATE IT CAN DO THAT FOR YOU.
SO LONG AS I CAN KEEP FINDING THOSE SPECIAL BATTERIES.
QUITE TRUE.
BUT FOR THAT TO HAPPEN--

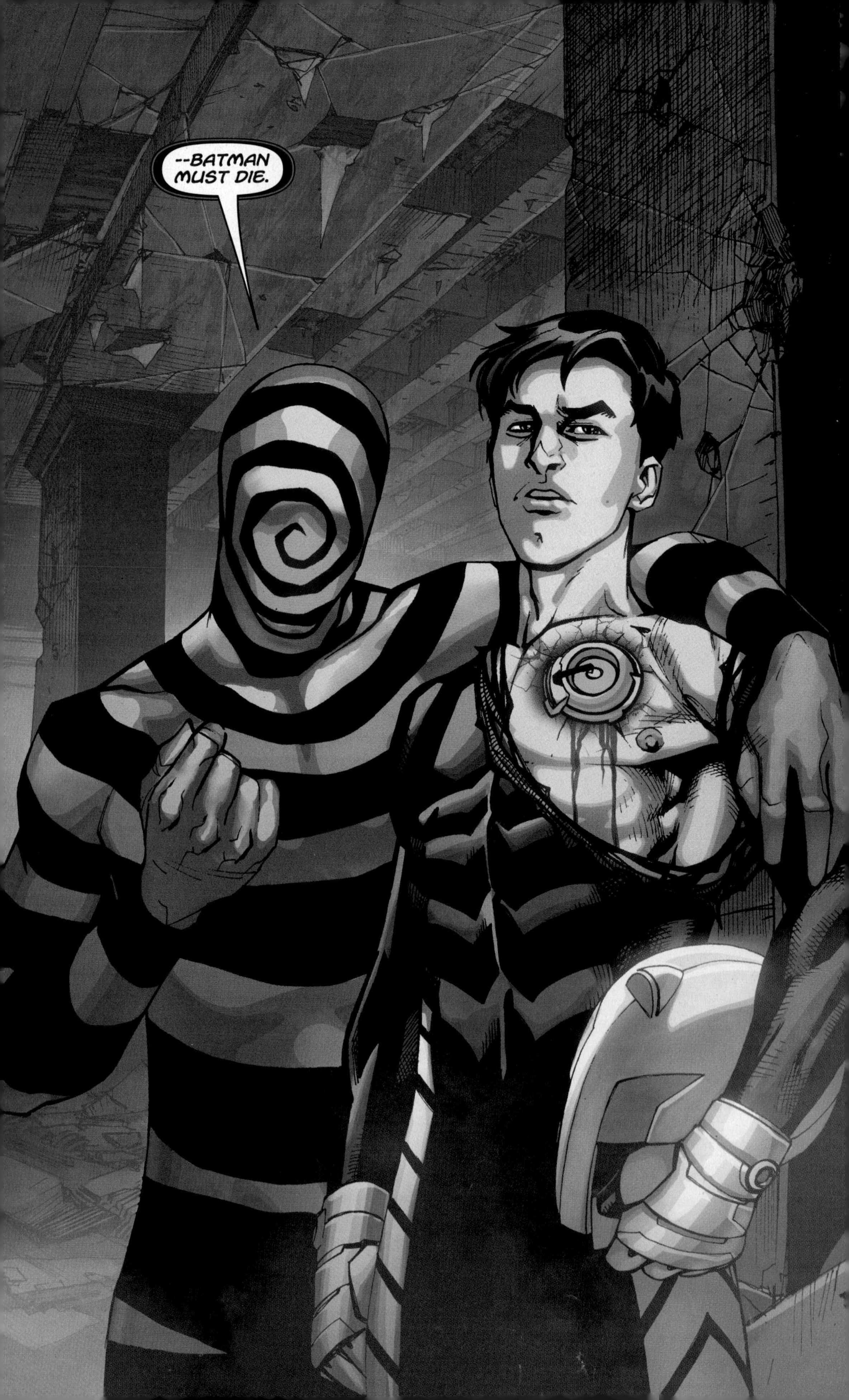
--BATMAN MUST DIE.

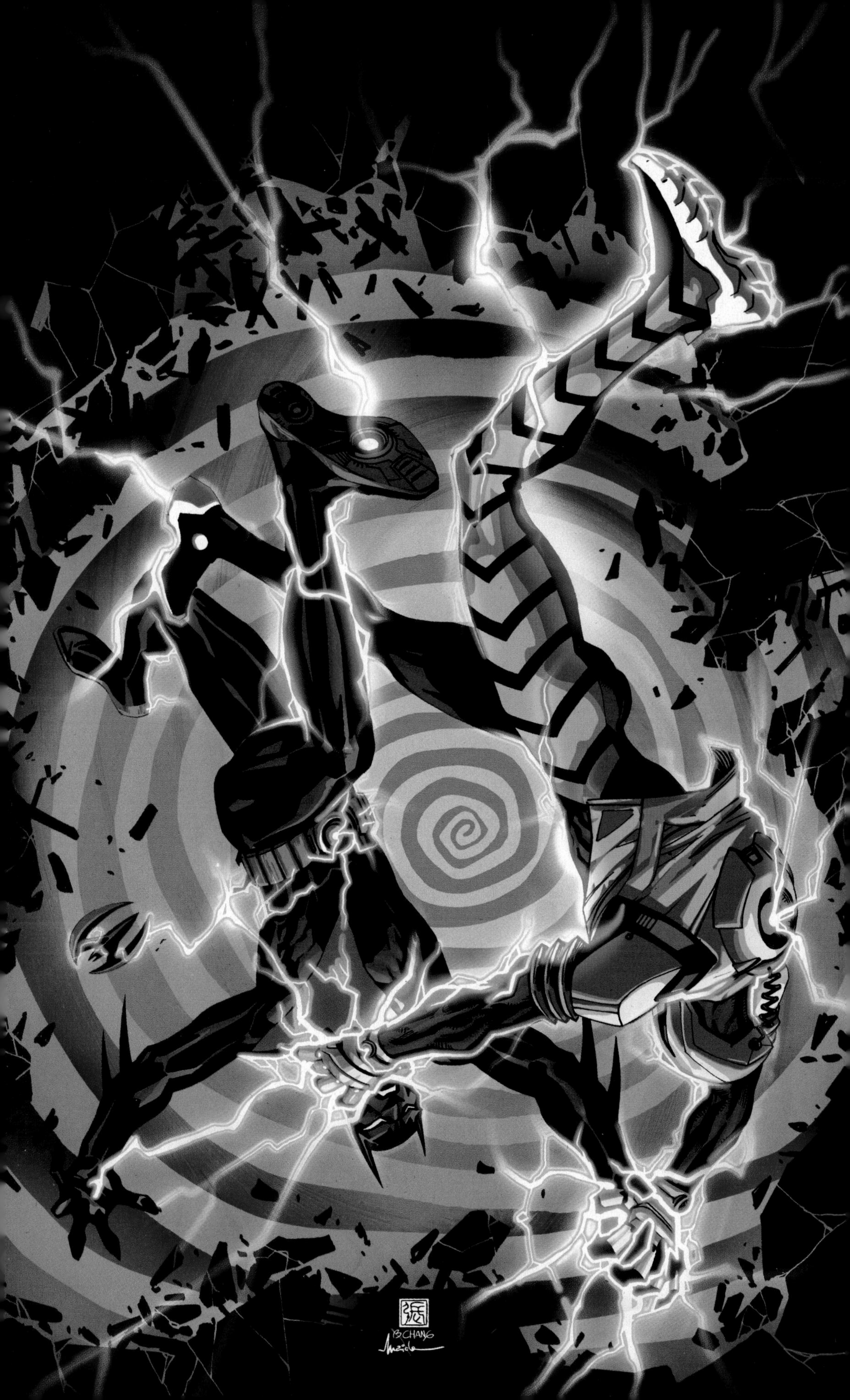
B CHANG

BERNARD CHANG artist   MARCELO MAIOLO colorist   BERNARD CHANG & MARCELO MAIOLO cover

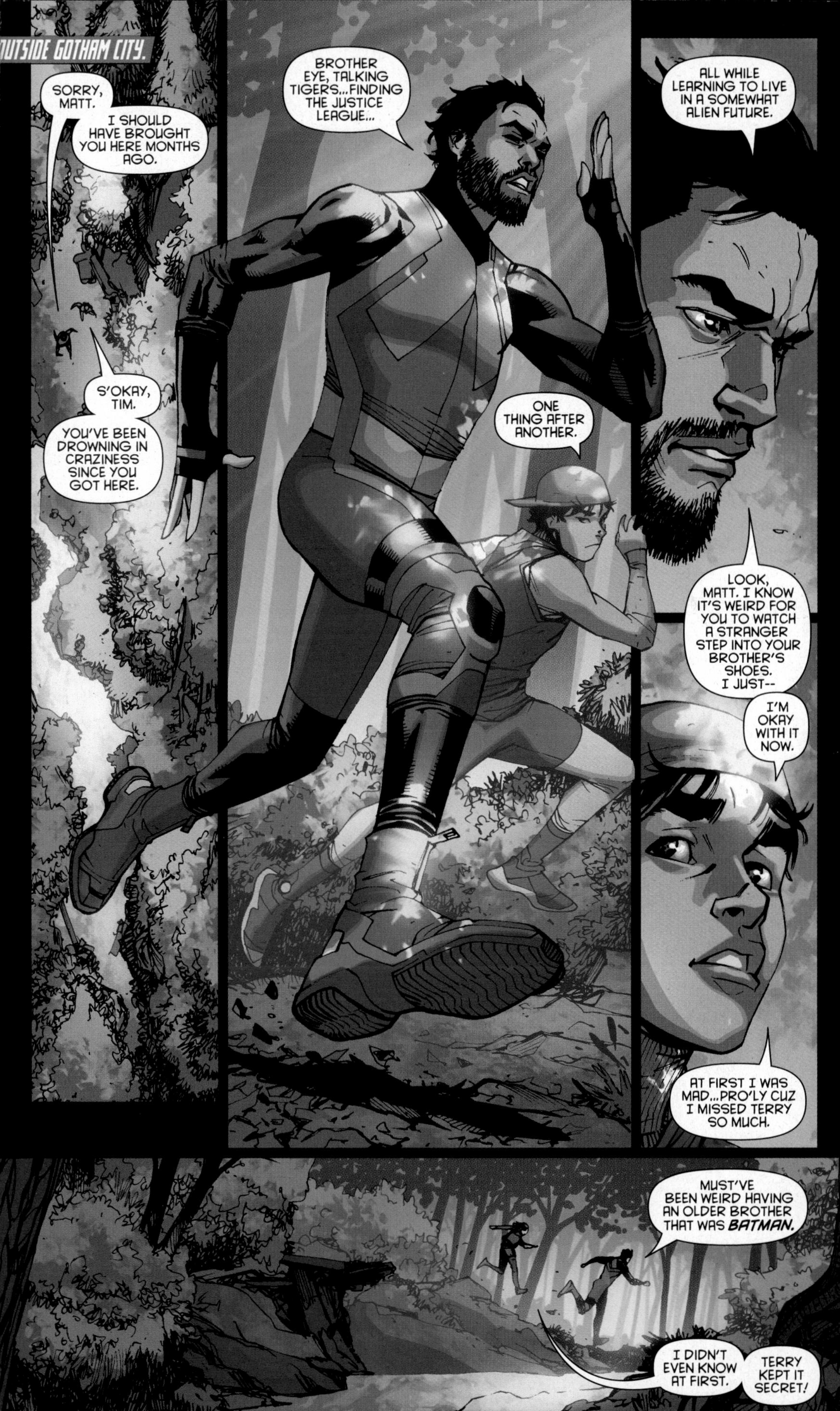
OUTSIDE GOTHAM CITY.
SORRY, MATT.
I SHOULD HAVE BROUGHT YOU HERE MONTHS AGO.
S'OKAY, TIM.
YOU'VE BEEN DROWNING IN CRAZINESS SINCE YOU GOT HERE.
BROTHER EYE, TALKING TIGERS...FINDING THE JUSTICE LEAGUE...
ONE THING AFTER ANOTHER.
ALL WHILE LEARNING TO LIVE IN A SOMEWHAT ALIEN FUTURE.
LOOK, MATT. I KNOW IT'S WEIRD FOR YOU TO WATCH A STRANGER STEP INTO YOUR BROTHER'S SHOES. I JUST--
I'M OKAY WITH IT NOW.
AT FIRST I WAS MAD...PRO'LY CUZ I MISSED TERRY SO MUCH.
MUST'VE BEEN WEIRD HAVING AN OLDER BROTHER THAT WAS BATMAN.
I DIDN'T EVEN KNOW AT FIRST.
TERRY KEPT IT SECRET!

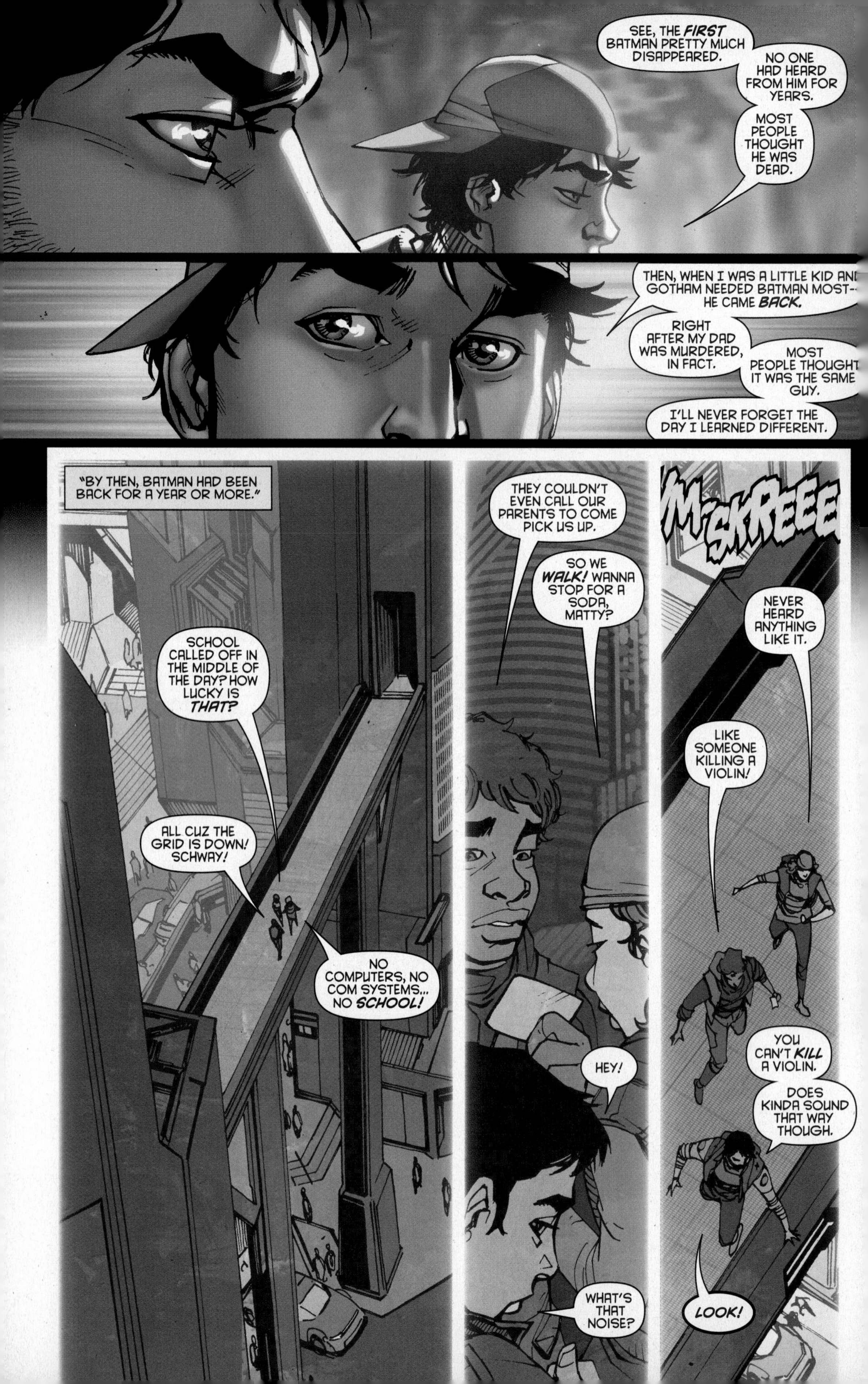
SEE, THE FIRST BATMAN PRETTY MUCH DISAPPEARED.
NO ONE HAD HEARD FROM HIM FOR YEARS.
MOST PEOPLE THOUGHT HE WAS DEAD.
THEN, WHEN I WAS A LITTLE KID AND GOTHAM NEEDED BATMAN MOST-- HE CAME BACK.
RIGHT AFTER MY DAD WAS MURDERED, IN FACT.
MOST PEOPLE THOUGHT IT WAS THE SAME GUY.
I'LL NEVER FORGET THE DAY I LEARNED DIFFERENT.
"BY THEN, BATMAN HAD BEEN BACK FOR A YEAR OR MORE."
SCHOOL CALLED OFF IN THE MIDDLE OF THE DAY? HOW LUCKY IS THAT?
ALL CUZ THE GRID IS DOWN! SCHWAY!
NO COMPUTERS, NO COM SYSTEMS... NO SCHOOL!
THEY COULDN'T EVEN CALL OUR PARENTS TO COME PICK US UP.
SO WE WALK! WANNA STOP FOR A SODA, MATTY?
HEY!
WHAT'S THAT NOISE?
M-SKREEE
NEVER HEARD ANYTHING LIKE IT.
LIKE SOMEONE KILLING A VIOLIN!
YOU CAN'T KILL A VIOLIN.
DOES KINDA SOUND THAT WAY THOUGH.
LOOK!

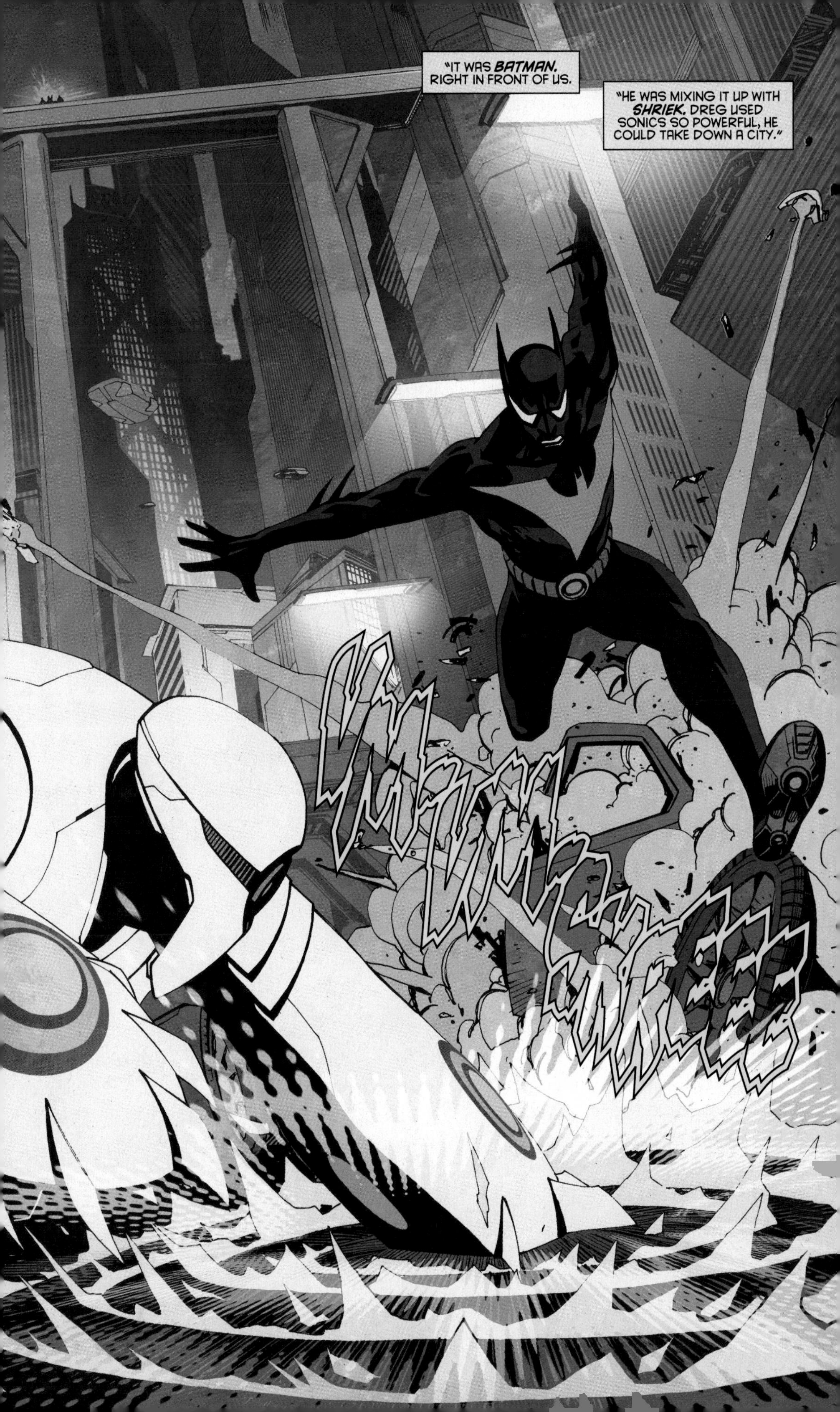
"IT WAS **BATMAN.** RIGHT IN FRONT OF US.
"HE WAS MIXING IT UP WITH **SHRIEK.** DREG USED SONICS SO POWERFUL, HE COULD TAKE DOWN A CITY."

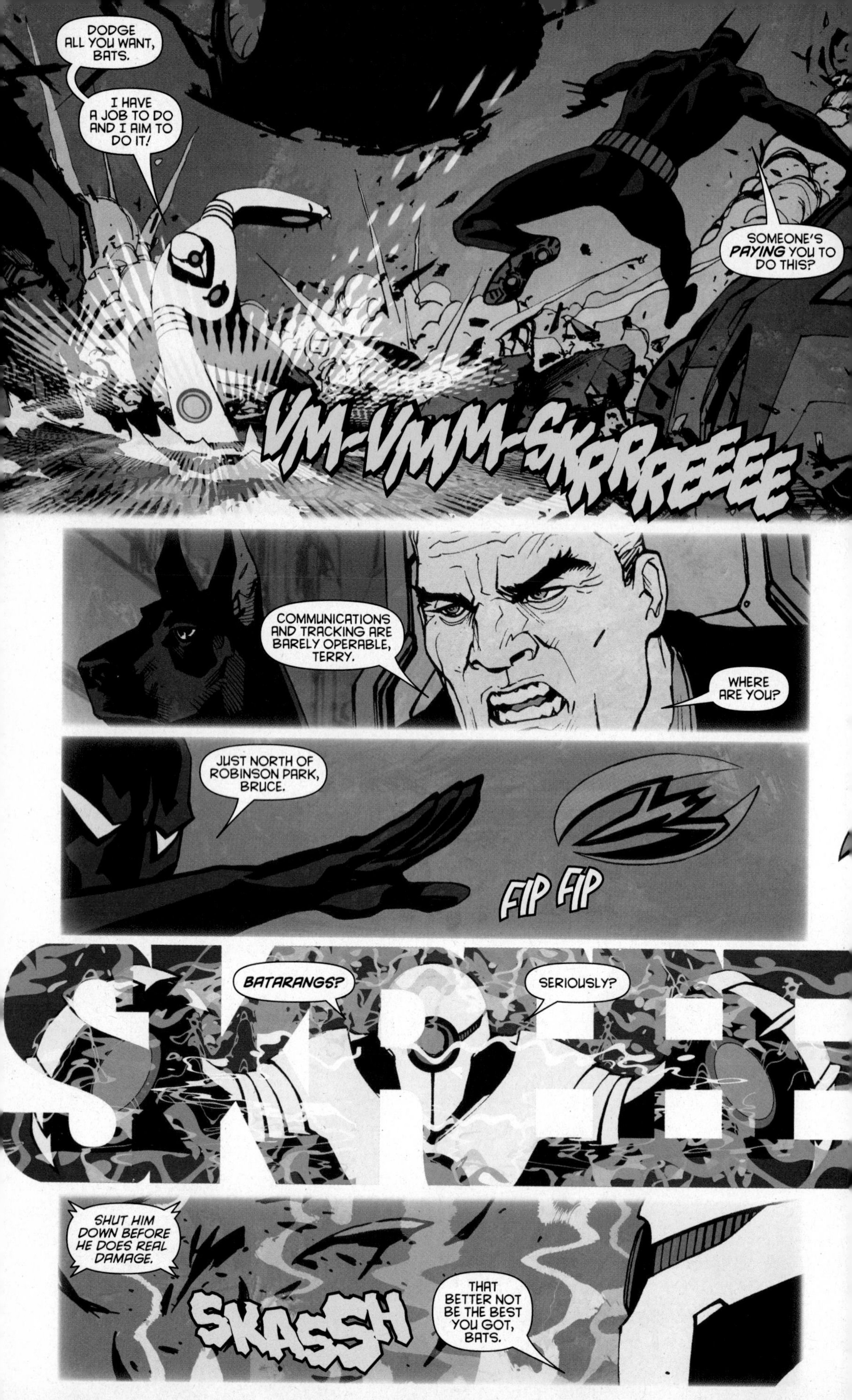
DODGE ALL YOU WANT, BATS.
I HAVE A JOB TO DO AND I AIM TO DO IT!
SOMEONE'S *PAYING* YOU TO DO THIS?
VM-VMM-SKRRREEEEE
COMMUNICATIONS AND TRACKING ARE BARELY OPERABLE, TERRY.
WHERE ARE YOU?
JUST NORTH OF ROBINSON PARK, BRUCE.
FIP FIP
BATARANGS?
SERIOUSLY?
SHUT HIM DOWN BEFORE HE DOES REAL DAMAGE.
SKASSH
THAT BETTER NOT BE THE BEST YOU GOT, BATS.

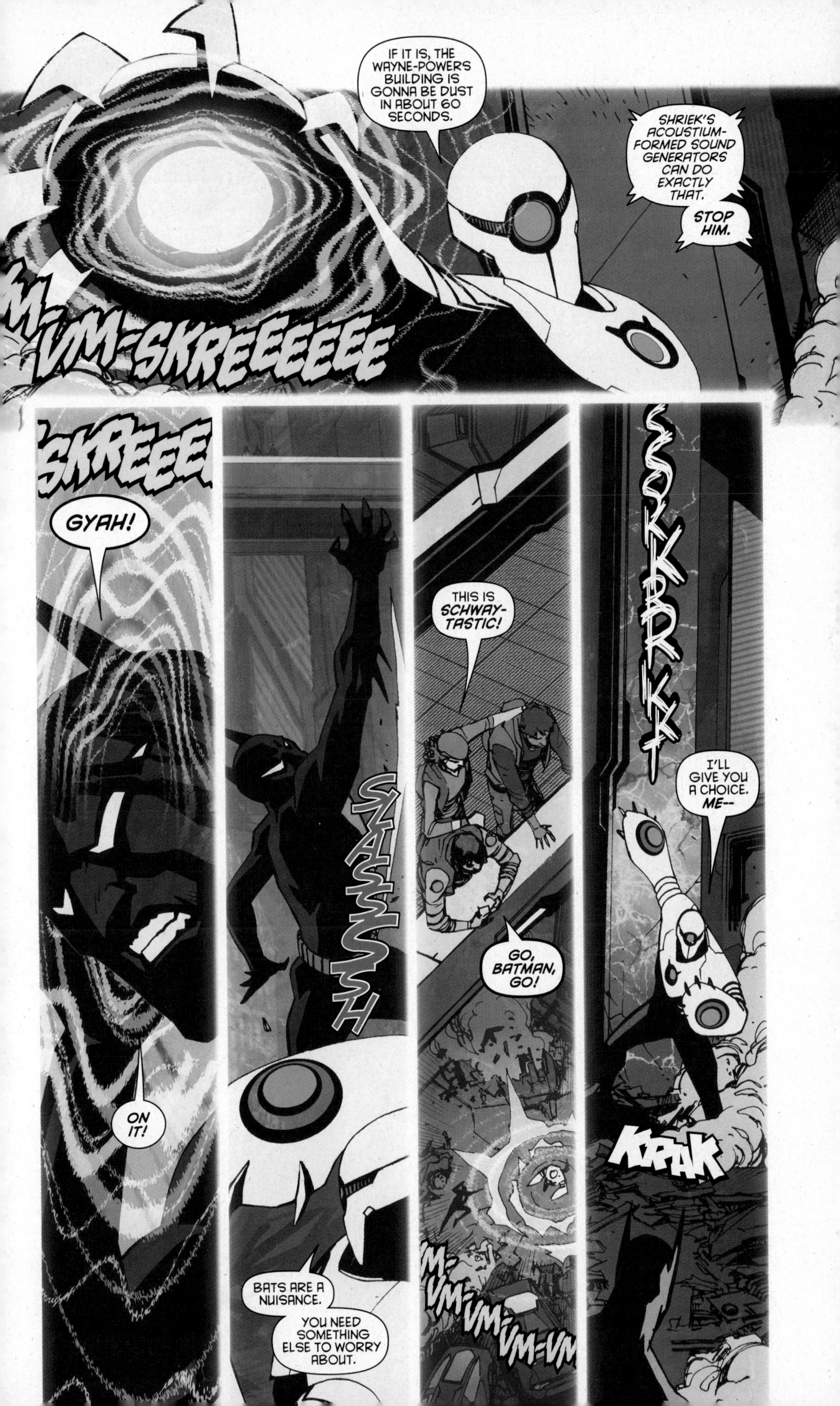

IF IT IS, THE WAYNE-POWERS BUILDING IS GONNA BE DUST IN ABOUT 60 SECONDS.
SHRIEK'S ACOUSTIUM-FORMED SOUND GENERATORS CAN DO EXACTLY THAT.
STOP HIM.
VM-VM-SKREEEEEEE
SKREEEE
GYAH!
ON IT!
SLASSSSH
THIS IS SCHWAY-TASTIC!
GO, BATMAN, GO!
BATS ARE A NUISANCE.
YOU NEED SOMETHING ELSE TO WORRY ABOUT.
VM-VM-VM-VM-VM
SKKRKKKT
I'LL GIVE YOU A CHOICE. ME--
KRAK

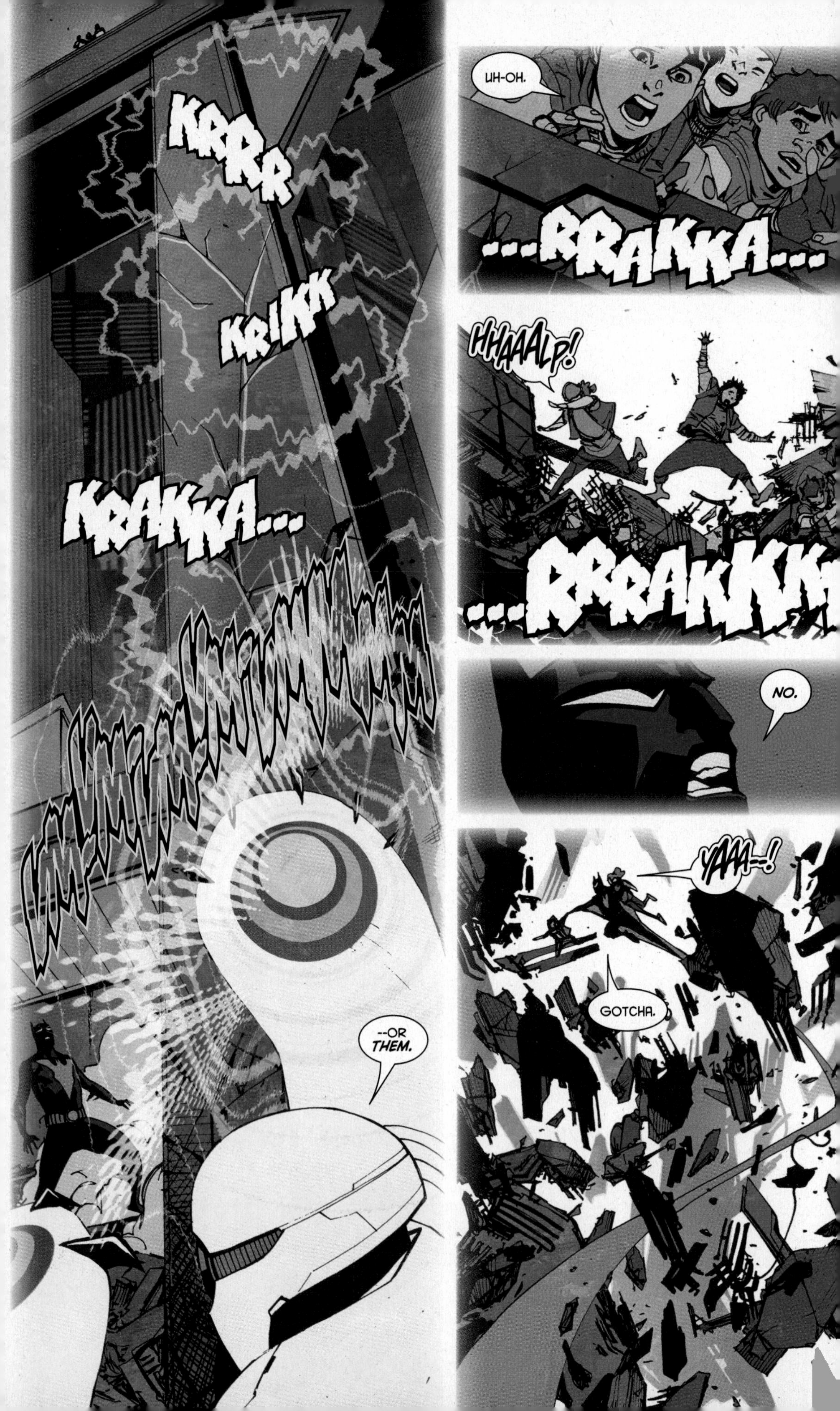
KRRRR
KRIKK
KRAKKA...
--OR THEM.
UH-OH.
...RRAKKA...
HHAAALP!
...RRRAKKK
NO.
YAAA--!
GOTCHA.

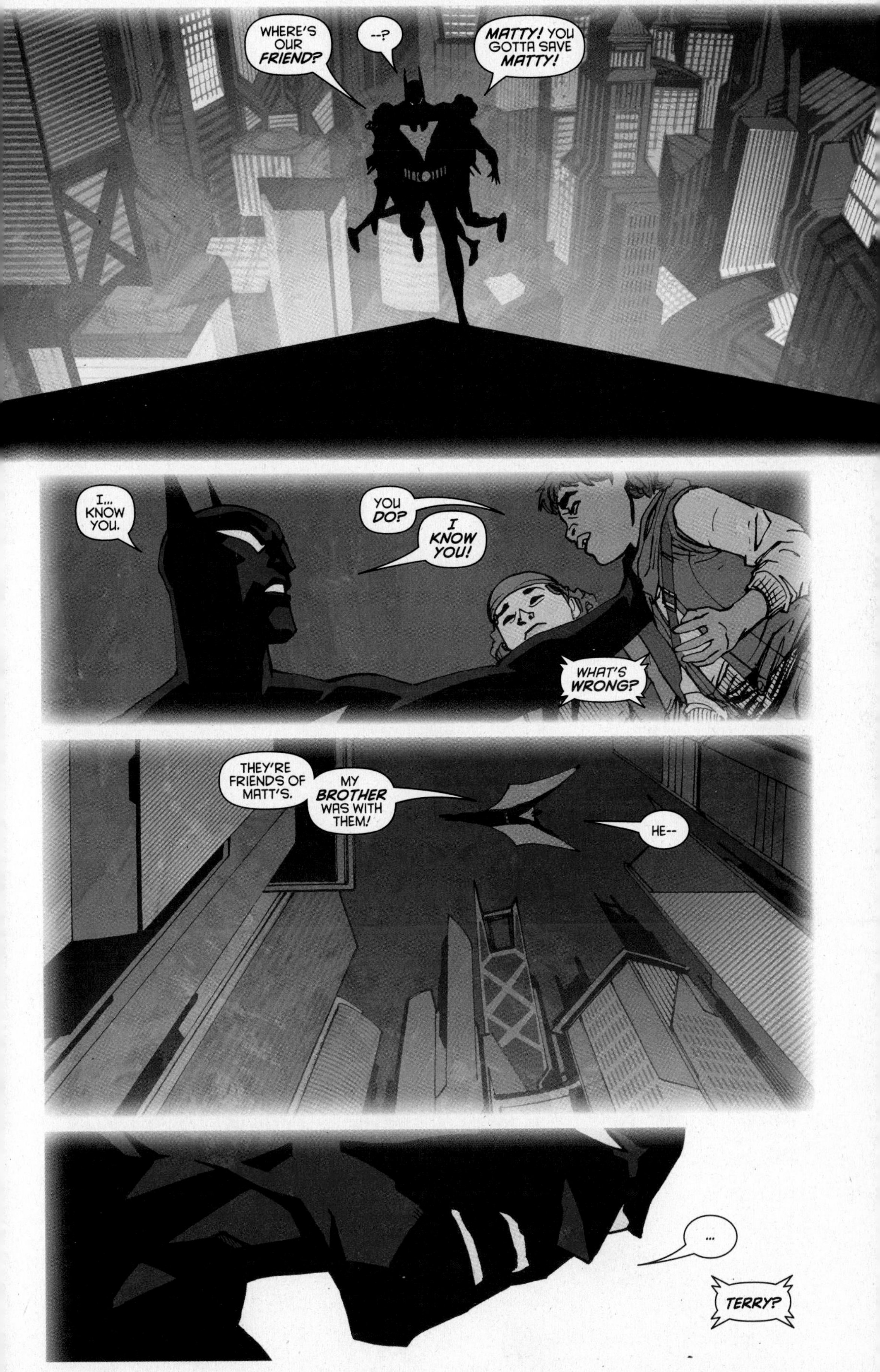

WHERE'S OUR FRIEND?
--?
MATTY! YOU GOTTA SAVE MATTY!
I... KNOW YOU.
YOU DO?
I KNOW YOU!
WHAT'S WRONG?
THEY'RE FRIENDS OF MATT'S.
MY BROTHER WAS WITH THEM!
HE--
...
TERRY?

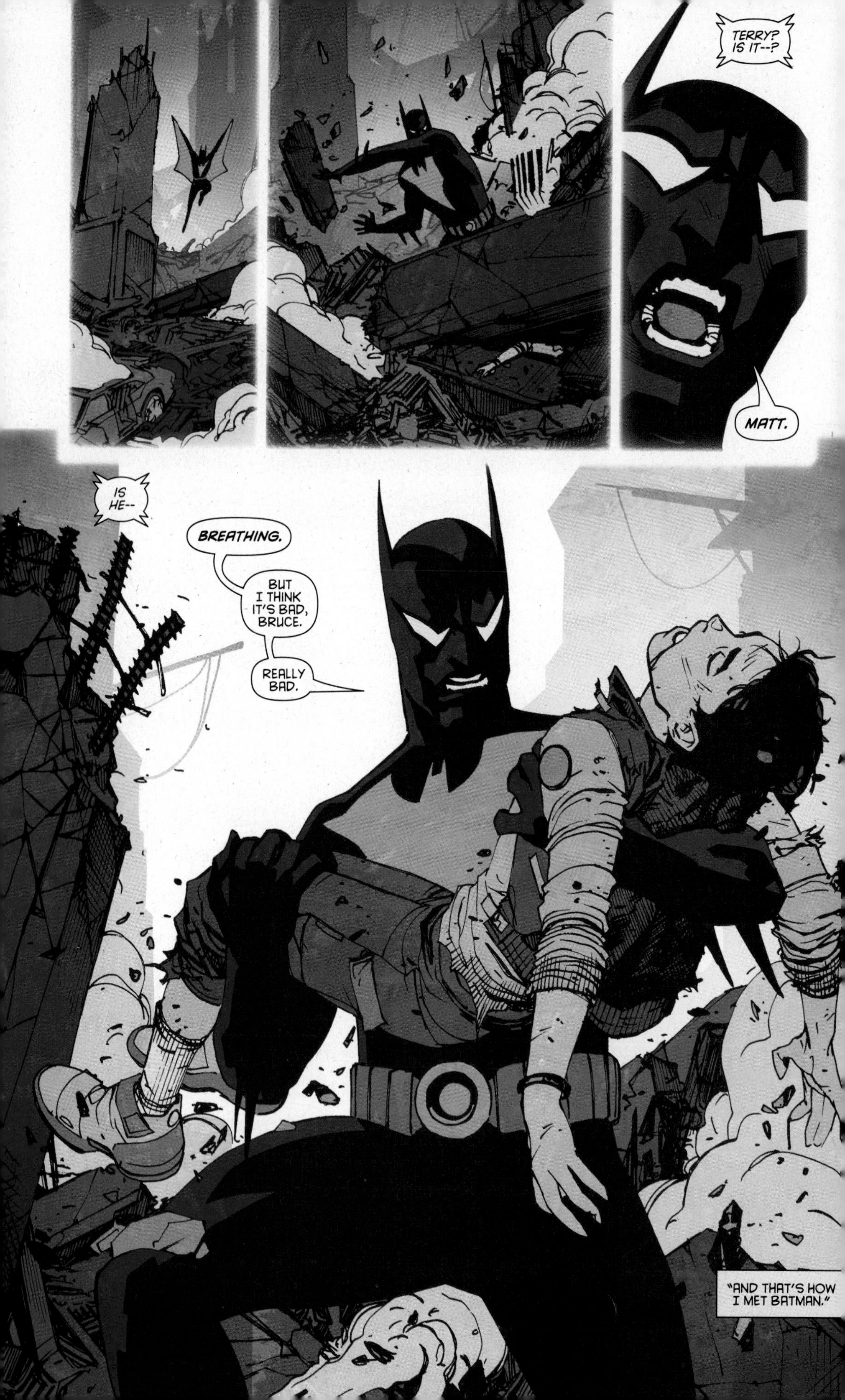
TERRY? IS IT--?
MATT.
IS HE--
BREATHING.
BUT I THINK IT'S BAD, BRUCE.
REALLY BAD.
"AND THAT'S HOW I MET BATMAN."

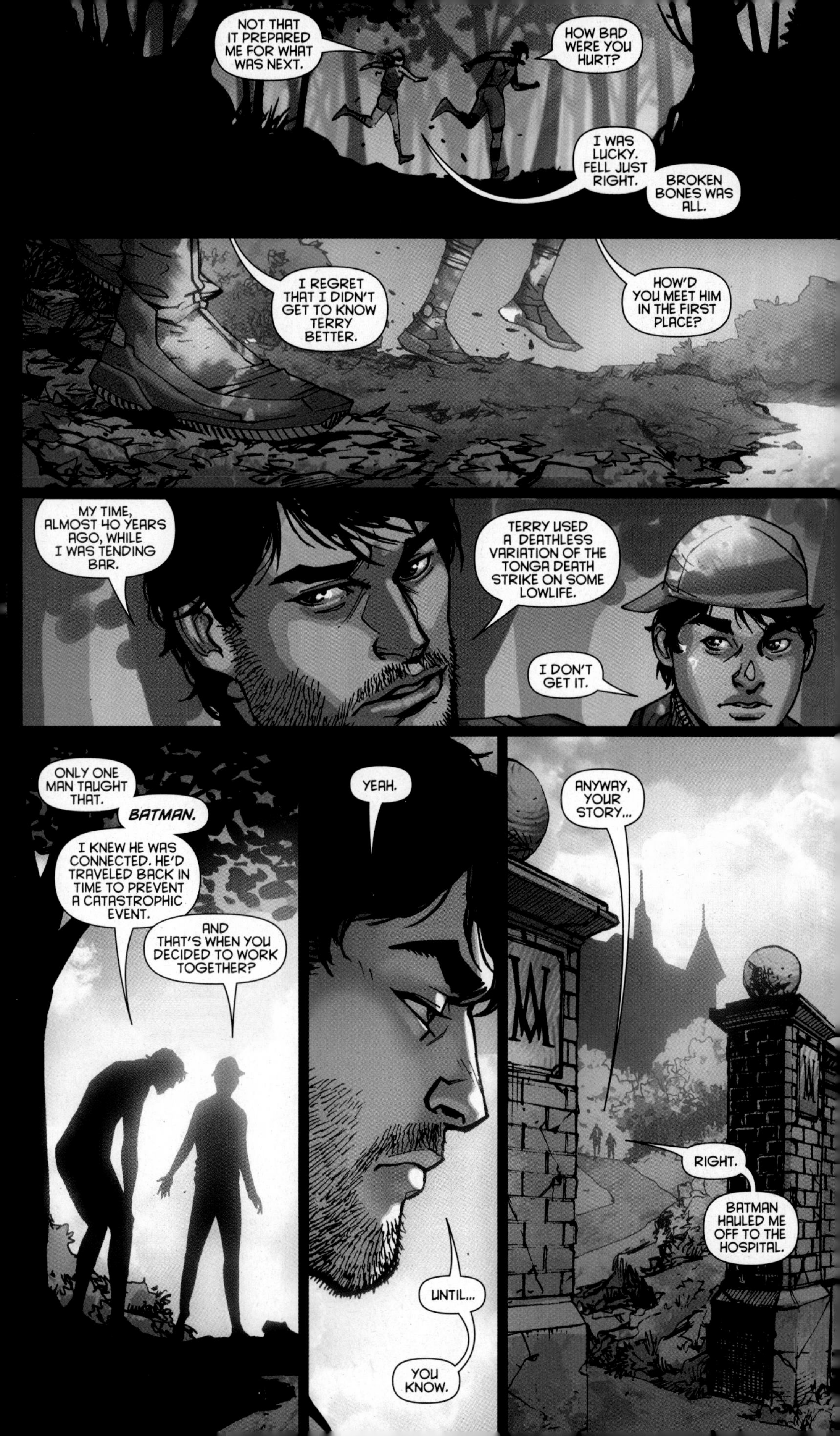
NOT THAT IT PREPARED ME FOR WHAT WAS NEXT.
HOW BAD WERE YOU HURT?
I WAS LUCKY. FELL JUST RIGHT.
BROKEN BONES WAS ALL.
I REGRET THAT I DIDN'T GET TO KNOW TERRY BETTER.
HOW'D YOU MEET HIM IN THE FIRST PLACE?
MY TIME, ALMOST 40 YEARS AGO, WHILE I WAS TENDING BAR.
TERRY USED A DEATHLESS VARIATION OF THE TONGA DEATH STRIKE ON SOME LOWLIFE.
I DON'T GET IT.
ONLY ONE MAN TAUGHT THAT.
BATMAN.
I KNEW HE WAS CONNECTED. HE'D TRAVELED BACK IN TIME TO PREVENT A CATASTROPHIC EVENT.
AND THAT'S WHEN YOU DECIDED TO WORK TOGETHER?
YEAH.
UNTIL...
YOU KNOW.
ANYWAY, YOUR STORY...
RIGHT.
BATMAN HAULED ME OFF TO THE HOSPITAL.

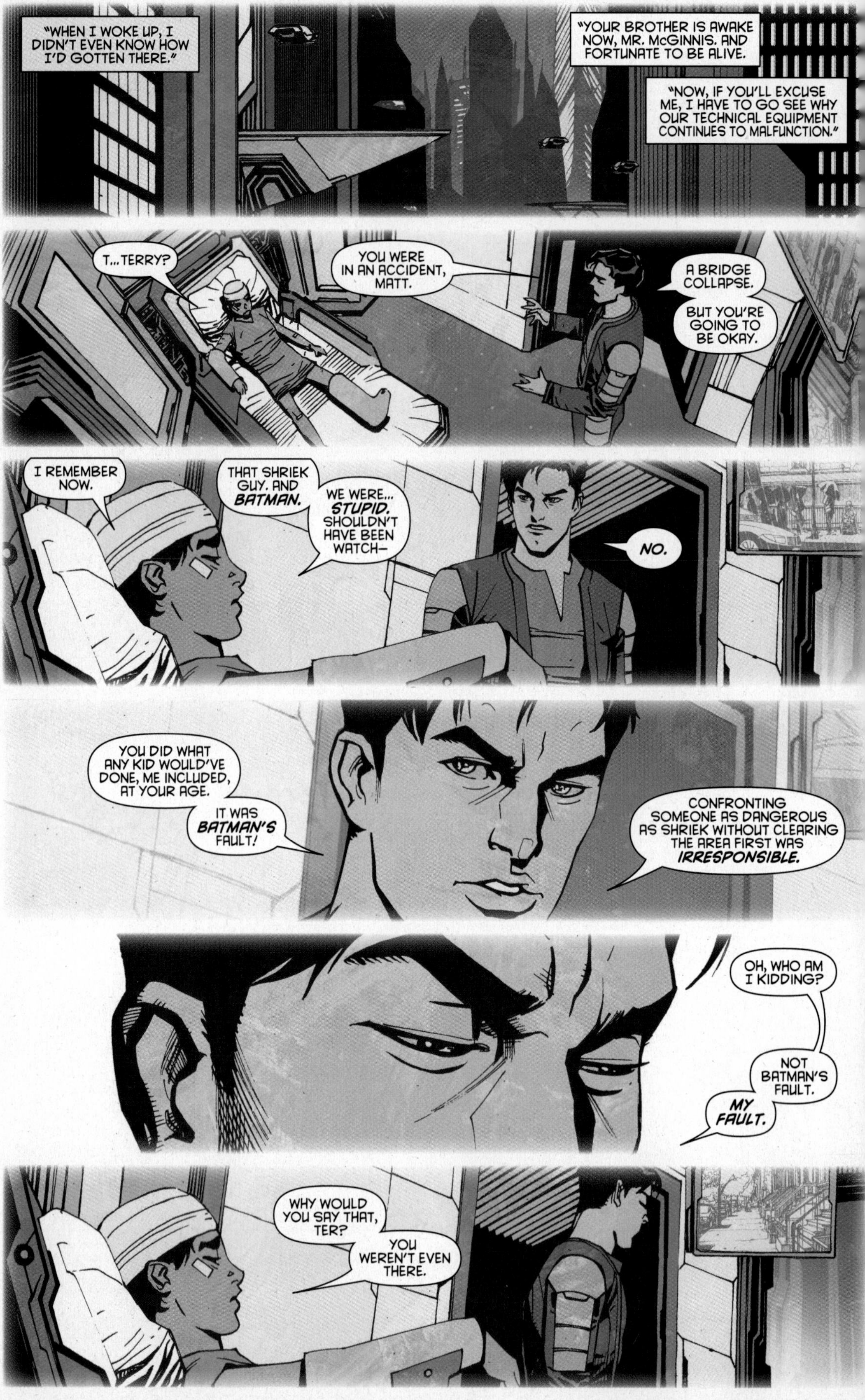
"WHEN I WOKE UP, I DIDN'T EVEN KNOW HOW I'D GOTTEN THERE."
"YOUR BROTHER IS AWAKE NOW, MR. McGINNIS. AND FORTUNATE TO BE ALIVE.
"NOW, IF YOU'LL EXCUSE ME, I HAVE TO GO SEE WHY OUR TECHNICAL EQUIPMENT CONTINUES TO MALFUNCTION."
T... TERRY?
YOU WERE IN AN ACCIDENT, MATT.
A BRIDGE COLLAPSE.
BUT YOU'RE GOING TO BE OKAY.
I REMEMBER NOW.
THAT SHRIEK GUY. AND BATMAN.
WE WERE... STUPID. SHOULDN'T HAVE BEEN WATCH—
NO.
YOU DID WHAT ANY KID WOULD'VE DONE, ME INCLUDED, AT YOUR AGE.
IT WAS BATMAN'S FAULT!
CONFRONTING SOMEONE AS DANGEROUS AS SHRIEK WITHOUT CLEARING THE AREA FIRST WAS IRRESPONSIBLE.
OH, WHO AM I KIDDING?
NOT BATMAN'S FAULT.
MY FAULT.
WHY WOULD YOU SAY THAT, TER?
YOU WEREN'T EVEN THERE.

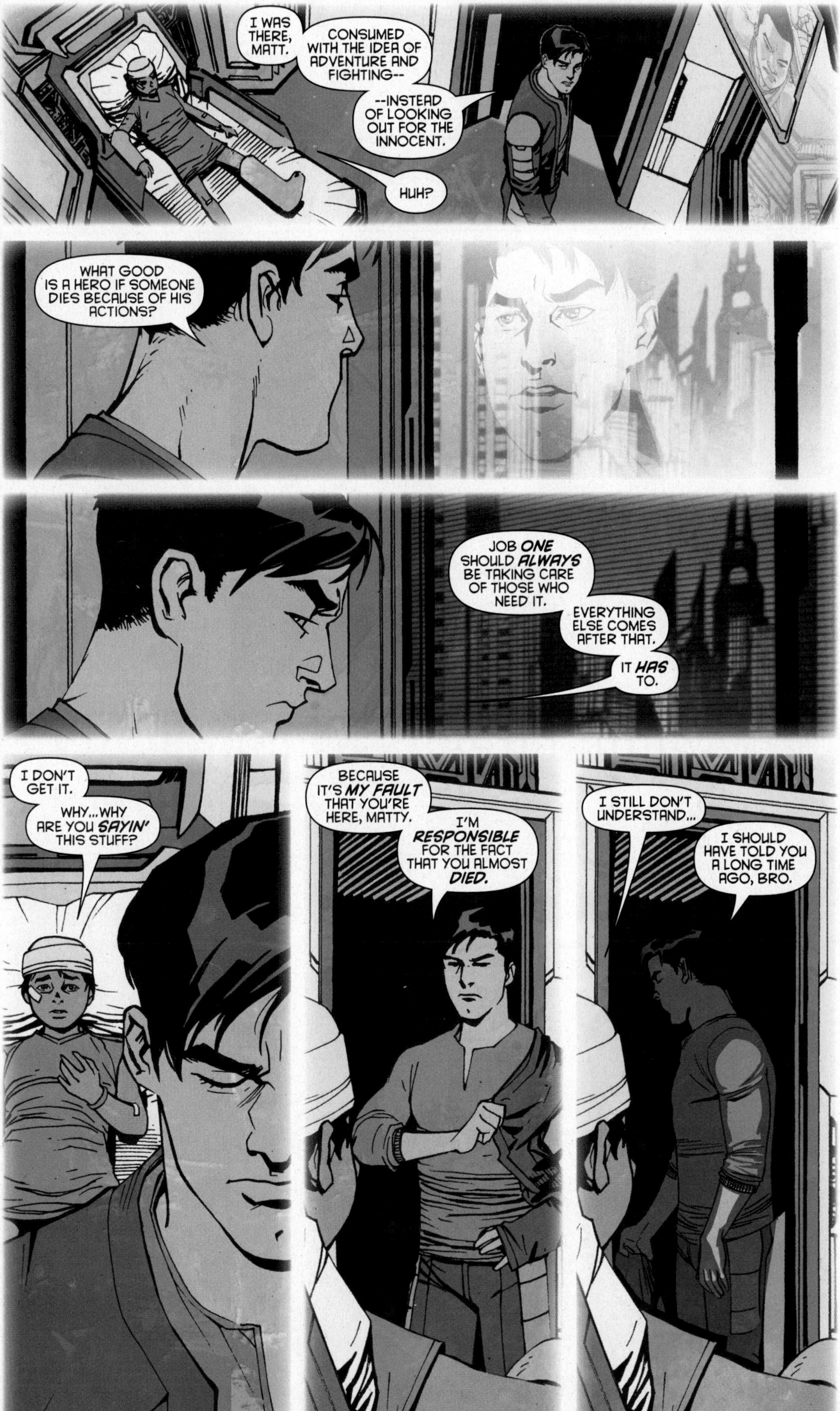
I WAS THERE, MATT.
CONSUMED WITH THE IDEA OF ADVENTURE AND FIGHTING--
--INSTEAD OF LOOKING OUT FOR THE INNOCENT.
HUH?
WHAT GOOD IS A HERO IF SOMEONE DIES BECAUSE OF HIS ACTIONS?
JOB ONE SHOULD ALWAYS BE TAKING CARE OF THOSE WHO NEED IT.
EVERYTHING ELSE COMES AFTER THAT.
IT HAS TO.
I DON'T GET IT.
WHY...WHY ARE YOU SAYIN' THIS STUFF?
BECAUSE IT'S MY FAULT THAT YOU'RE HERE, MATTY.
I'M RESPONSIBLE FOR THE FACT THAT YOU ALMOST DIED.
I STILL DON'T UNDERSTAND...
I SHOULD HAVE TOLD YOU A LONG TIME AGO, BRO.

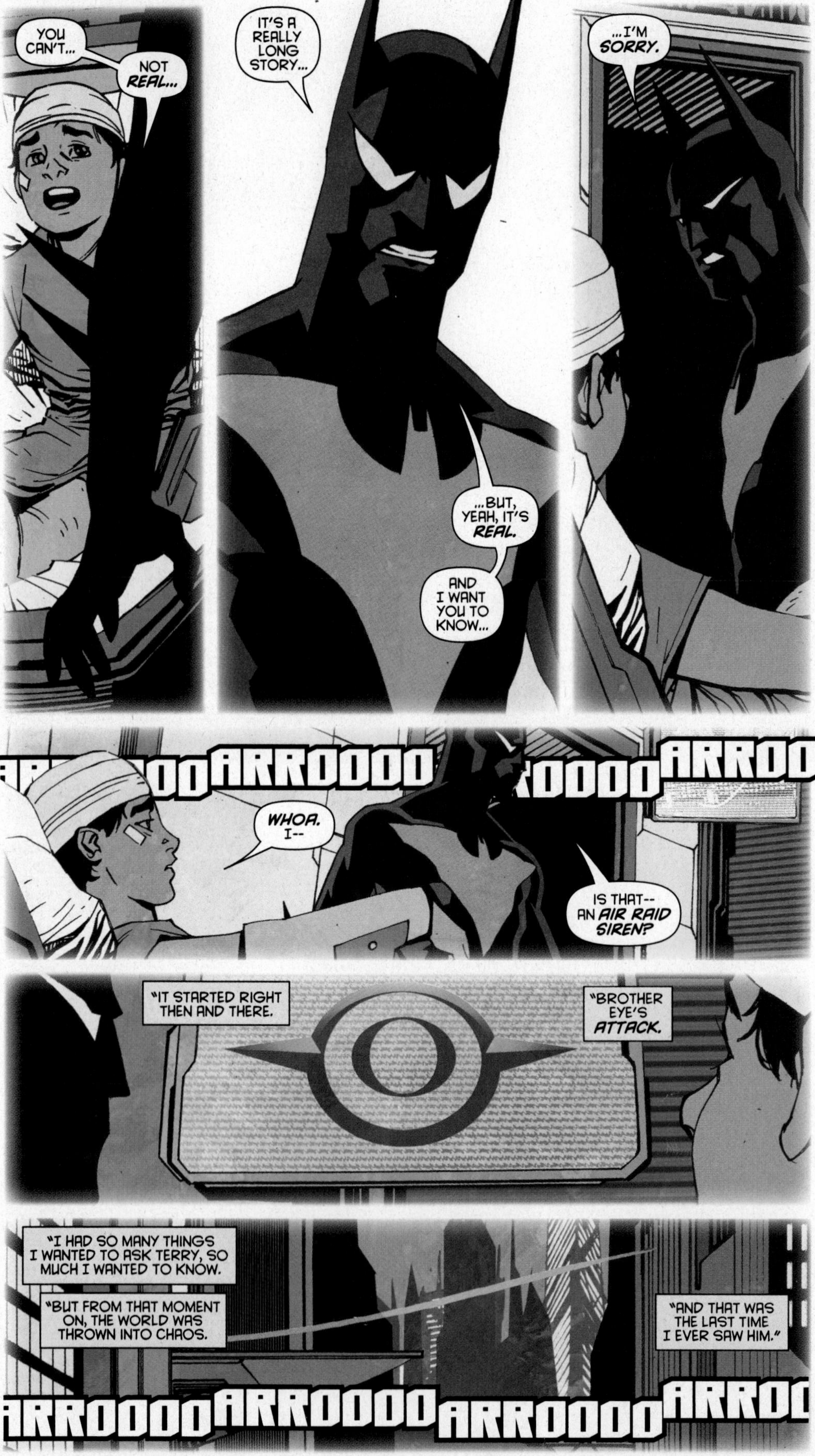
YOU CAN'T...
NOT REAL...
IT'S A REALLY LONG STORY...
...BUT, YEAH, IT'S REAL.
AND I WANT YOU TO KNOW...
...I'M SORRY.
ARROOOO ARROOOO ARROOOO ARROO
WHOA. I--
IS THAT-- AN AIR RAID SIREN?
"IT STARTED RIGHT THEN AND THERE.
"BROTHER EYE'S ATTACK.
"I HAD SO MANY THINGS I WANTED TO ASK TERRY, SO MUCH I WANTED TO KNOW.
"BUT FROM THAT MOMENT ON, THE WORLD WAS THROWN INTO CHAOS.
"AND THAT WAS THE LAST TIME I EVER SAW HIM."
ARROOOO ARROOOO ARROOOO ARROO

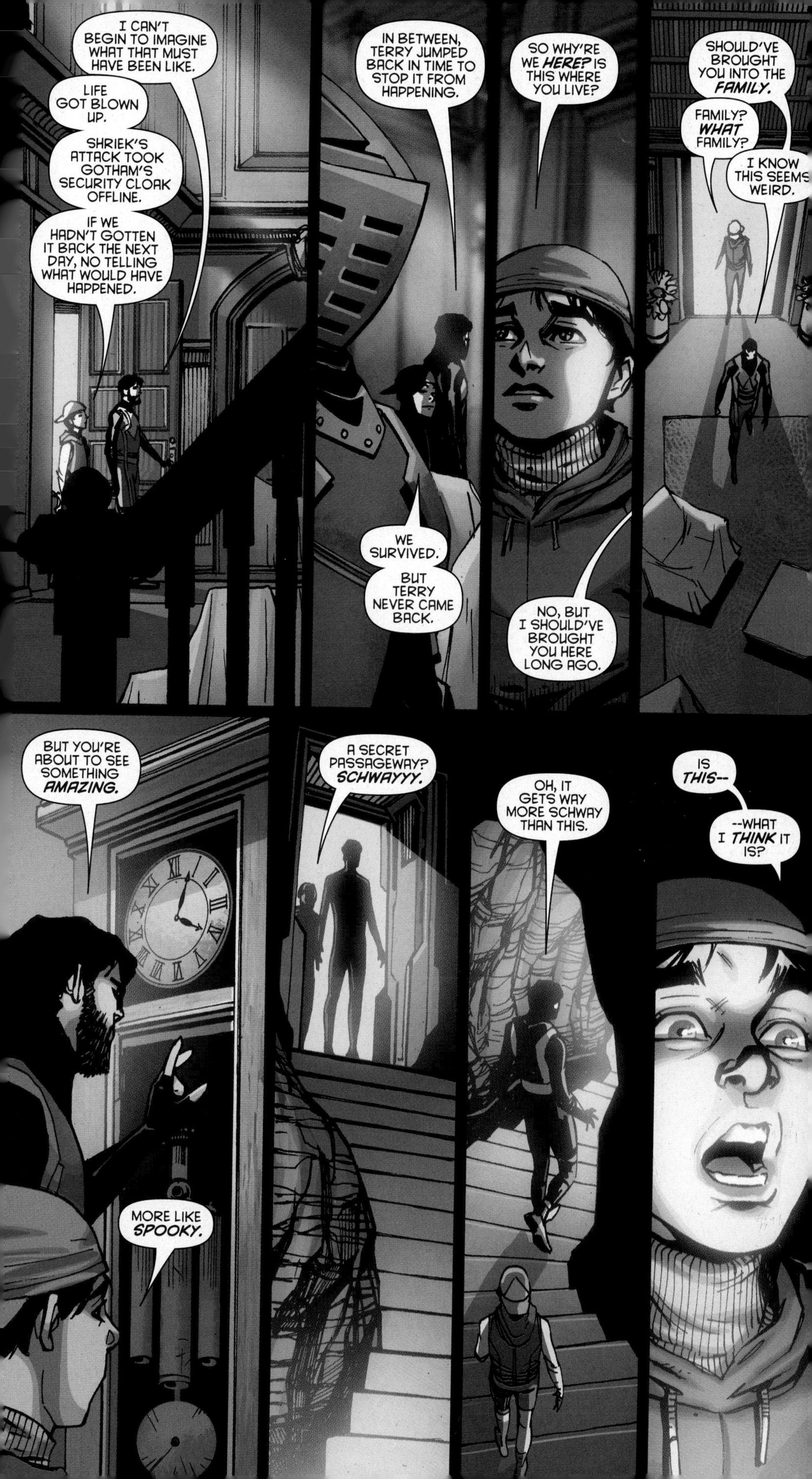
I CAN'T BEGIN TO IMAGINE WHAT THAT MUST HAVE BEEN LIKE.
LIFE GOT BLOWN UP.
SHRIEK'S ATTACK TOOK GOTHAM'S SECURITY CLOAK OFFLINE.
IF WE HADN'T GOTTEN IT BACK THE NEXT DAY, NO TELLING WHAT WOULD HAVE HAPPENED.
IN BETWEEN, TERRY JUMPED BACK IN TIME TO STOP IT FROM HAPPENING.
WE SURVIVED.
BUT TERRY NEVER CAME BACK.
SO WHY'RE WE *HERE?* IS THIS WHERE YOU LIVE?
NO, BUT I SHOULD'VE BROUGHT YOU HERE LONG AGO.
SHOULD'VE BROUGHT YOU INTO THE *FAMILY.*
FAMILY? *WHAT* FAMILY?
I KNOW THIS SEEMS WEIRD.
BUT YOU'RE ABOUT TO SEE SOMETHING *AMAZING.*
MORE LIKE *SPOOKY.*
A SECRET PASSAGEWAY? *SCHWAYYY.*
OH, IT GETS WAY MORE SCHWAY THAN THIS.
IS *THIS*--
--WHAT I *THINK* IT IS?

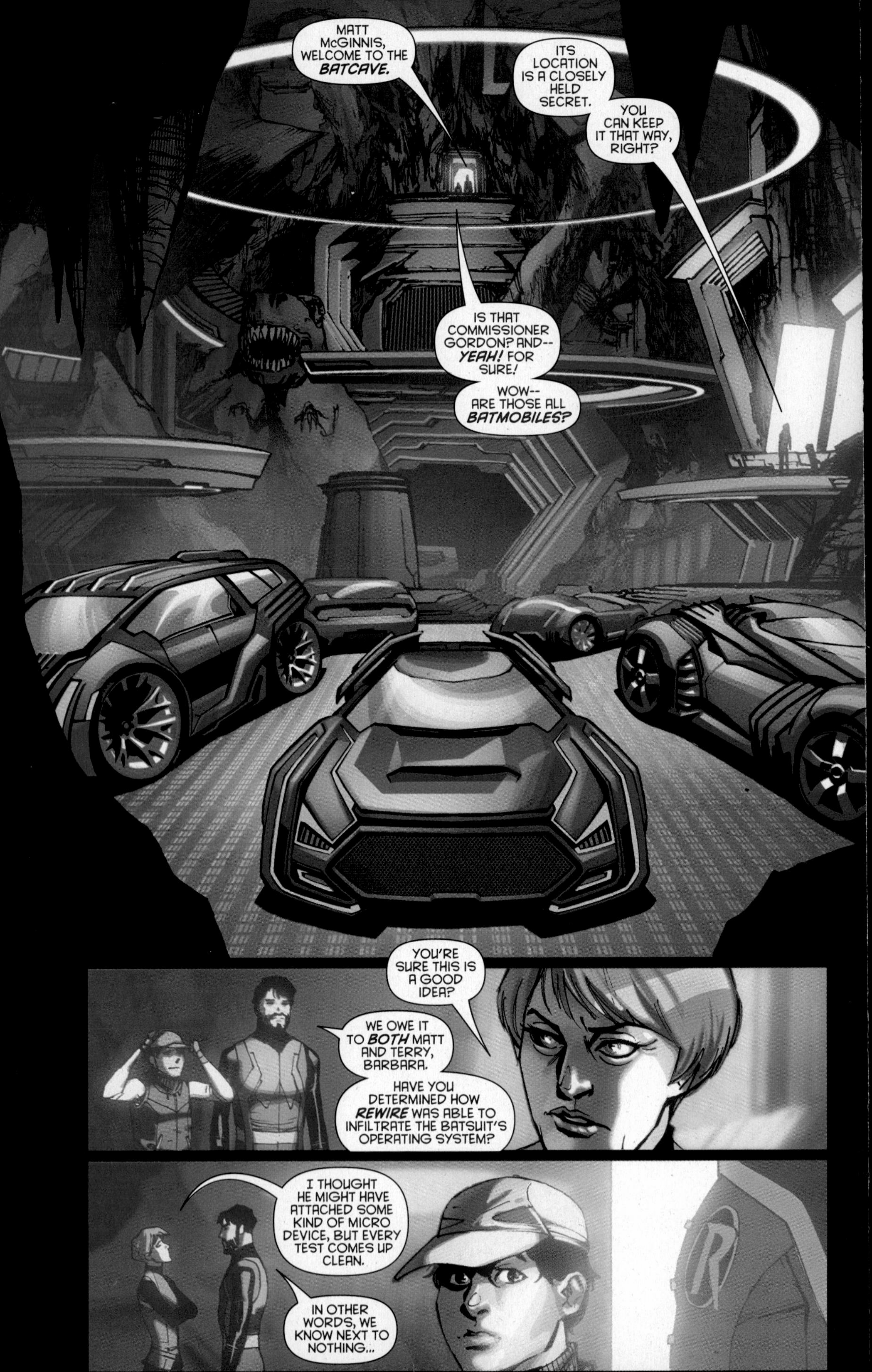
MATT McGINNIS, WELCOME TO THE BATCAVE.
ITS LOCATION IS A CLOSELY HELD SECRET.
YOU CAN KEEP IT THAT WAY, RIGHT?
IS THAT COMMISSIONER GORDON? AND-- YEAH! FOR SURE!
WOW-- ARE THOSE ALL BATMOBILES?
YOU'RE SURE THIS IS A GOOD IDEA?
WE OWE IT TO BOTH MATT AND TERRY, BARBARA.
HAVE YOU DETERMINED HOW REWIRE WAS ABLE TO INFILTRATE THE BATSUIT'S OPERATING SYSTEM?
I THOUGHT HE MIGHT HAVE ATTACHED SOME KIND OF MICRO DEVICE, BUT EVERY TEST COMES UP CLEAN.
IN OTHER WORDS, WE KNOW NEXT TO NOTHING...

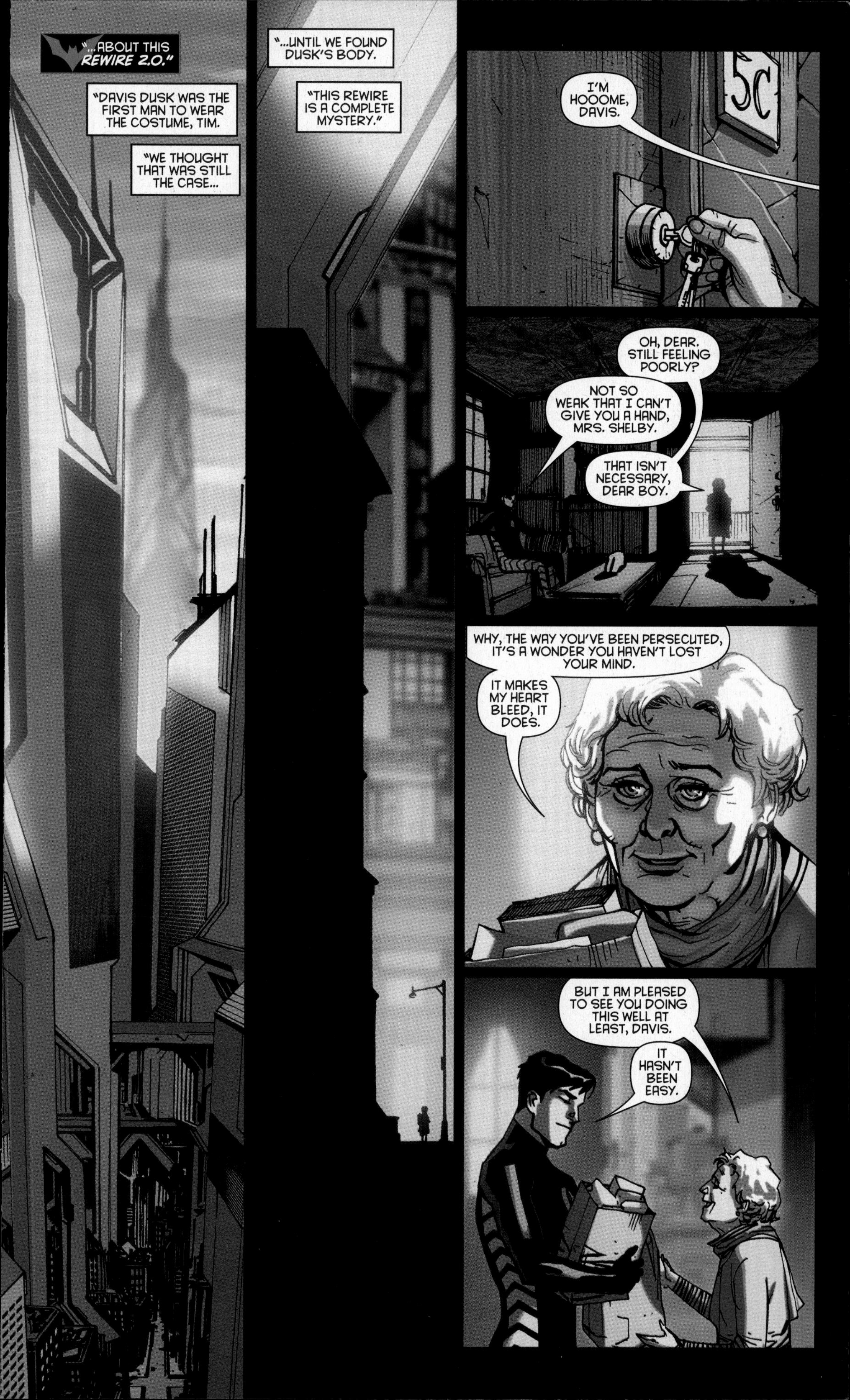
"...ABOUT THIS REWIRE 2.0."
"DAVIS DUSK WAS THE FIRST MAN TO WEAR THE COSTUME, TIM.
"WE THOUGHT THAT WAS STILL THE CASE...
"...UNTIL WE FOUND DUSK'S BODY.
"THIS REWIRE IS A COMPLETE MYSTERY."
5C
I'M HOOOME, DAVIS.
OH, DEAR. STILL FEELING POORLY?
NOT SO WEAK THAT I CAN'T GIVE YOU A HAND, MRS. SHELBY.
THAT ISN'T NECESSARY, DEAR BOY.
WHY, THE WAY YOU'VE BEEN PERSECUTED, IT'S A WONDER YOU HAVEN'T LOST YOUR MIND.
IT MAKES MY HEART BLEED, IT DOES.
BUT I AM PLEASED TO SEE YOU DOING THIS WELL AT LEAST, DAVIS.
IT HASN'T BEEN EASY.

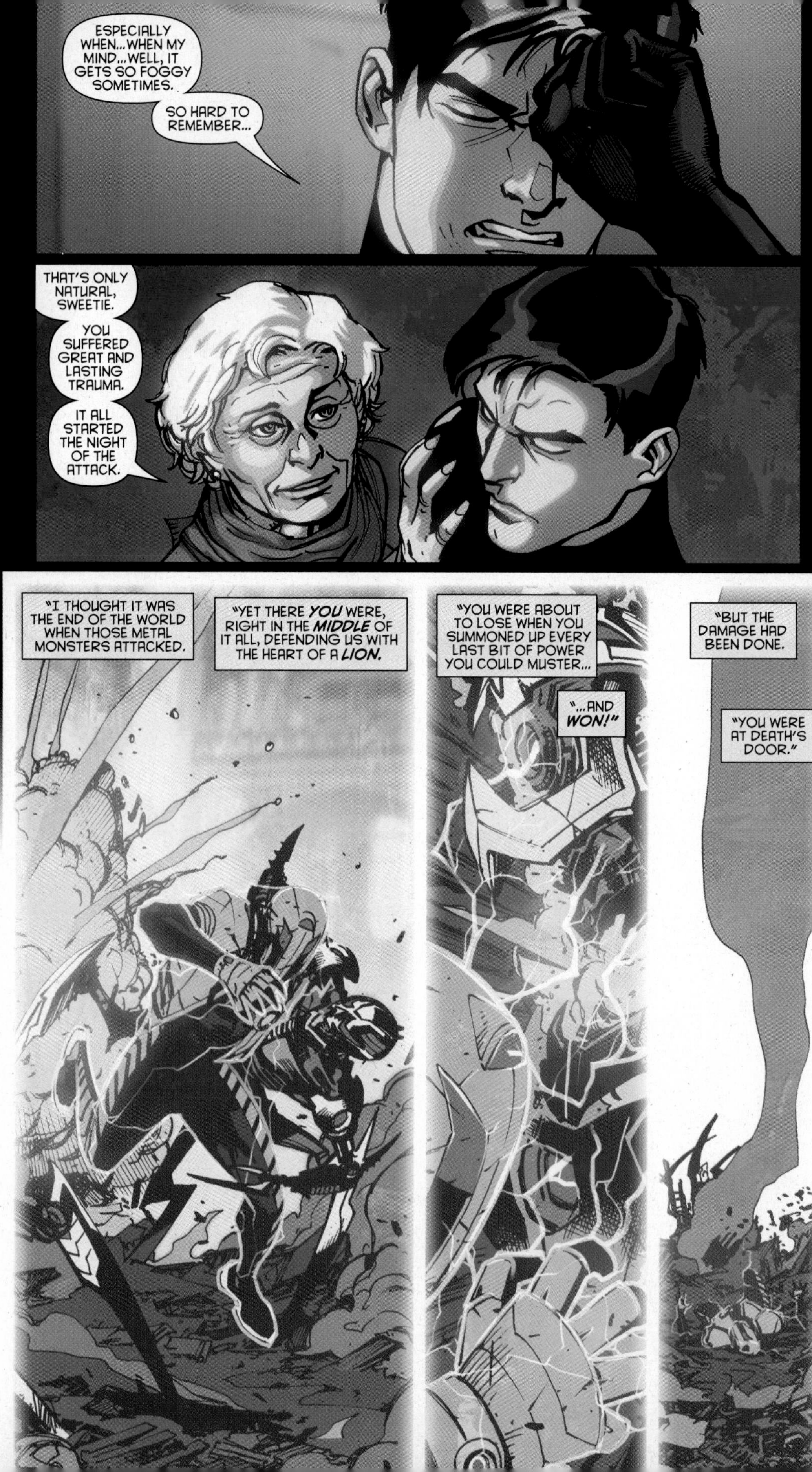
ESPECIALLY WHEN...WHEN MY MIND...WELL, IT GETS SO FOGGY SOMETIMES.
SO HARD TO REMEMBER...
THAT'S ONLY NATURAL, SWEETIE.
YOU SUFFERED GREAT AND LASTING TRAUMA.
IT ALL STARTED THE NIGHT OF THE ATTACK.
"I THOUGHT IT WAS THE END OF THE WORLD WHEN THOSE METAL MONSTERS ATTACKED.
"YET THERE *YOU* WERE, RIGHT IN THE *MIDDLE* OF IT ALL, DEFENDING US WITH THE HEART OF A *LION.*
"YOU WERE ABOUT TO LOSE WHEN YOU SUMMONED UP EVERY LAST BIT OF POWER YOU COULD MUSTER...
"...AND *WON!*"
"BUT THE DAMAGE HAD BEEN DONE.
"YOU WERE AT DEATH'S DOOR."

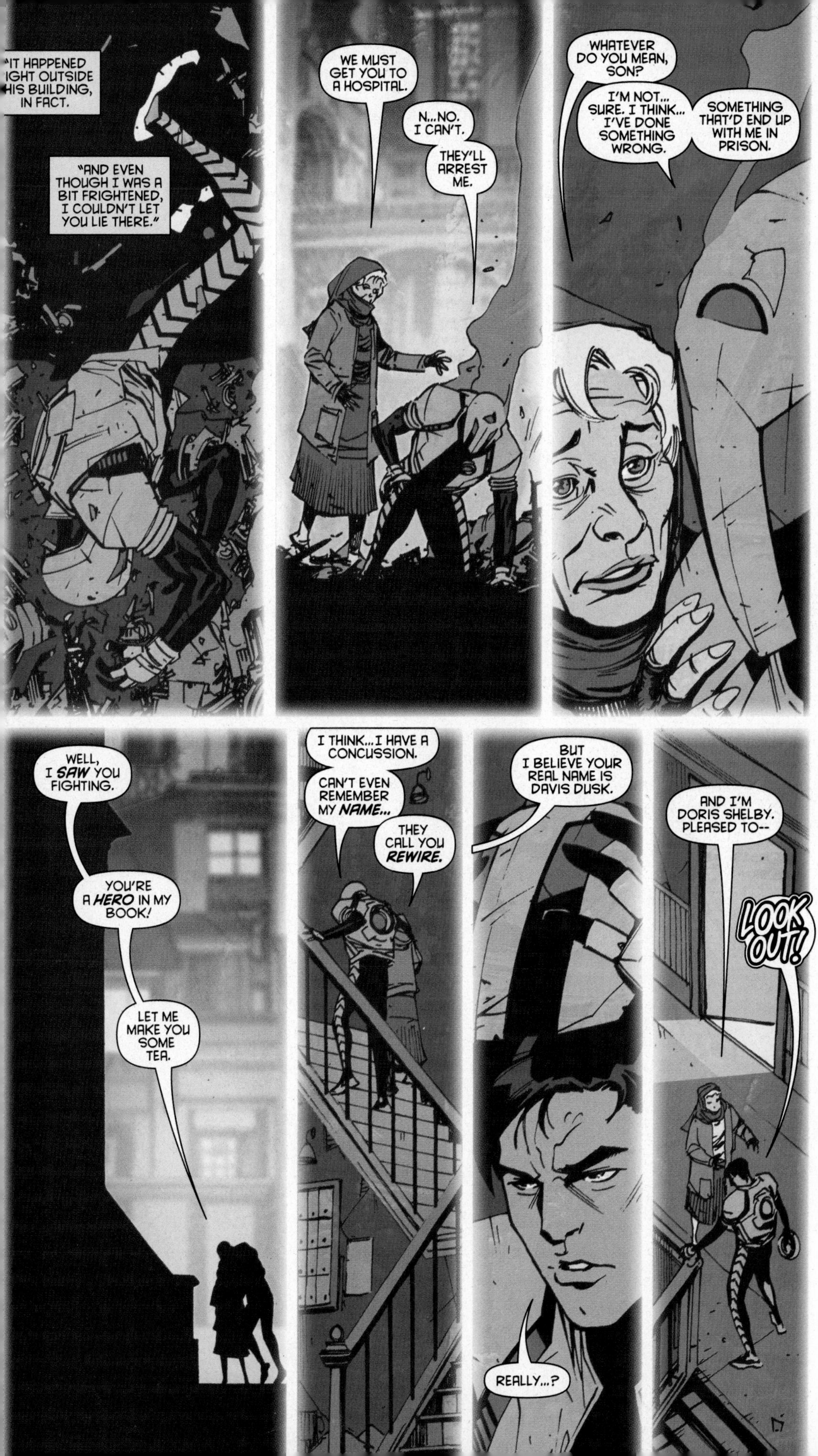
"IT HAPPENED
IGHT OUTSIDE
HIS BUILDING,
IN FACT.
"AND EVEN THOUGH I WAS A BIT FRIGHTENED, I COULDN'T LET YOU LIE THERE."
WE MUST GET YOU TO A HOSPITAL.
N...NO. I CAN'T.
THEY'LL ARREST ME.
WHATEVER DO YOU MEAN, SON?
I'M NOT... SURE. I THINK... I'VE DONE SOMETHING WRONG.
SOMETHING THAT'D END UP WITH ME IN PRISON.
WELL, I SAW YOU FIGHTING.
YOU'RE A HERO IN MY BOOK!
LET ME MAKE YOU SOME TEA.
I THINK...I HAVE A CONCUSSION.
CAN'T EVEN REMEMBER MY NAME...
THEY CALL YOU REWIRE.
BUT I BELIEVE YOUR REAL NAME IS DAVIS DUSK.
REALLY...?
AND I'M DORIS SHELBY. PLEASED TO--
LOOK OUT!

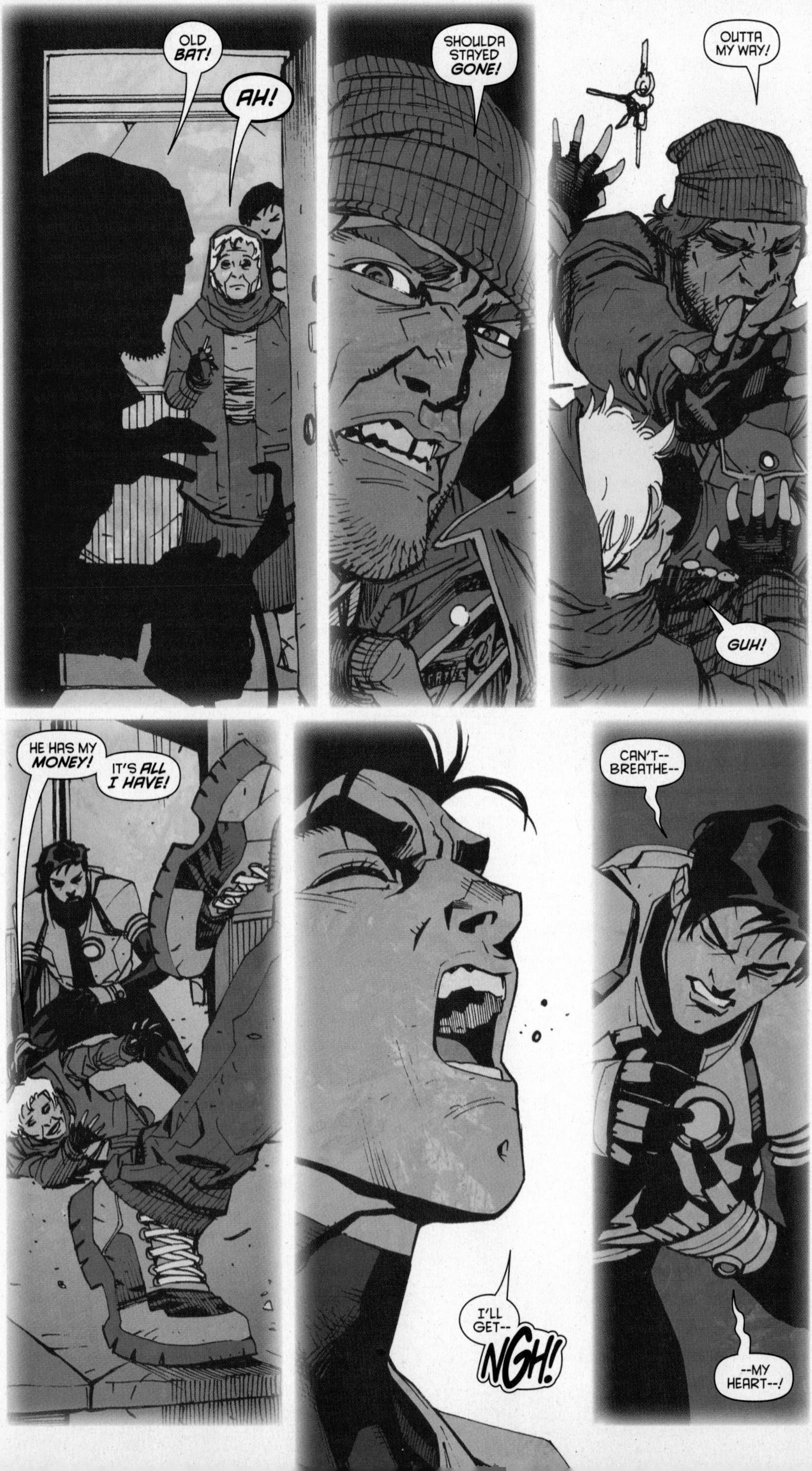
OLD BAT!
AH!
SHOULDA STAYED GONE!
OUTTA MY WAY!
GUH!
HE HAS MY MONEY!
IT'S ALL I HAVE!
I'LL GET--
NGH!
CAN'T-- BREATHE--
--MY HEART--!

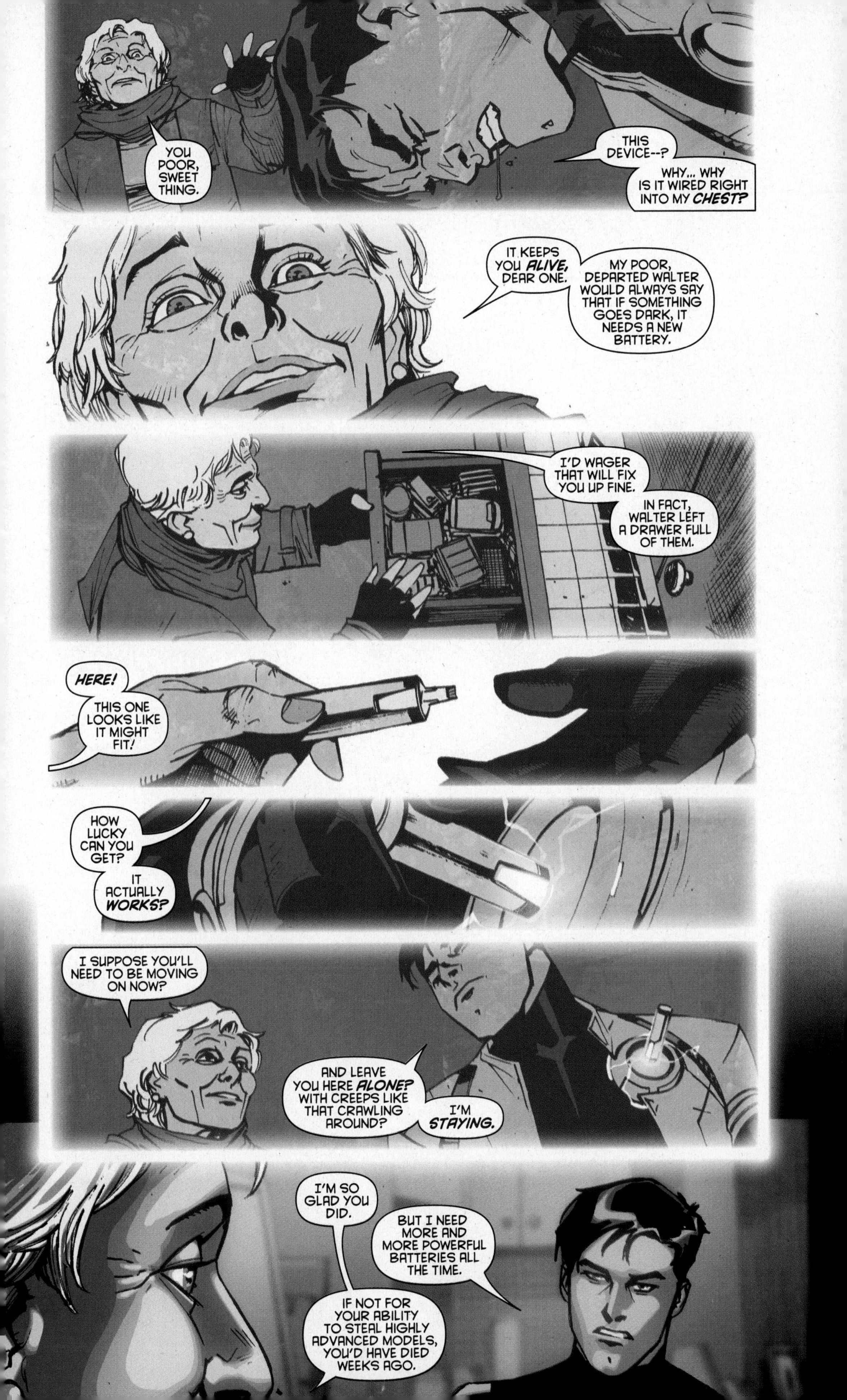
YOU POOR, SWEET THING.
THIS DEVICE--?
WHY... WHY IS IT WIRED RIGHT INTO MY CHEST?
IT KEEPS YOU ALIVE, DEAR ONE.
MY POOR, DEPARTED WALTER WOULD ALWAYS SAY THAT IF SOMETHING GOES DARK, IT NEEDS A NEW BATTERY.
I'D WAGER THAT WILL FIX YOU UP FINE.
IN FACT, WALTER LEFT A DRAWER FULL OF THEM.
HERE!
THIS ONE LOOKS LIKE IT MIGHT FIT!
HOW LUCKY CAN YOU GET?
IT ACTUALLY WORKS?
I SUPPOSE YOU'LL NEED TO BE MOVING ON NOW?
AND LEAVE YOU HERE ALONE? WITH CREEPS LIKE THAT CRAWLING AROUND?
I'M STAYING.
I'M SO GLAD YOU DID.
BUT I NEED MORE AND MORE POWERFUL BATTERIES ALL THE TIME.
IF NOT FOR YOUR ABILITY TO STEAL HIGHLY ADVANCED MODELS, YOU'D HAVE DIED WEEKS AGO.

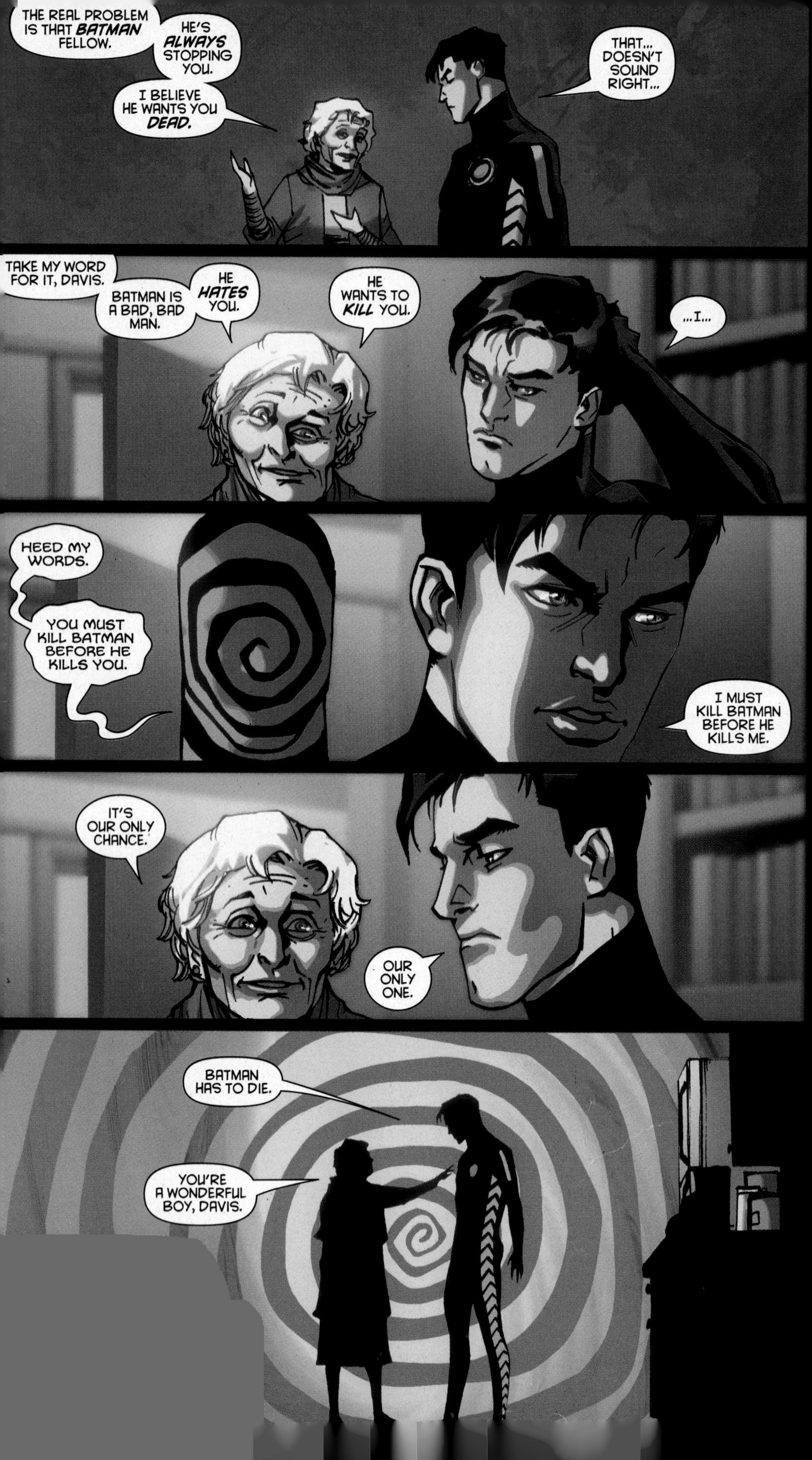
THE REAL PROBLEM IS THAT BATMAN FELLOW.
HE'S ALWAYS STOPPING YOU.
I BELIEVE HE WANTS YOU DEAD.
THAT... DOESN'T SOUND RIGHT...
TAKE MY WORD FOR IT, DAVIS.
BATMAN IS A BAD, BAD MAN.
HE HATES YOU.
HE WANTS TO KILL YOU.
...I...
HEED MY WORDS.
YOU MUST KILL BATMAN BEFORE HE KILLS YOU.
I MUST KILL BATMAN BEFORE HE KILLS ME.
IT'S OUR ONLY CHANCE.
OUR ONLY ONE.
BATMAN HAS TO DIE.
YOU'RE A WONDERFUL BOY, DAVIS.

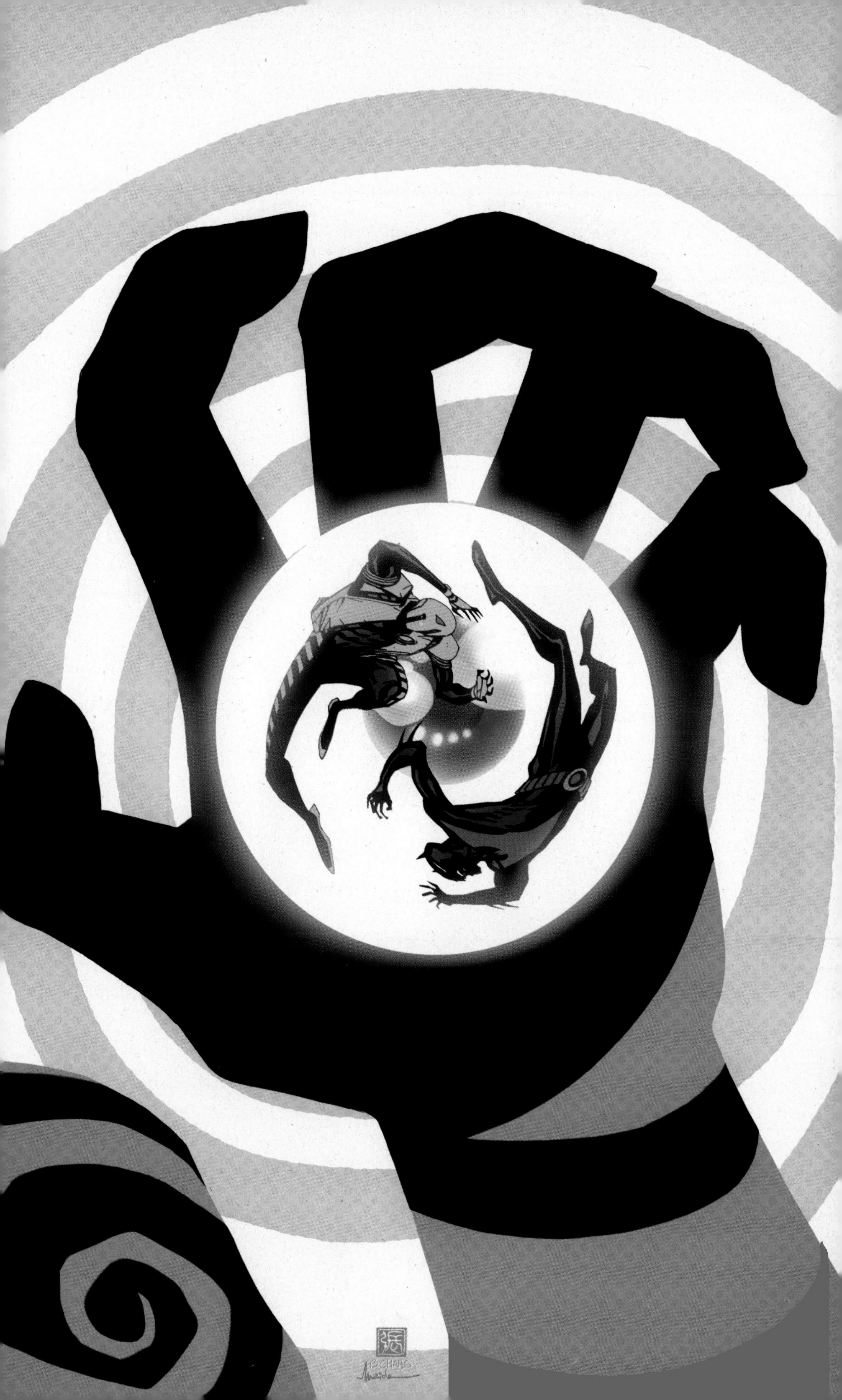

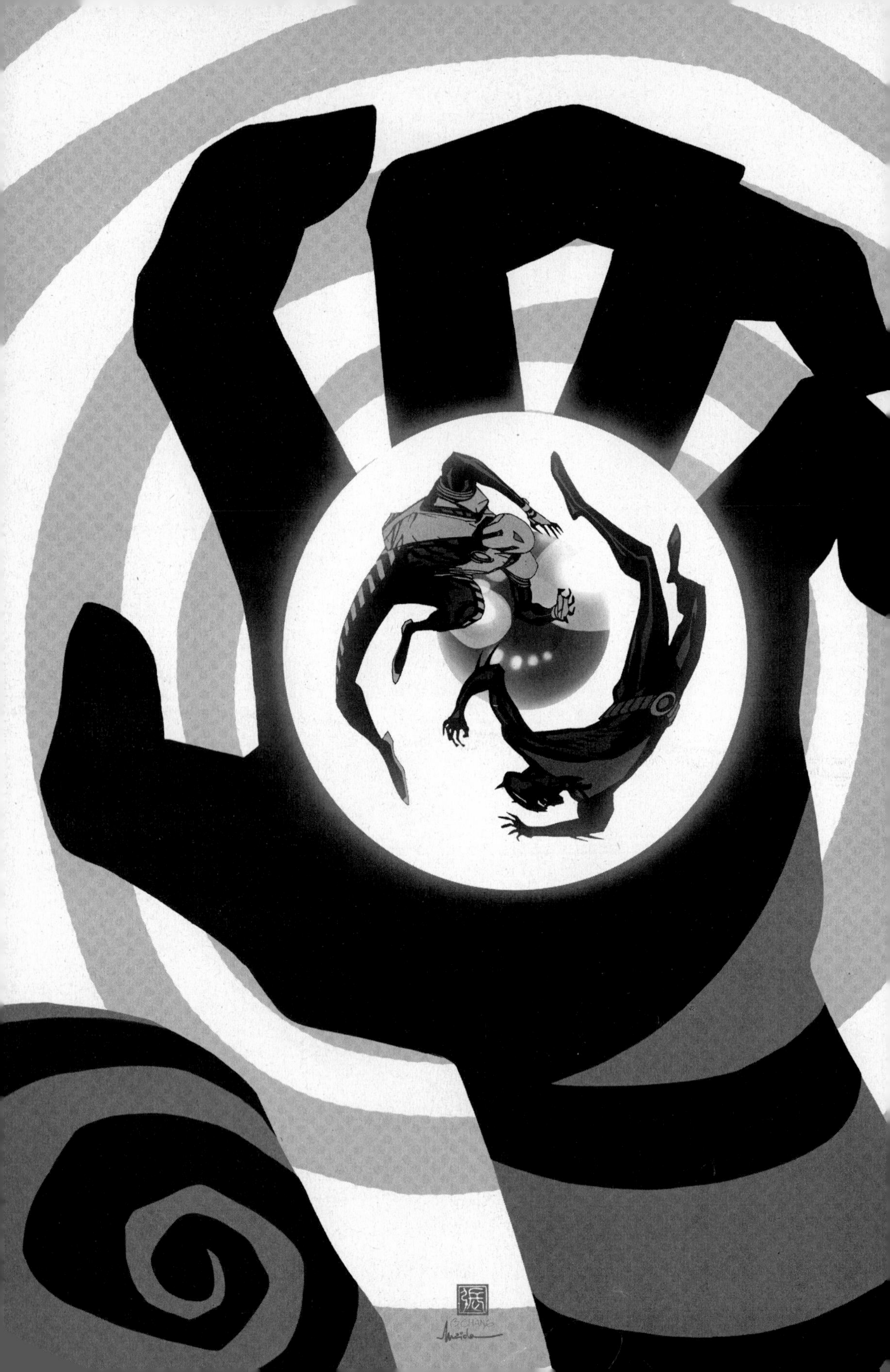

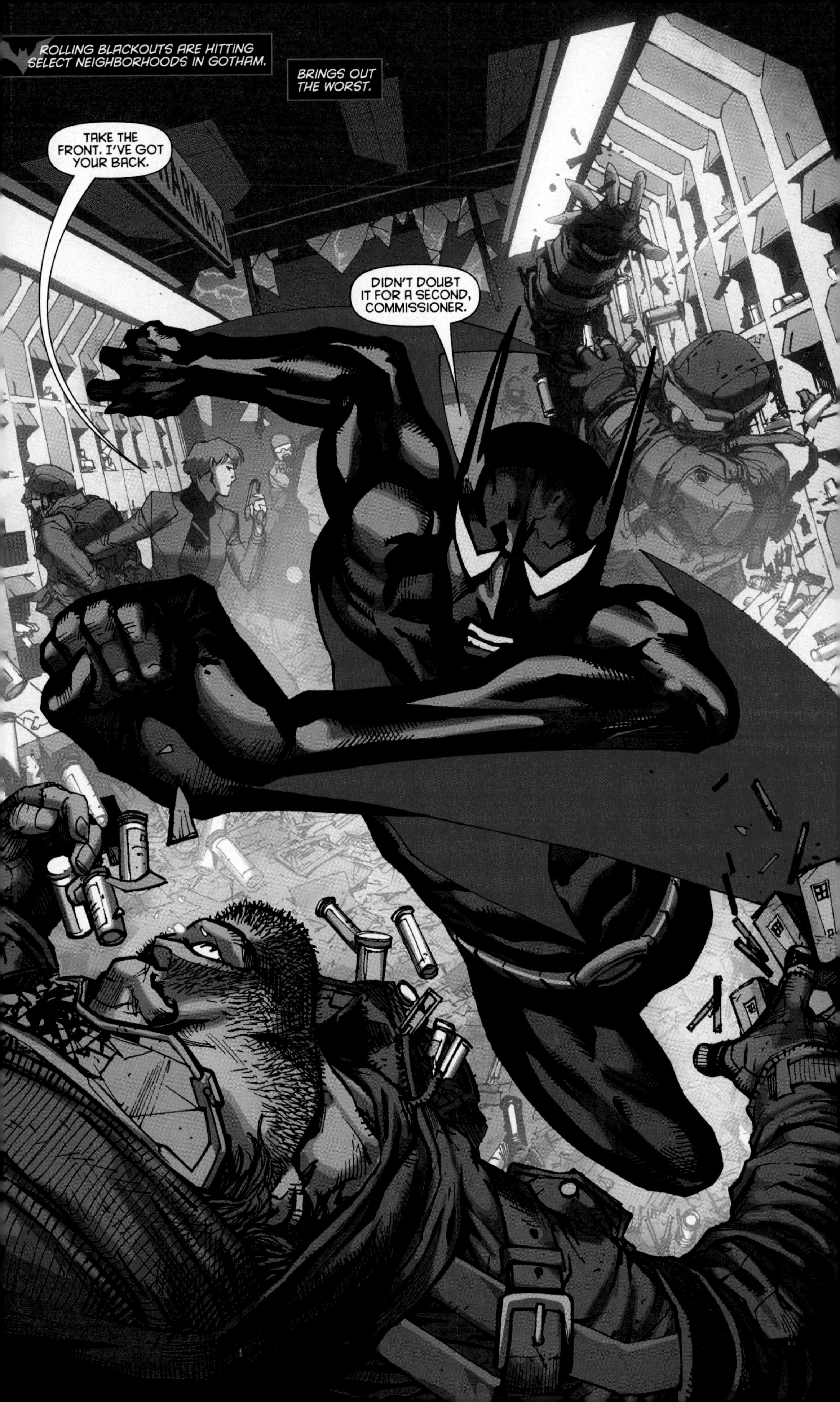
ROLLING BLACKOUTS ARE HITTING SELECT NEIGHBORHOODS IN GOTHAM.
BRINGS OUT THE WORST.
TAKE THE FRONT. I'VE GOT YOUR BACK.
DIDN'T DOUBT IT FOR A SECOND, COMMISSIONER.

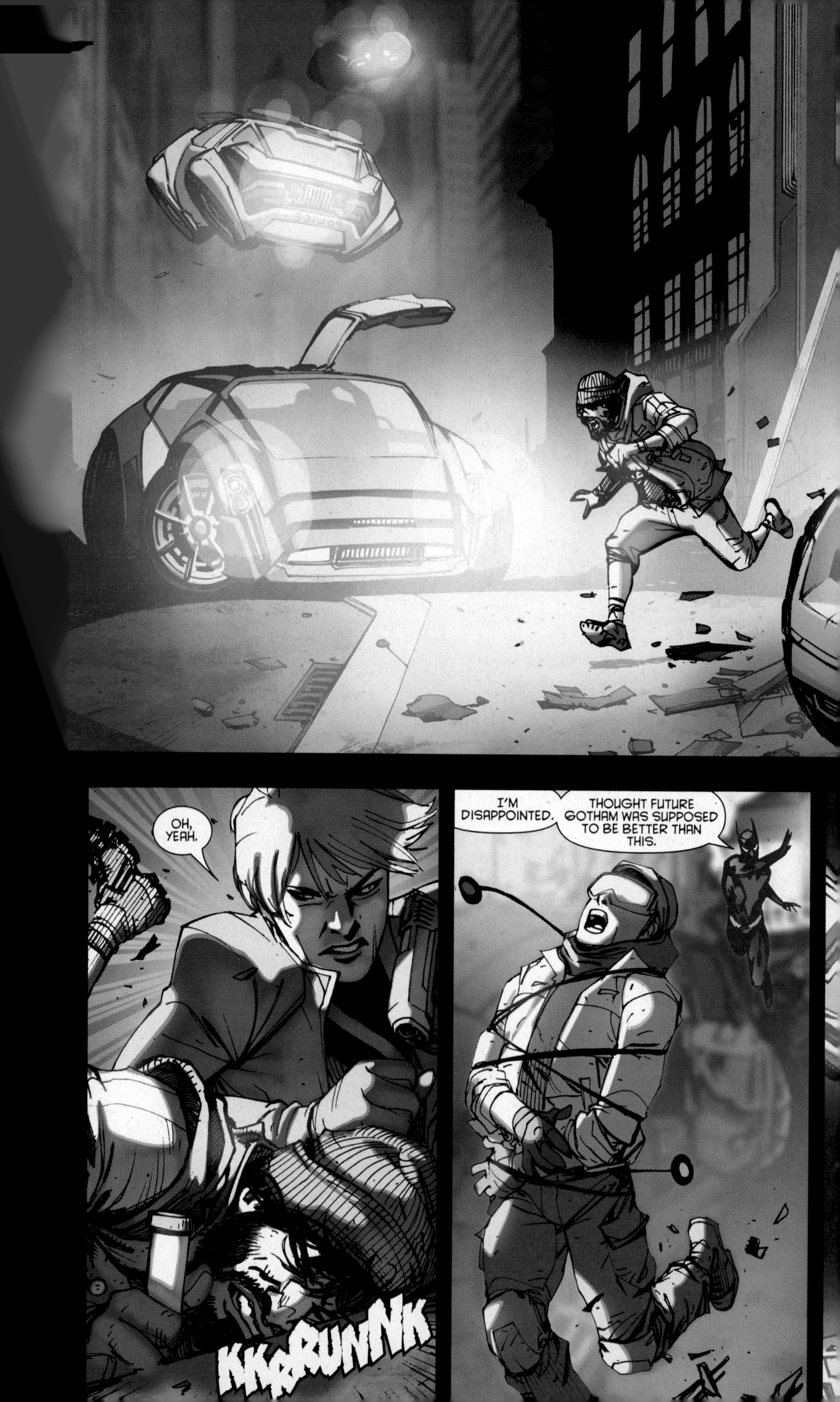
OH, YEAH.
KKRRUNNK
I'M DISAPPOINTED.
THOUGHT FUTURE GOTHAM WAS SUPPOSED TO BE BETTER THAN THIS.

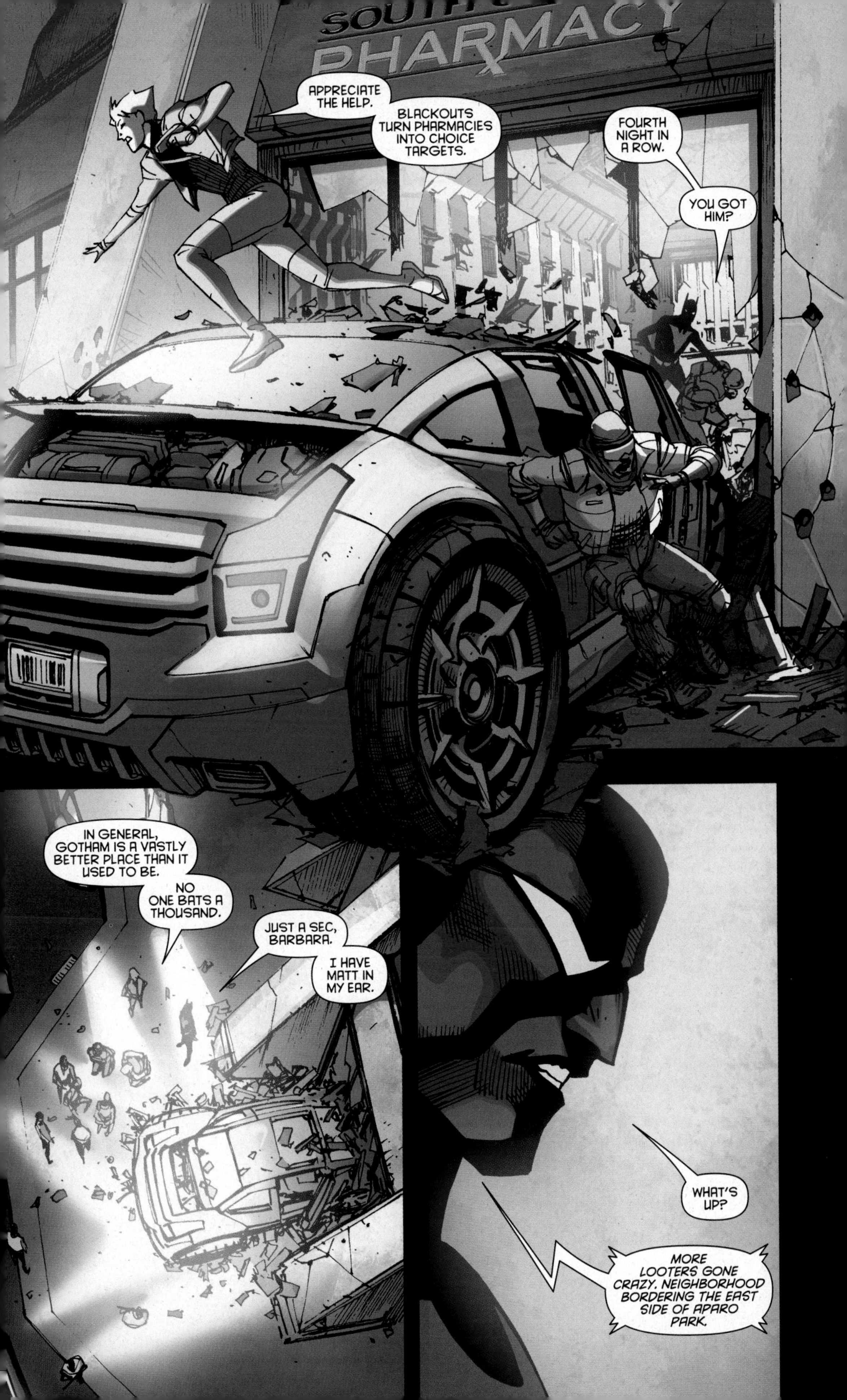
SOUTH
PHARMACY
APPRECIATE THE HELP.
BLACKOUTS TURN PHARMACIES INTO CHOICE TARGETS.
FOURTH NIGHT IN A ROW.
YOU GOT HIM?
IN GENERAL, GOTHAM IS A VASTLY BETTER PLACE THAN IT USED TO BE.
NO ONE BATS A THOUSAND.
JUST A SEC, BARBARA.
I HAVE MATT IN MY EAR.
WHAT'S UP?
MORE LOOTERS GONE CRAZY. NEIGHBORHOOD BORDERING THE EAST SIDE OF APARO PARK.

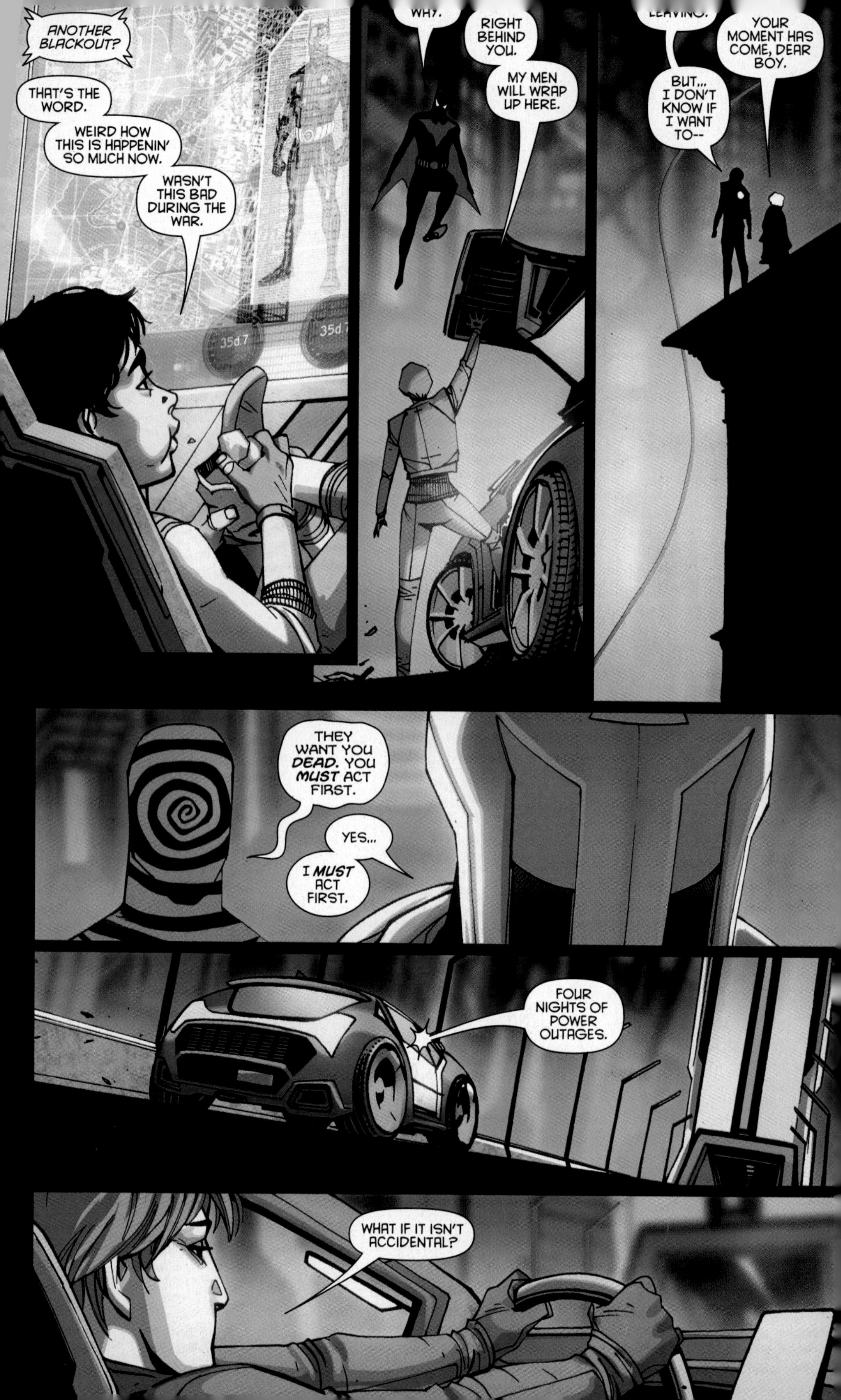
ANOTHER BLACKOUT?
THAT'S THE WORD.
WEIRD HOW THIS IS HAPPENIN' SO MUCH NOW.
WASN'T THIS BAD DURING THE WAR.
RIGHT BEHIND YOU.
MY MEN WILL WRAP UP HERE.
BUT... I DON'T KNOW IF I WANT TO--
YOUR MOMENT HAS COME, DEAR BOY.
THEY WANT YOU DEAD. YOU MUST ACT FIRST.
YES...
I MUST ACT FIRST.
FOUR NIGHTS OF POWER OUTAGES.
WHAT IF IT ISN'T ACCIDENTAL?

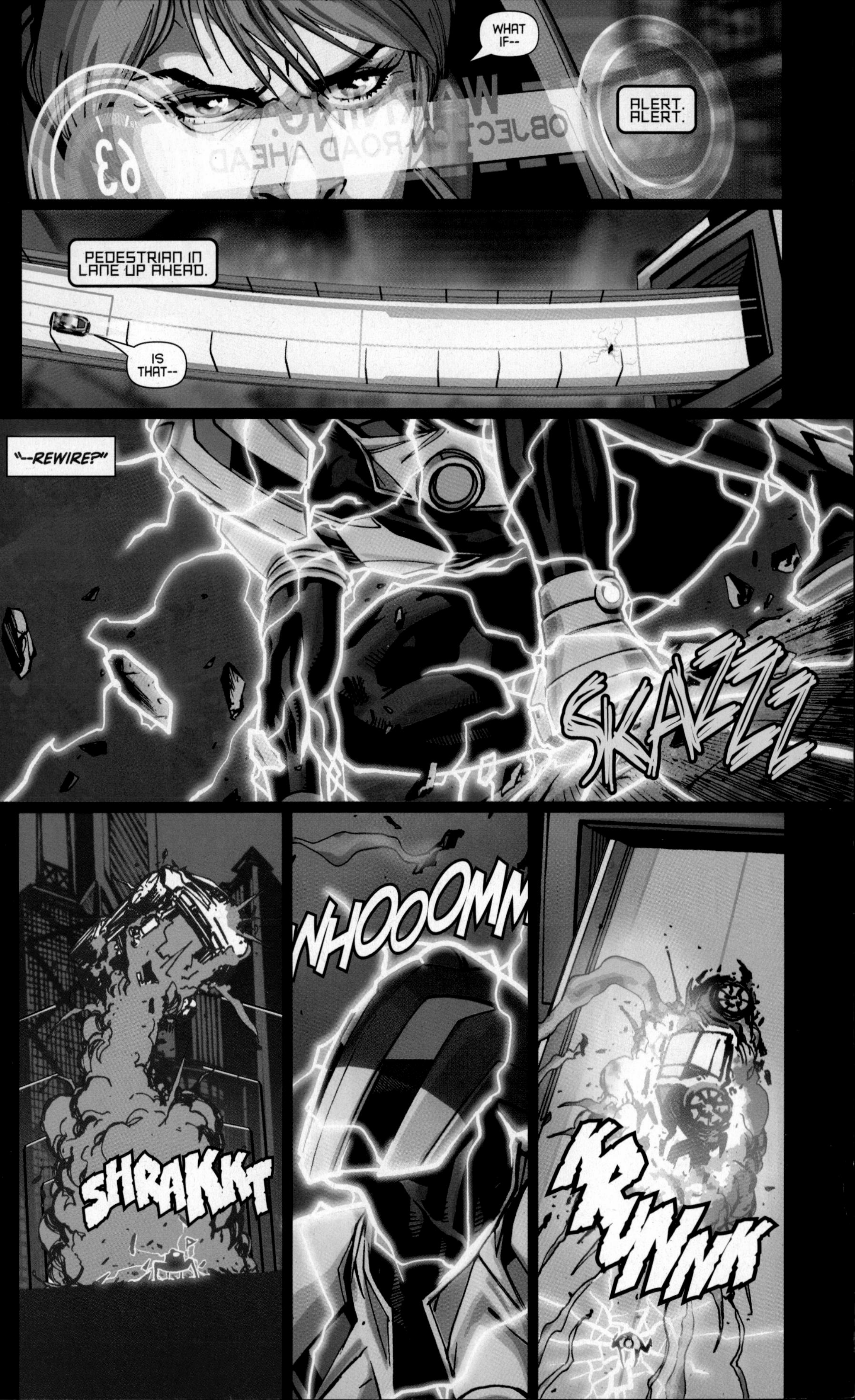
WHAT IF--
ALERT. ALERT.
PEDESTRIAN IN LANE UP AHEAD.
IS THAT--
"--REWIRE?"
SKAZZZ
SHRAKKT
WHOOOOMM
KRUNNK

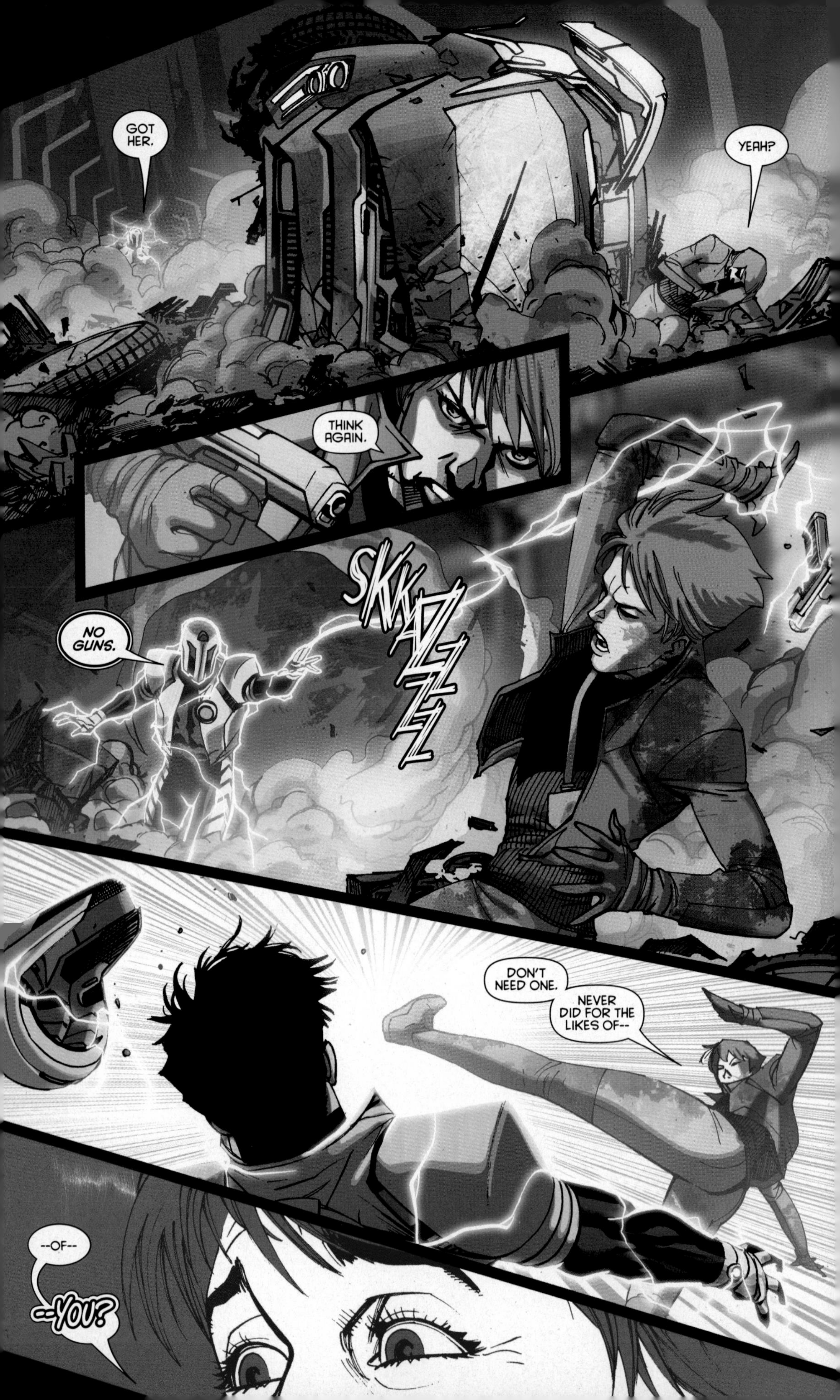
GOT HER.
YEAH?
THINK AGAIN.
NO GUNS.
SKKKAZZZZ
DON'T NEED ONE.
NEVER DID FOR THE LIKES OF--
--OF--
--YOU?

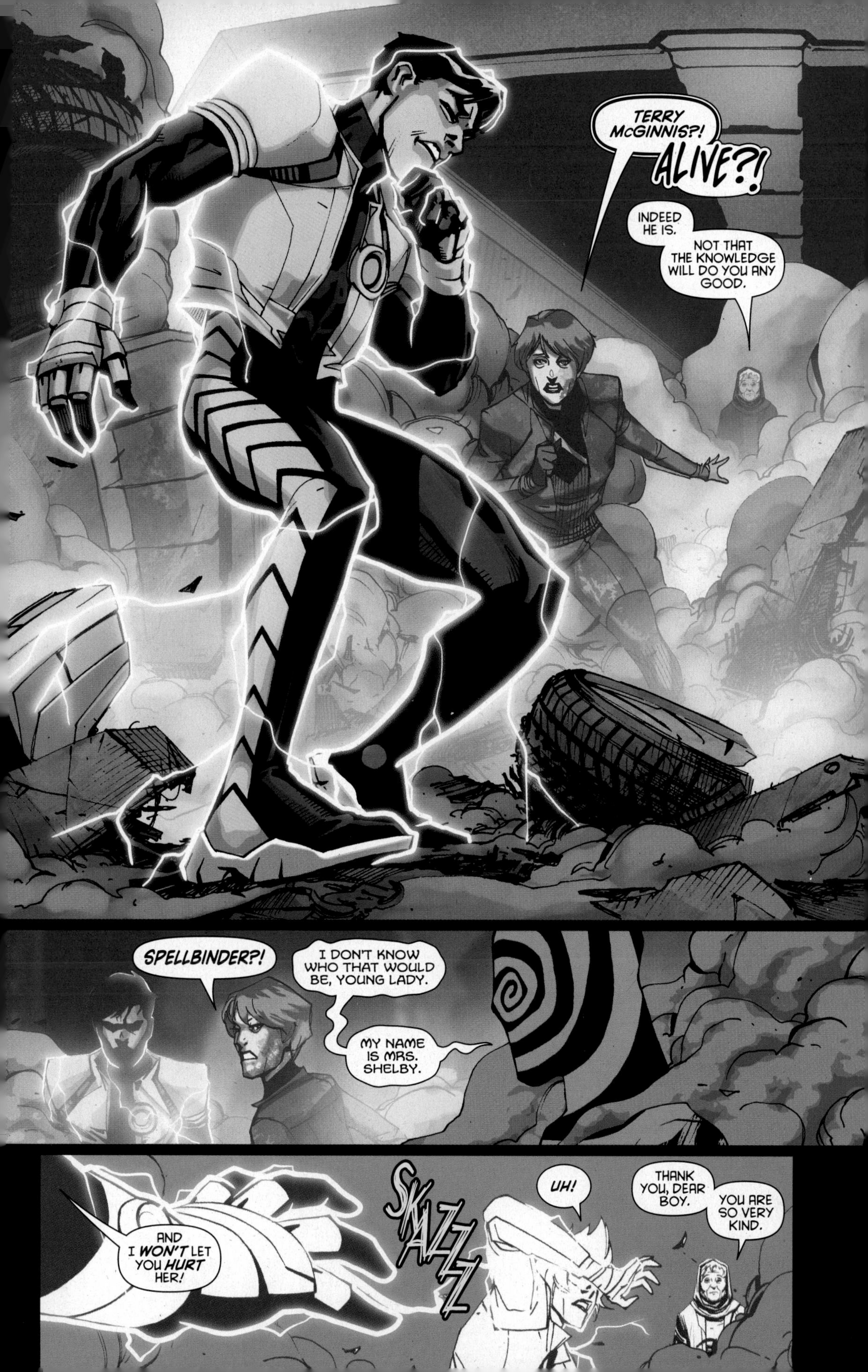
TERRY McGINNIS?! ALIVE?!
INDEED HE IS.
NOT THAT THE KNOWLEDGE WILL DO YOU ANY GOOD.
SPELLBINDER?!
I DON'T KNOW WHO THAT WOULD BE, YOUNG LADY.
MY NAME IS MRS. SHELBY.
AND I WON'T LET YOU HURT HER!
SKAZZZZ
UH!
THANK YOU, DEAR BOY.
YOU ARE SO VERY KIND.

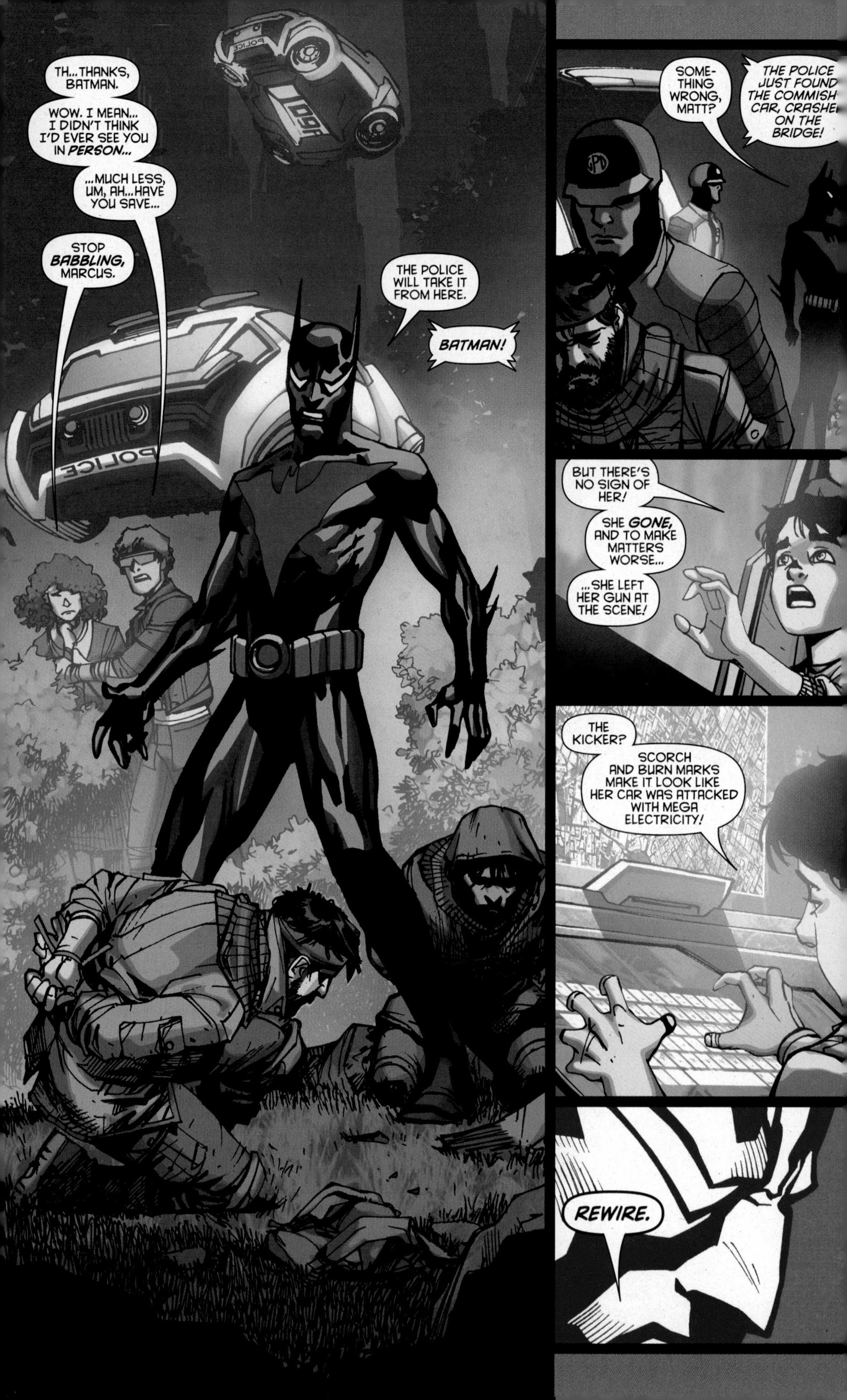
TH...THANKS, BATMAN.
WOW. I MEAN... I DIDN'T THINK I'D EVER SEE YOU IN PERSON...
...MUCH LESS, UM, AH...HAVE YOU SAVE...
STOP BABBLING, MARCUS.
THE POLICE WILL TAKE IT FROM HERE.
BATMAN!
SOME-THING WRONG, MATT?
THE POLICE JUST FOUND THE COMMISH CAR, CRASHE ON THE BRIDGE!
BUT THERE'S NO SIGN OF HER!
SHE GONE, AND TO MAKE MATTERS WORSE...
...SHE LEFT HER GUN AT THE SCENE!
THE KICKER?
SCORCH AND BURN MARKS MAKE IT LOOK LIKE HER CAR WAS ATTACKED WITH MEGA ELECTRICITY!
REWIRE.

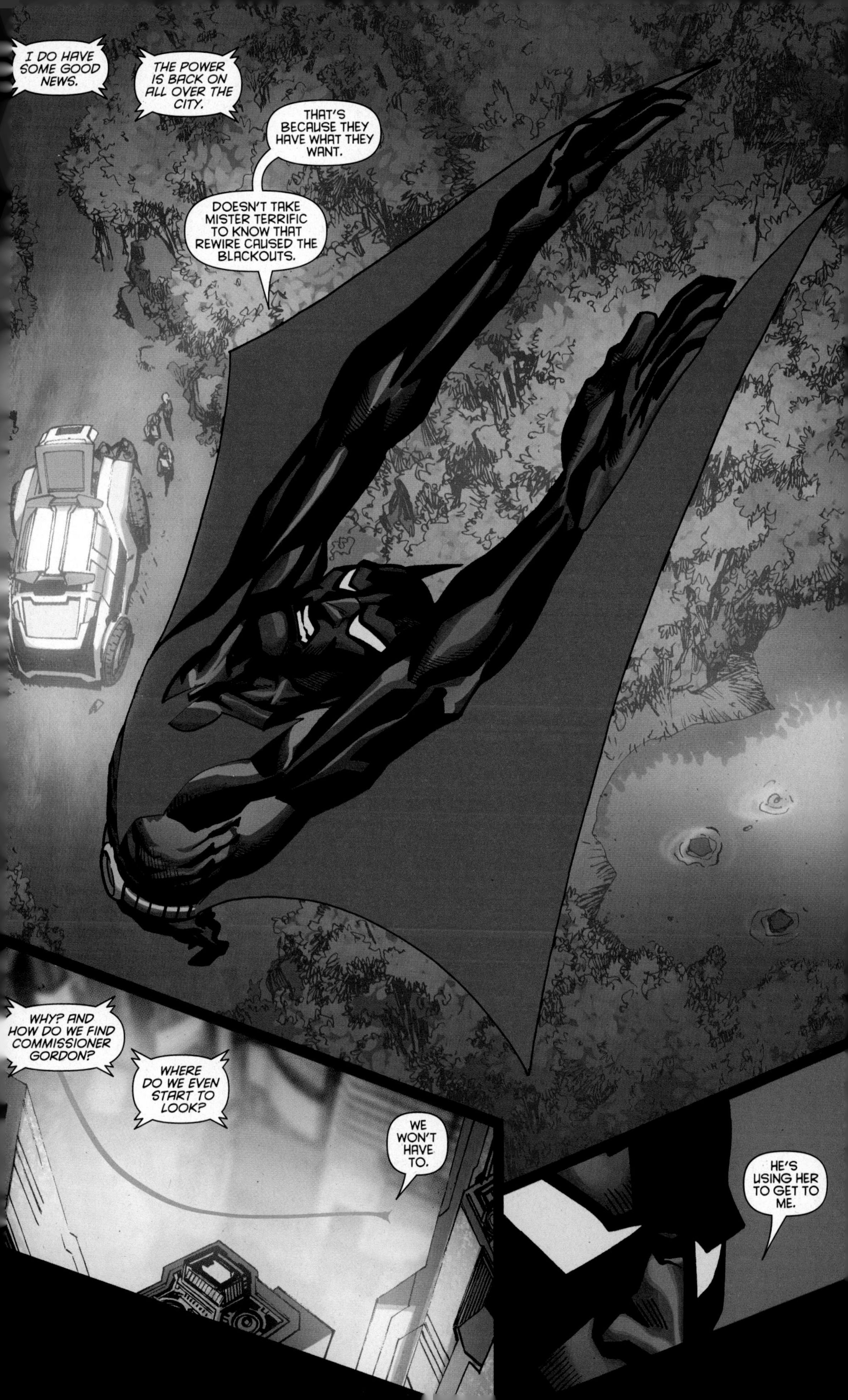
I DO HAVE SOME GOOD NEWS.
THE POWER IS BACK ON ALL OVER THE CITY.
THAT'S BECAUSE THEY HAVE WHAT THEY WANT.
DOESN'T TAKE MISTER TERRIFIC TO KNOW THAT REWIRE CAUSED THE BLACKOUTS.
WHY? AND HOW DO WE FIND COMMISSIONER GORDON?
WHERE DO WE EVEN START TO LOOK?
WE WON'T HAVE TO.
HE'S USING HER TO GET TO ME.

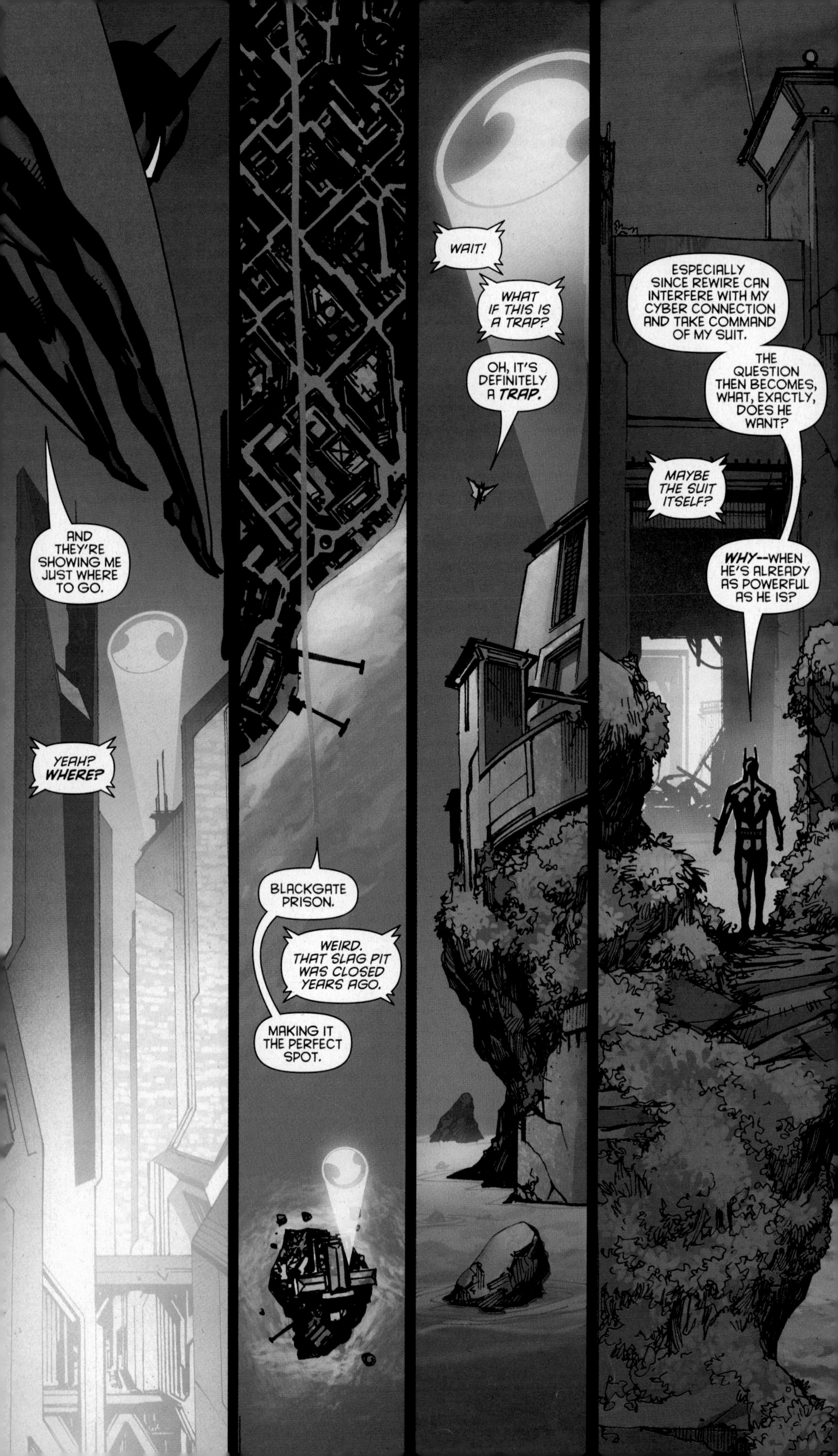
AND THEY'RE SHOWING ME JUST WHERE TO GO.
YEAH? WHERE?
BLACKGATE PRISON.
WEIRD. THAT SLAG PIT WAS CLOSED YEARS AGO.
MAKING IT THE PERFECT SPOT.
WAIT!
WHAT IF THIS IS A TRAP?
OH, IT'S DEFINITELY A TRAP.
ESPECIALLY SINCE REWIRE CAN INTERFERE WITH MY CYBER CONNECTION AND TAKE COMMAND OF MY SUIT.
THE QUESTION THEN BECOMES, WHAT, EXACTLY, DOES HE WANT?
MAYBE THE SUIT ITSELF?
WHY--WHEN HE'S ALREADY AS POWERFUL AS HE IS?

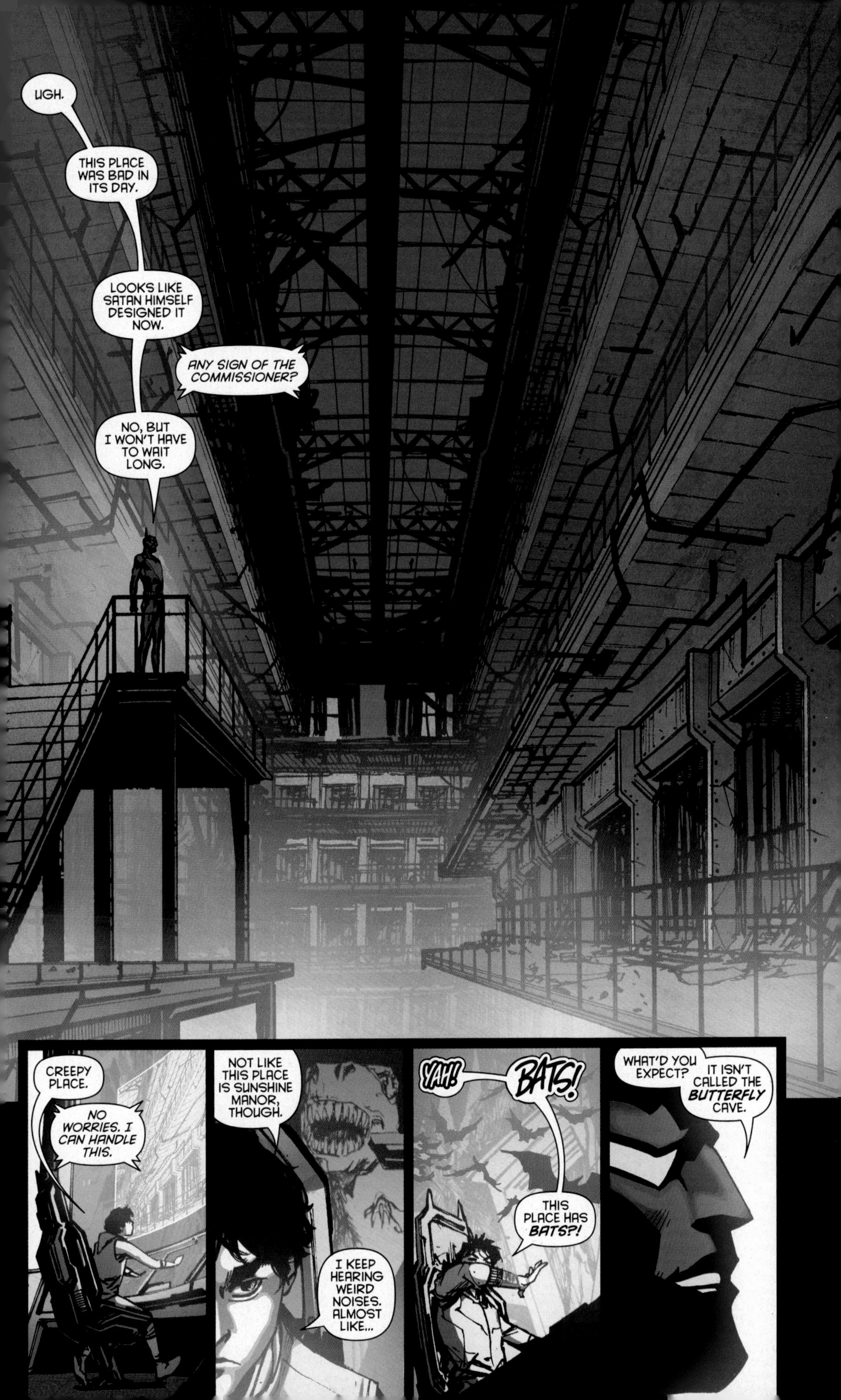
UGH.
THIS PLACE WAS BAD IN ITS DAY.
LOOKS LIKE SATAN HIMSELF DESIGNED IT NOW.
ANY SIGN OF THE COMMISSIONER?
NO, BUT I WON'T HAVE TO WAIT LONG.
CREEPY PLACE.
NO WORRIES. I CAN HANDLE THIS.
NOT LIKE THIS PLACE IS SUNSHINE MANOR, THOUGH.
I KEEP HEARING WEIRD NOISES. ALMOST LIKE...
YAH!
BATS!
THIS PLACE HAS BATS?!
WHAT'D YOU EXPECT?
IT ISN'T CALLED THE BUTTERFLY CAVE.

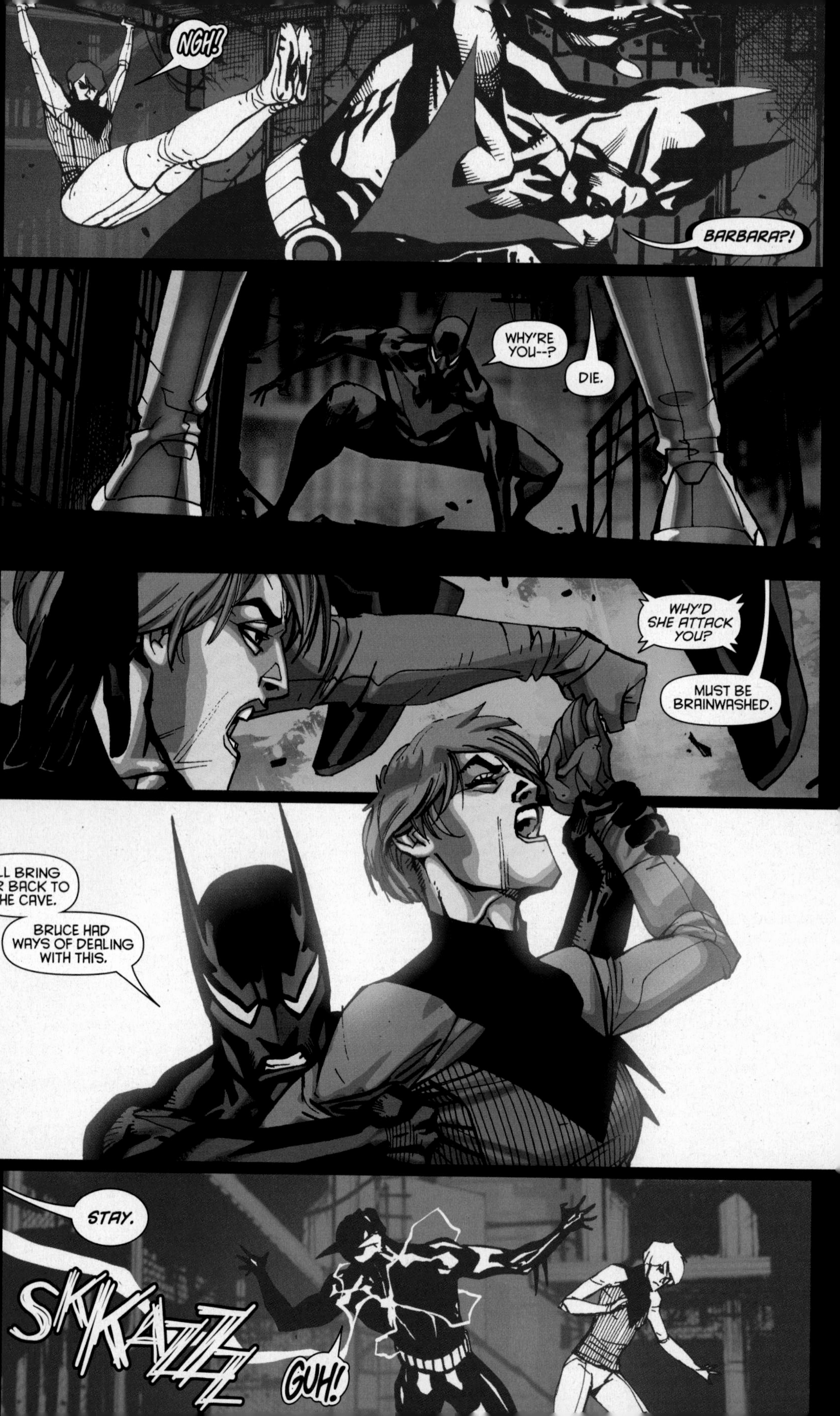
NGH!
BARBARA?!
WHY'RE YOU--?
DIE.
WHY'D SHE ATTACK YOU?
MUST BE BRAINWASHED.
I'LL BRING HER BACK TO THE CAVE.
BRUCE HAD WAYS OF DEALING WITH THIS.
STAY.
SKKAZZZZ
GUH!

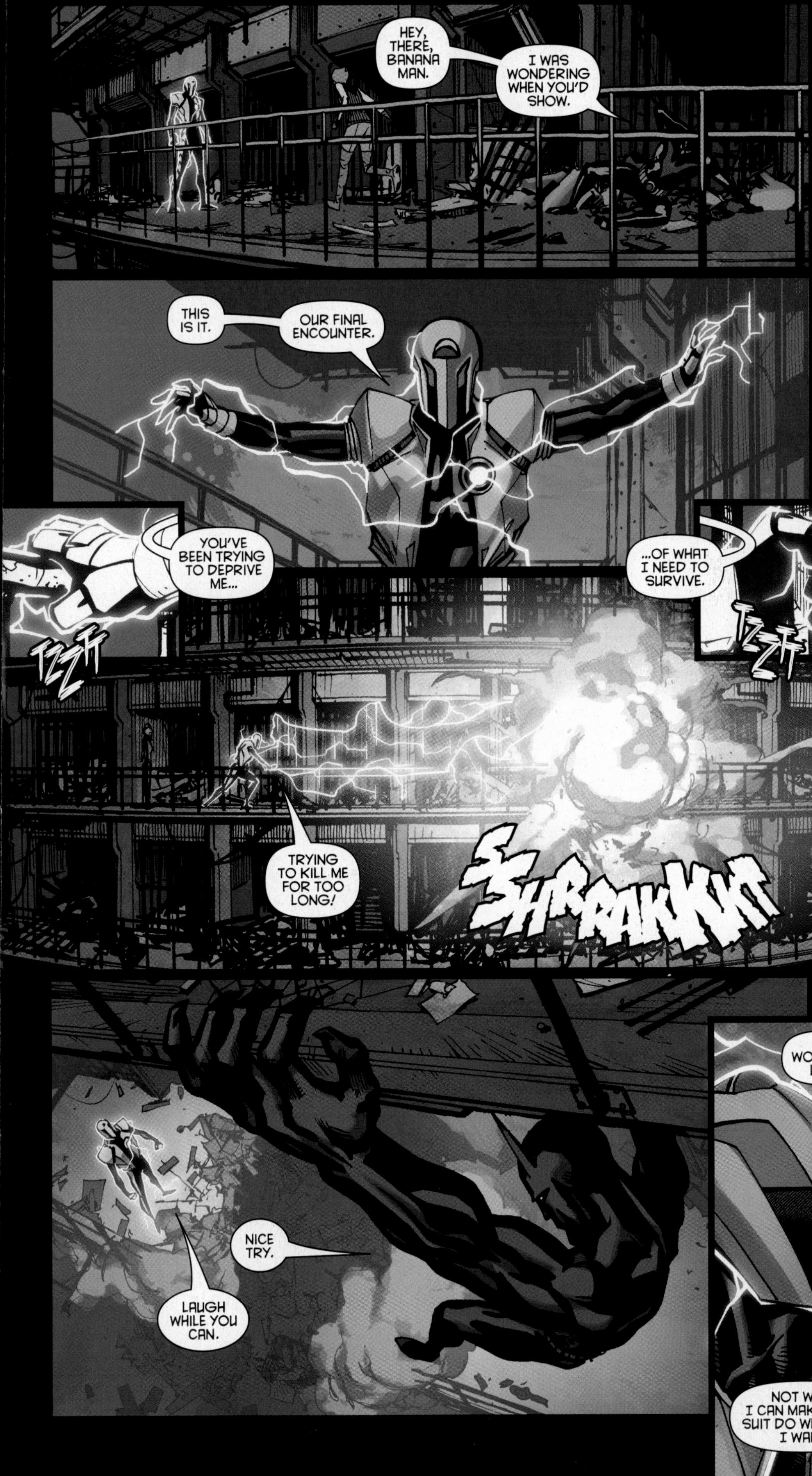

HEY, THERE, BANANA MAN.
I WAS WONDERING WHEN YOU'D SHOW.
THIS IS IT.
OUR FINAL ENCOUNTER.
YOU'VE BEEN TRYING TO DEPRIVE ME...
TZZZT
...OF WHAT I NEED TO SURVIVE.
TZZZT
TRYING TO KILL ME FOR TOO LONG!
SSHRAKKKT
NICE TRY.
LAUGH WHILE YOU CAN.
IT WON'T LAST LONG.
NOT WHEN I CAN MAKE YOUR SUIT DO WHATEVER I WANT.

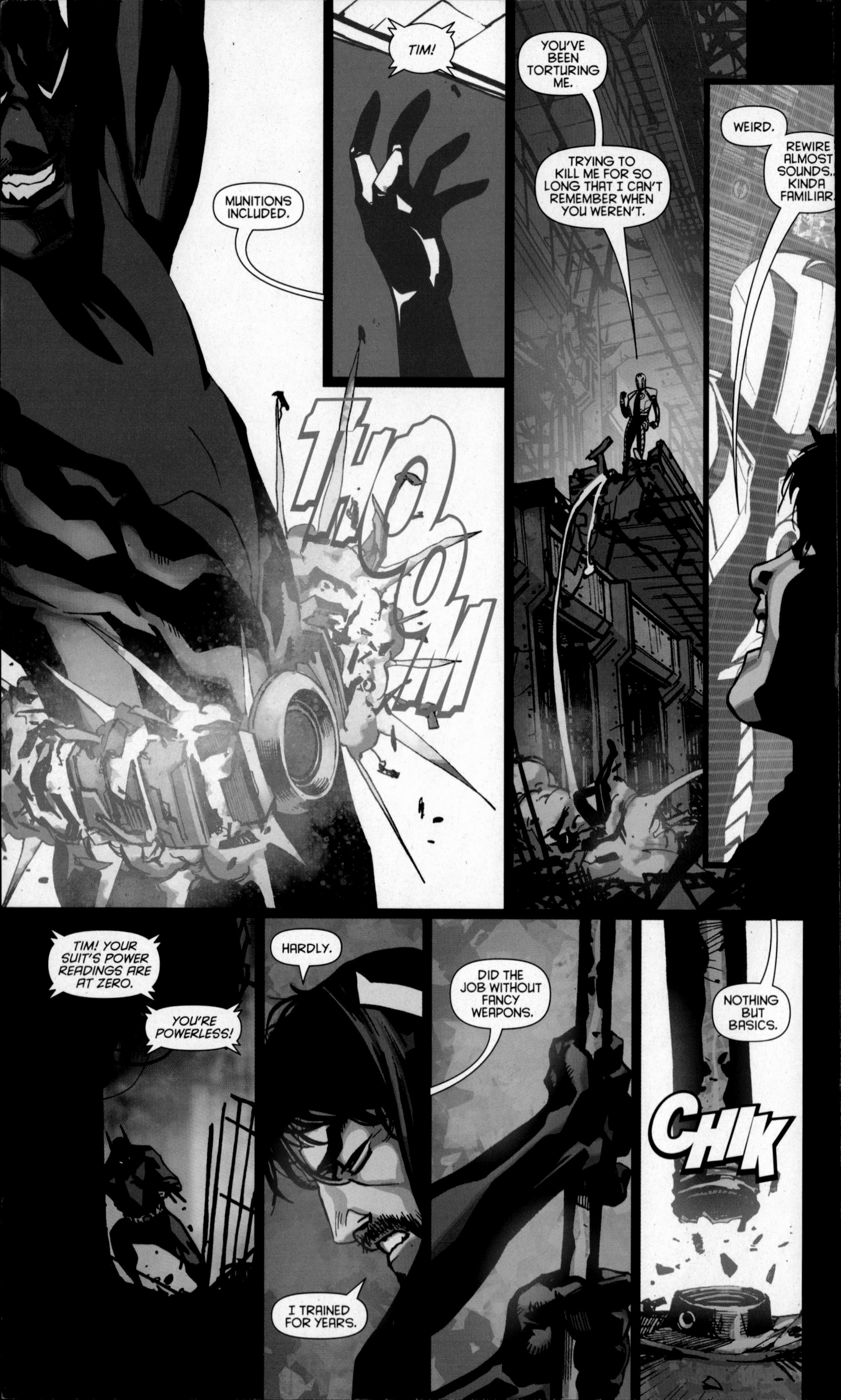

MUNITIONS INCLUDED.
TIM!
THOOM
YOU'VE BEEN TORTURING ME.
TRYING TO KILL ME FOR SO LONG THAT I CAN'T REMEMBER WHEN YOU WEREN'T.
WEIRD.
REWIRE ALMOST SOUNDS.. KINDA FAMILIAR.
TIM! YOUR SUIT'S POWER READINGS ARE AT ZERO.
YOU'RE POWERLESS!
HARDLY.
I TRAINED FOR YEARS.
DID THE JOB WITHOUT FANCY WEAPONS.
NOTHING BUT BASICS.
CHIK

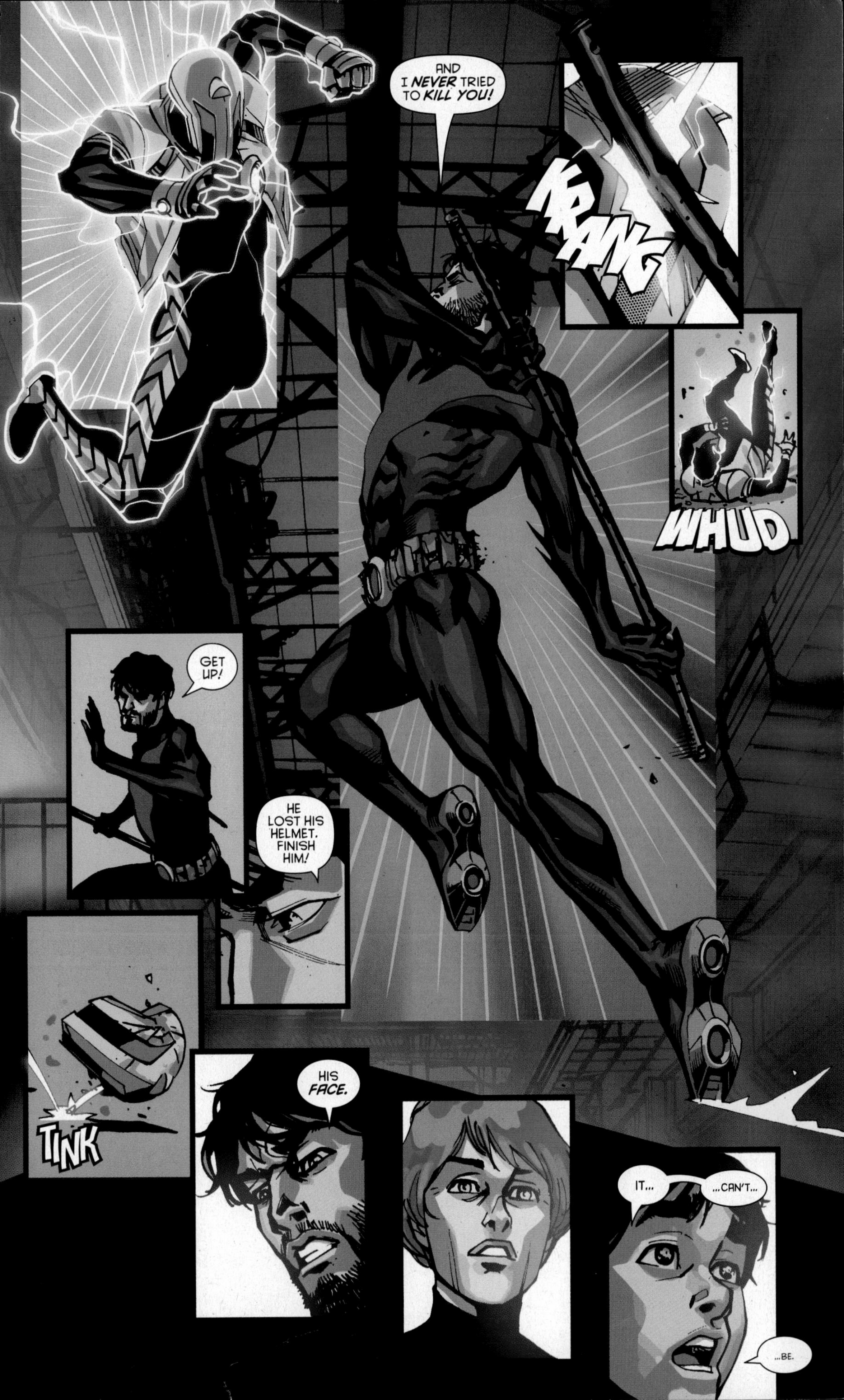
AND I NEVER TRIED TO KILL YOU!
KRANG
WHUD
GET UP!
HE LOST HIS HELMET. FINISH HIM!
TINK
HIS FACE.
IT...
...CAN'T...
...BE.

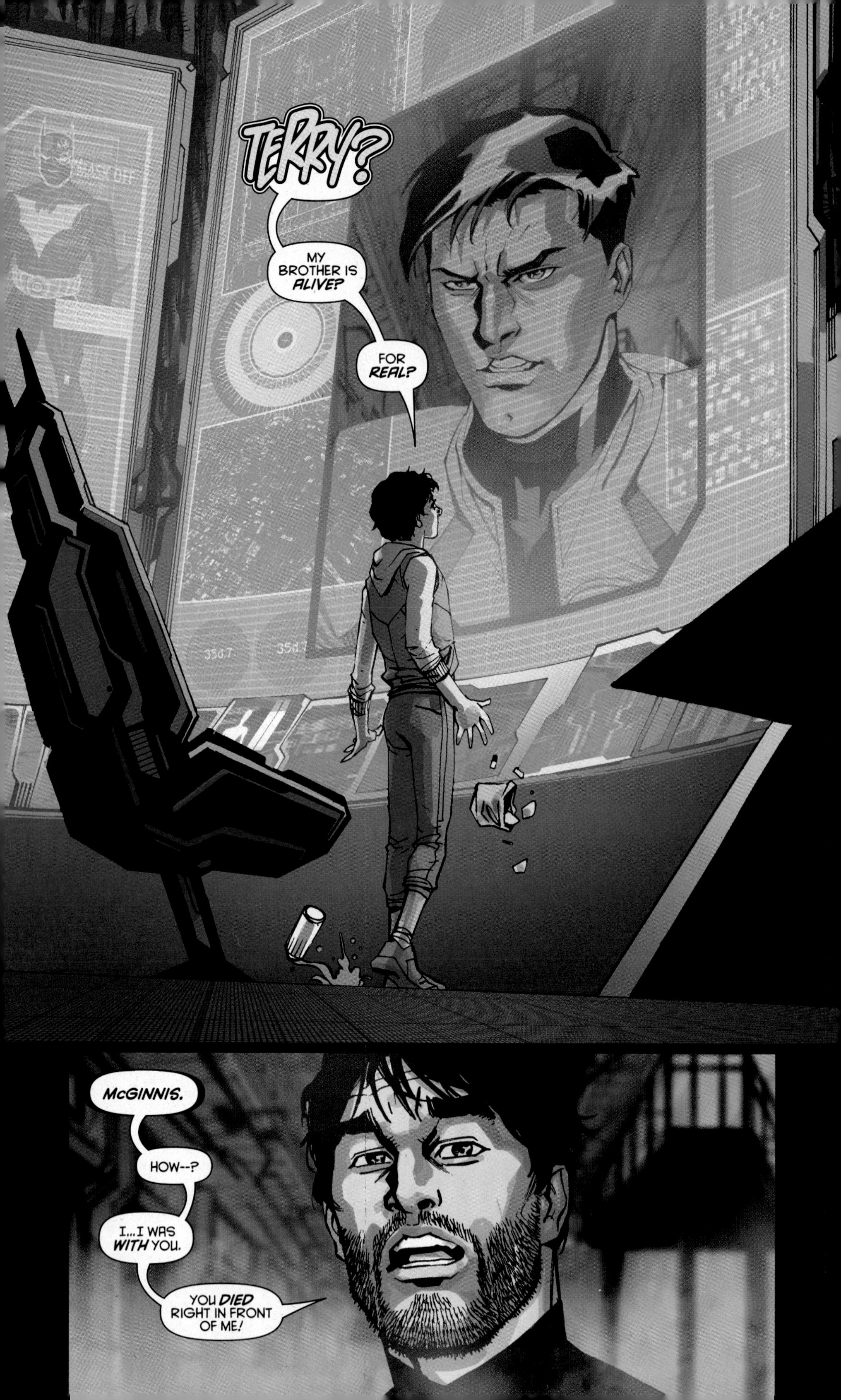

MASK OFF
TERRY?
MY BROTHER IS ***ALIVE?***
FOR ***REAL?***
McGINNIS.
HOW--?
I...I WAS ***WITH*** YOU.
YOU ***DIED*** RIGHT IN FRONT OF ME!

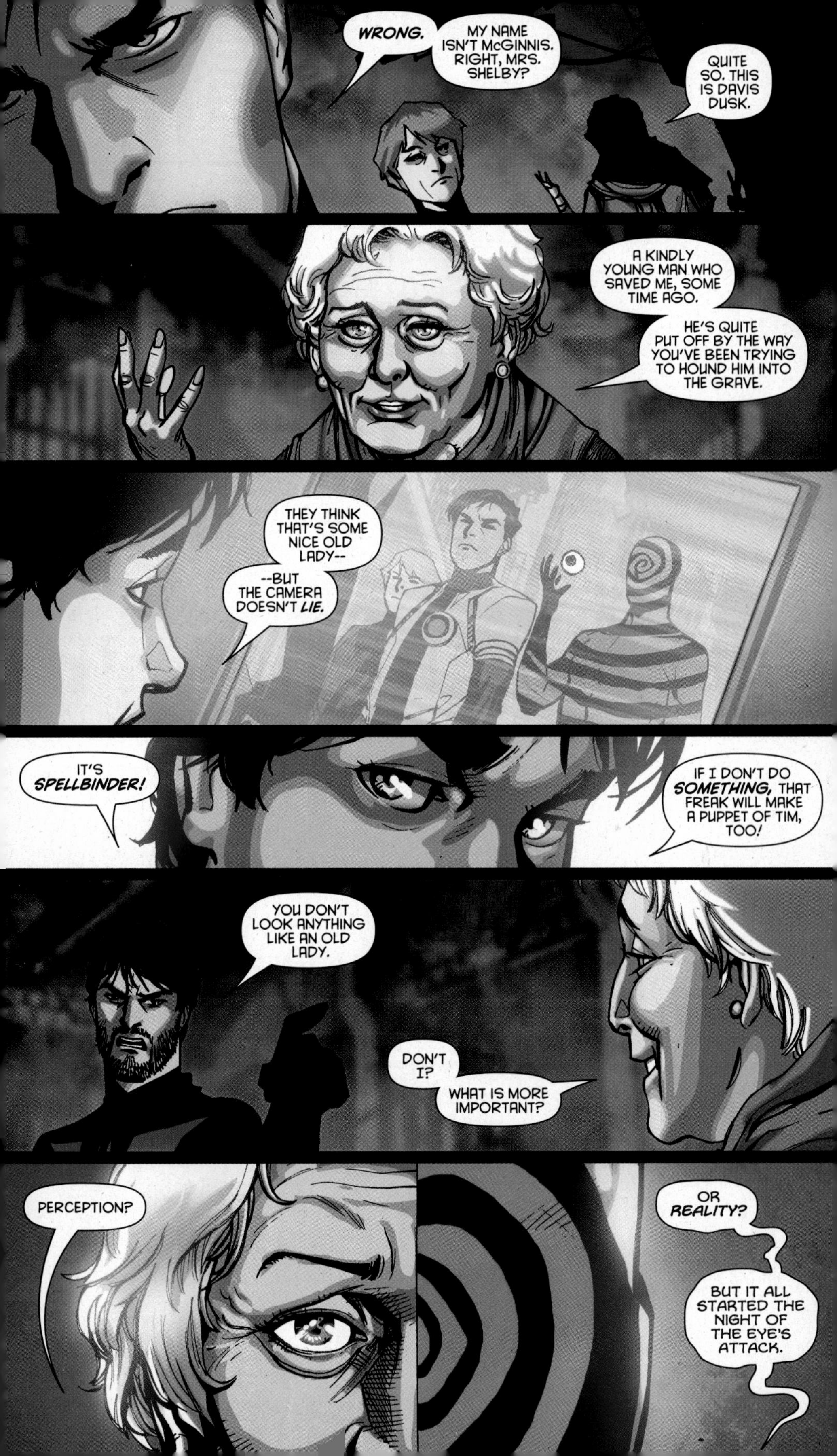
WRONG.
MY NAME ISN'T McGINNIS. RIGHT, MRS. SHELBY?
QUITE SO. THIS IS DAVIS DUSK.
A KINDLY YOUNG MAN WHO SAVED ME, SOME TIME AGO.
HE'S QUITE PUT OFF BY THE WAY YOU'VE BEEN TRYING TO HOUND HIM INTO THE GRAVE.
THEY THINK THAT'S SOME NICE OLD LADY--
--BUT THE CAMERA DOESN'T LIE.
IT'S SPELLBINDER!
IF I DON'T DO SOMETHING, THAT FREAK WILL MAKE A PUPPET OF TIM, TOO!
YOU DON'T LOOK ANYTHING LIKE AN OLD LADY.
DON'T I?
WHAT IS MORE IMPORTANT?
PERCEPTION?
OR REALITY?
BUT IT ALL STARTED THE NIGHT OF THE EYE'S ATTACK.

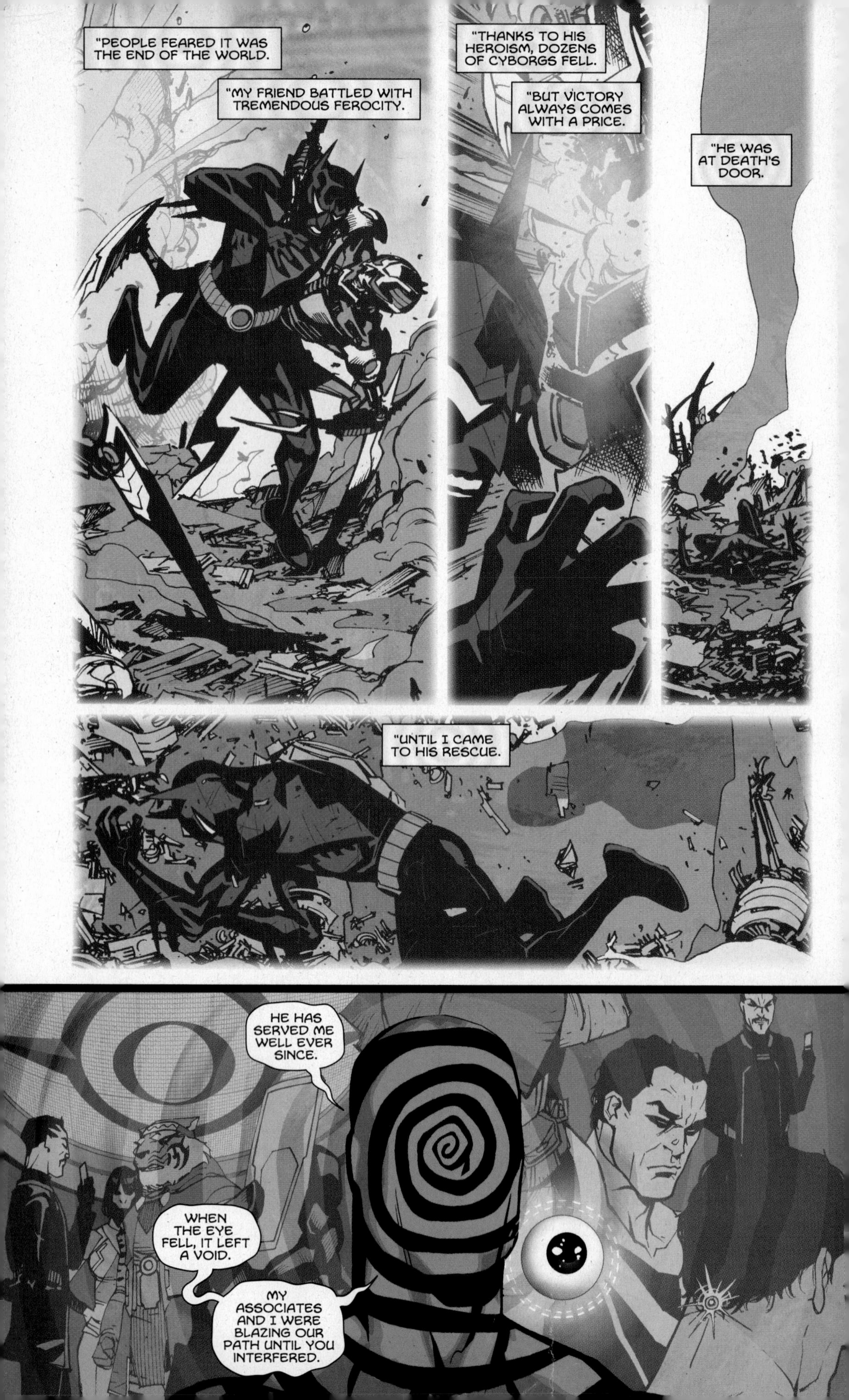
"PEOPLE FEARED IT WAS THE END OF THE WORLD.
"MY FRIEND BATTLED WITH TREMENDOUS FEROCITY.
"THANKS TO HIS HEROISM, DOZENS OF CYBORGS FELL.
"BUT VICTORY ALWAYS COMES WITH A PRICE.
"HE WAS AT DEATH'S DOOR.
"UNTIL I CAME TO HIS RESCUE.
HE HAS SERVED ME WELL EVER SINCE.
WHEN THE EYE FELL, IT LEFT A VOID.
MY ASSOCIATES AND I WERE BLAZING OUR PATH UNTIL YOU INTERFERED.

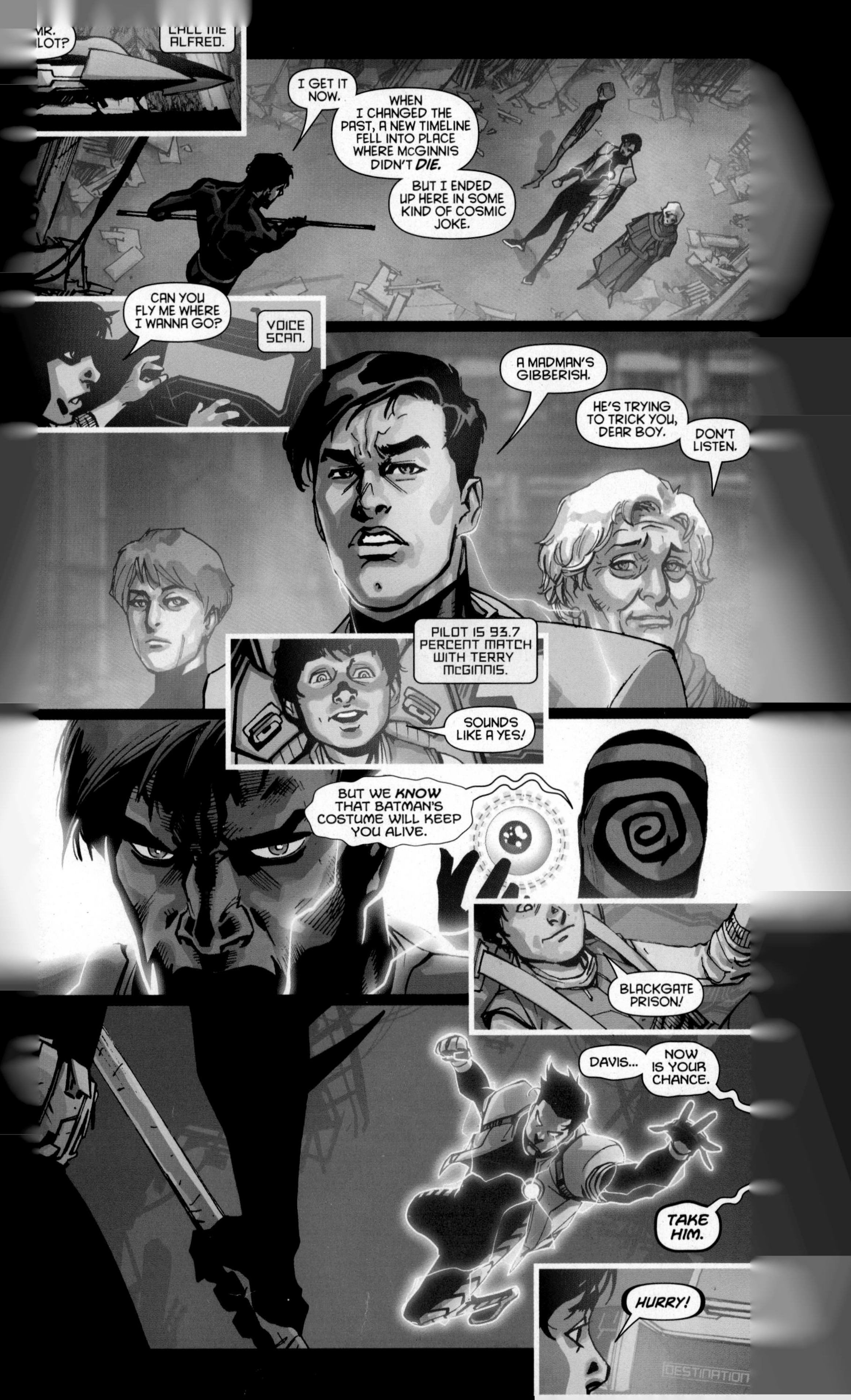
MR.
LOT?
ALFRED.
I GET IT NOW.
WHEN I CHANGED THE PAST, A NEW TIMELINE FELL INTO PLACE WHERE McGINNIS DIDN'T **DIE.**
BUT I ENDED UP HERE IN SOME KIND OF COSMIC JOKE.
CAN YOU FLY ME WHERE I WANNA GO?
VOICE SCAN.
A MADMAN'S GIBBERISH.
HE'S TRYING TO TRICK YOU, DEAR BOY.
DON'T LISTEN.
PILOT IS 93.7 PERCENT MATCH WITH TERRY McGINNIS.
SOUNDS LIKE A YES!
BUT WE **KNOW** THAT BATMAN'S COSTUME WILL KEEP YOU ALIVE.
BLACKGATE PRISON!
DAVIS...
NOW IS YOUR CHANCE.
TAKE HIM.
HURRY!
DESTINATION

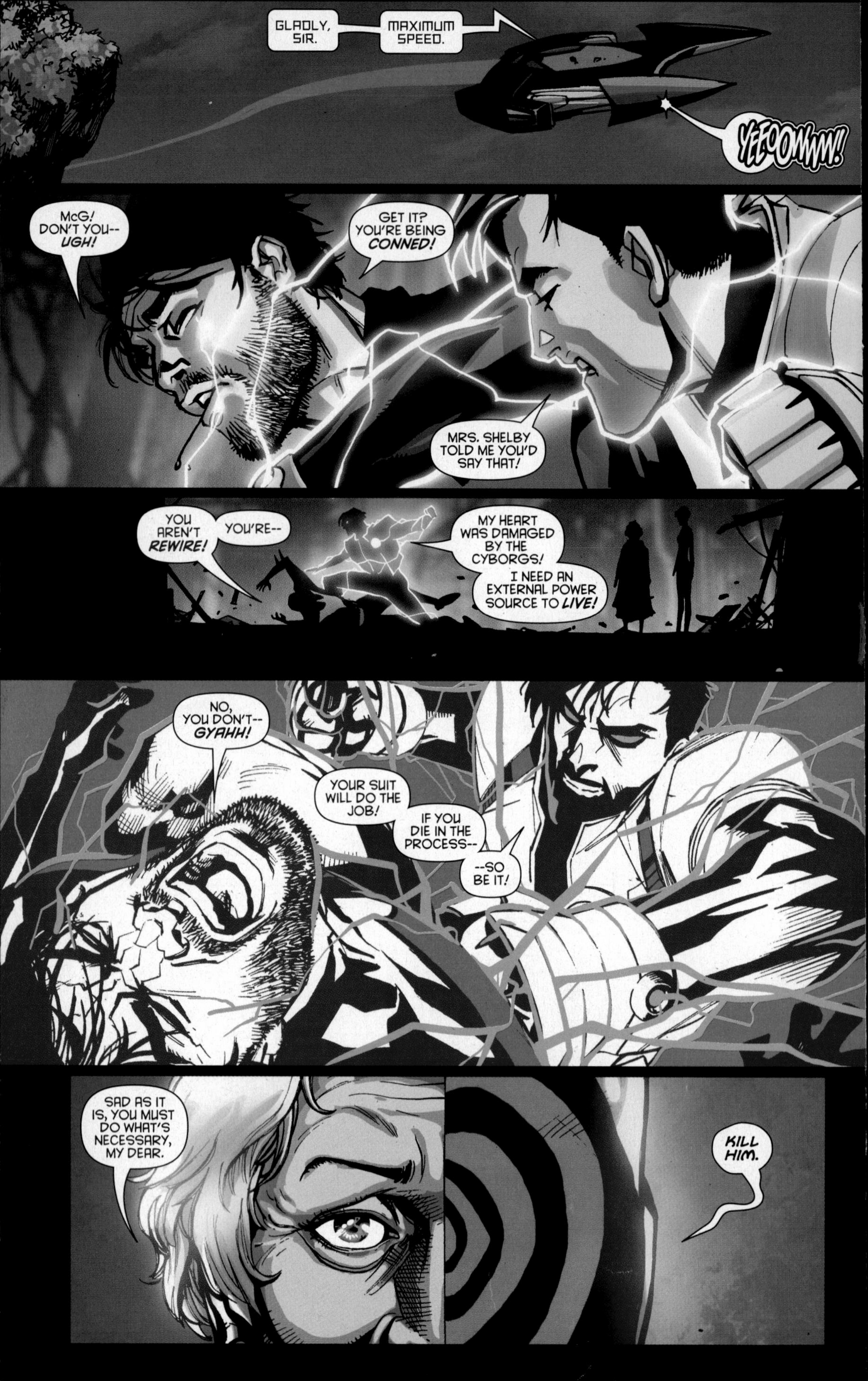
GLADLY, SIR.
MAXIMUM SPEED.
YEEOOWWW!
McG! DON'T YOU-- UGH!
GET IT? YOU'RE BEING CONNED!
MRS. SHELBY TOLD ME YOU'D SAY THAT!
YOU AREN'T REWIRE!
YOU'RE--
MY HEART WAS DAMAGED BY THE CYBORGS!
I NEED AN EXTERNAL POWER SOURCE TO LIVE!
NO, YOU DON'T-- GYAHH!
YOUR SUIT WILL DO THE JOB!
IF YOU DIE IN THE PROCESS--
--SO BE IT!
SAD AS IT IS, YOU MUST DO WHAT'S NECESSARY, MY DEAR.
KILL HIM.

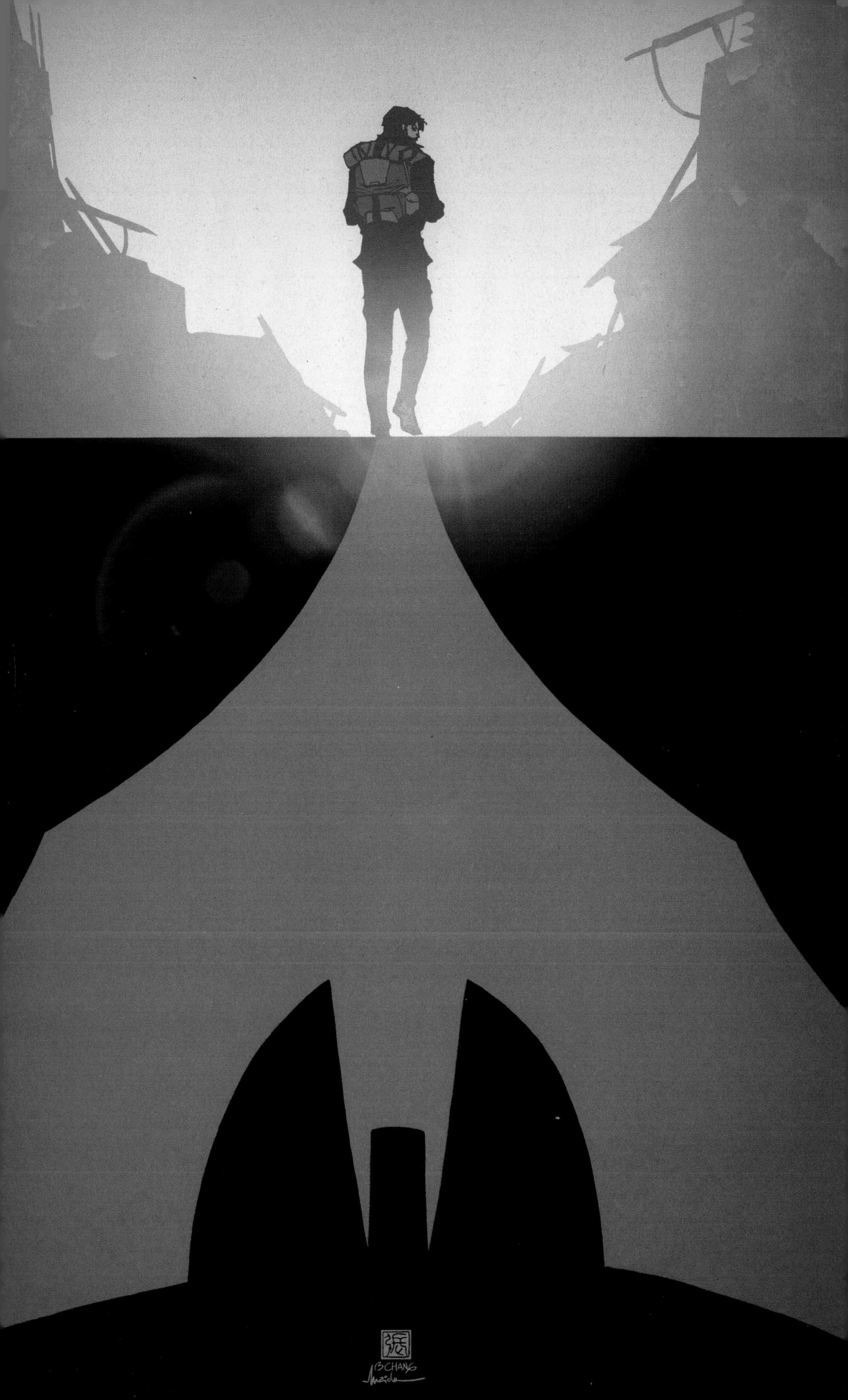
BCHANG

STEPHEN THOMPSON artist LISA JACKSON colorist BERNARD CHANG & MARCELO MAIOLO cover

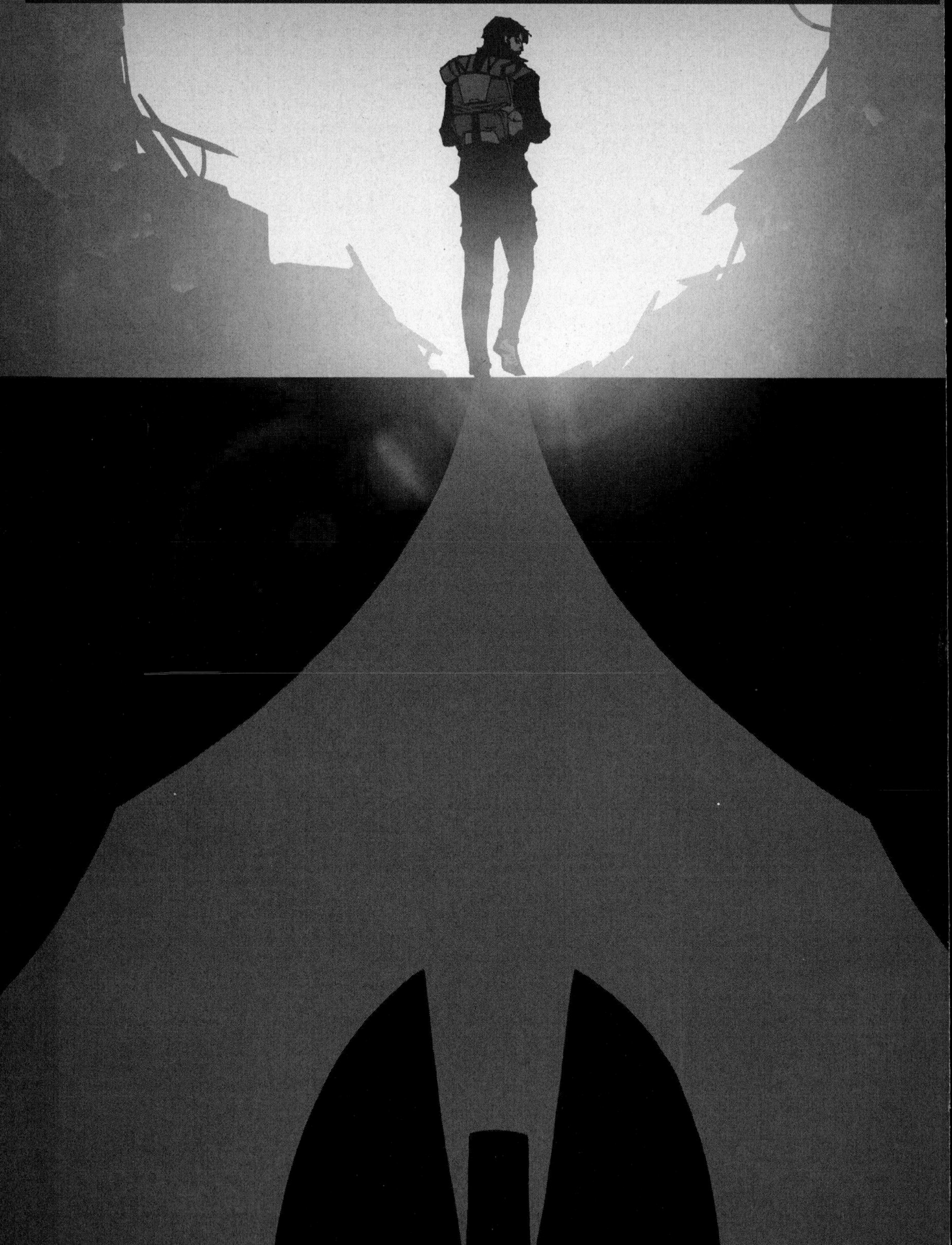

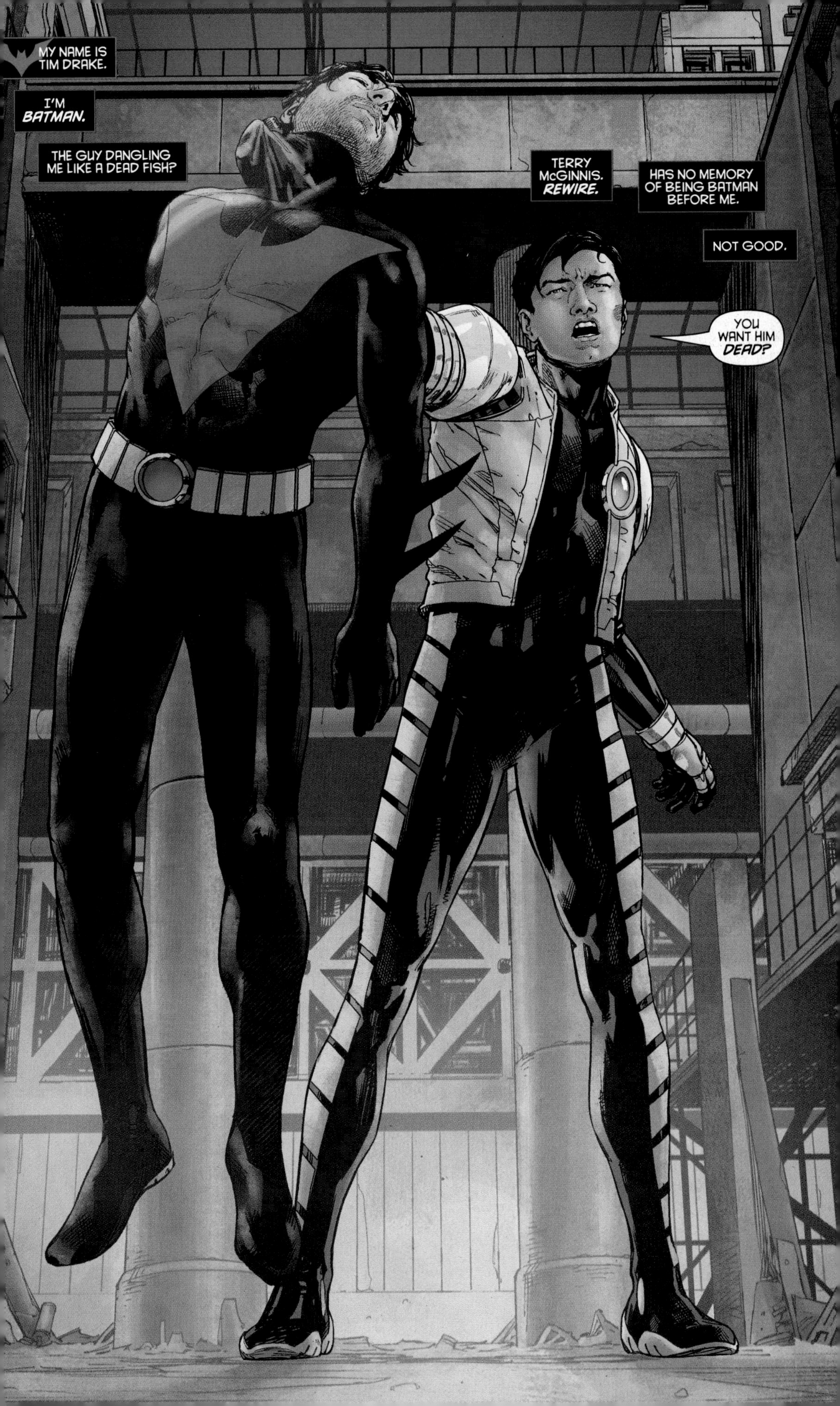
MY NAME IS TIM DRAKE.
I'M *BATMAN.*
THE GUY DANGLING ME LIKE A DEAD FISH?
TERRY McGINNIS. *REWIRE.*
HAS NO MEMORY OF BEING BATMAN BEFORE ME.
NOT GOOD.
YOU WANT HIM *DEAD?*

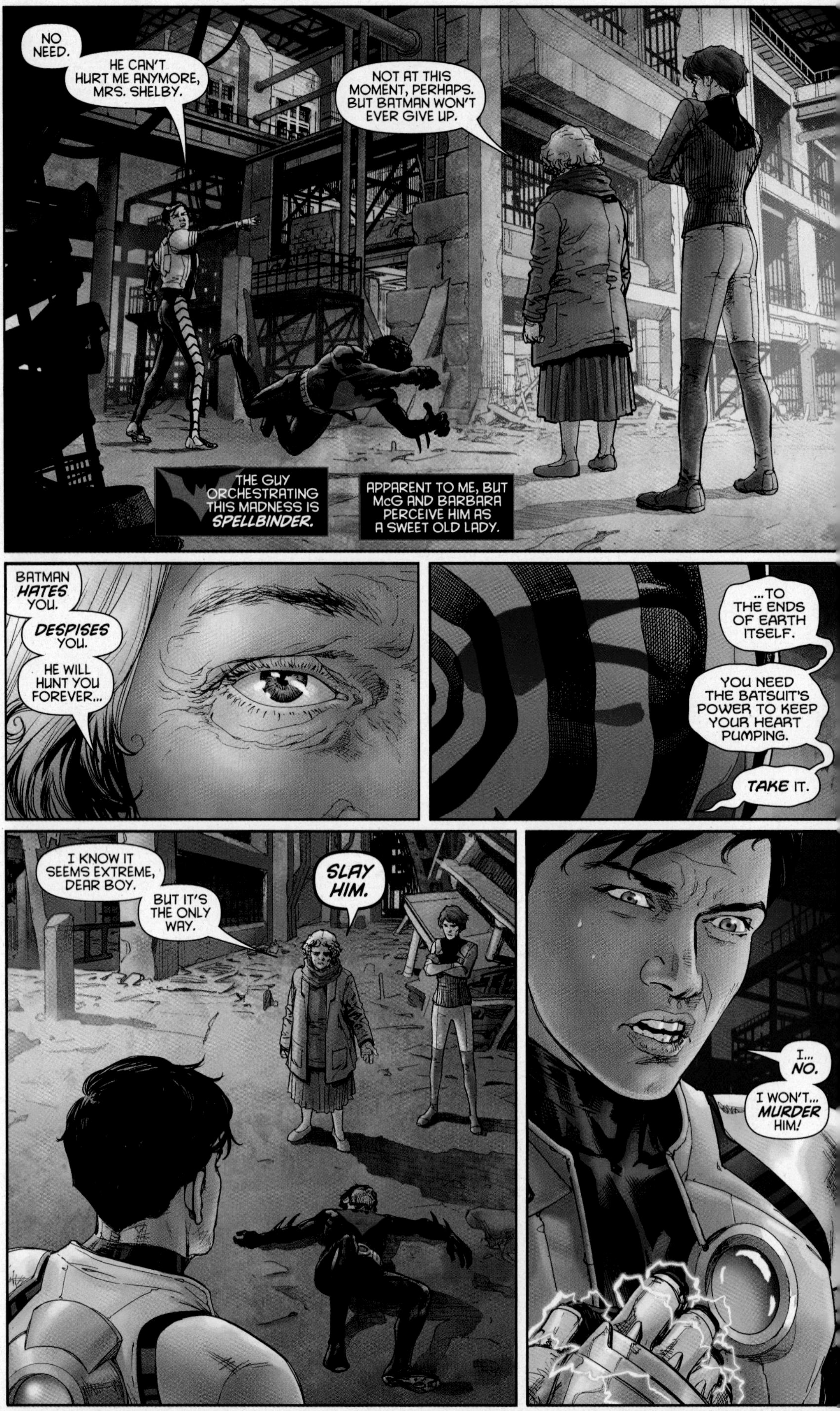

NO NEED.
HE CAN'T HURT ME ANYMORE, MRS. SHELBY.
NOT AT THIS MOMENT, PERHAPS. BUT BATMAN WON'T EVER GIVE UP.
THE GUY ORCHESTRATING THIS MADNESS IS SPELLBINDER.
APPARENT TO ME, BUT McG AND BARBARA PERCEIVE HIM AS A SWEET OLD LADY.
BATMAN HATES YOU.
DESPISES YOU.
HE WILL HUNT YOU FOREVER...
...TO THE ENDS OF EARTH ITSELF.
YOU NEED THE BATSUIT'S POWER TO KEEP YOUR HEART PUMPING.
TAKE IT.
I KNOW IT SEEMS EXTREME, DEAR BOY.
BUT IT'S THE ONLY WAY.
SLAY HIM.
I... NO.
I WON'T... MURDER HIM!

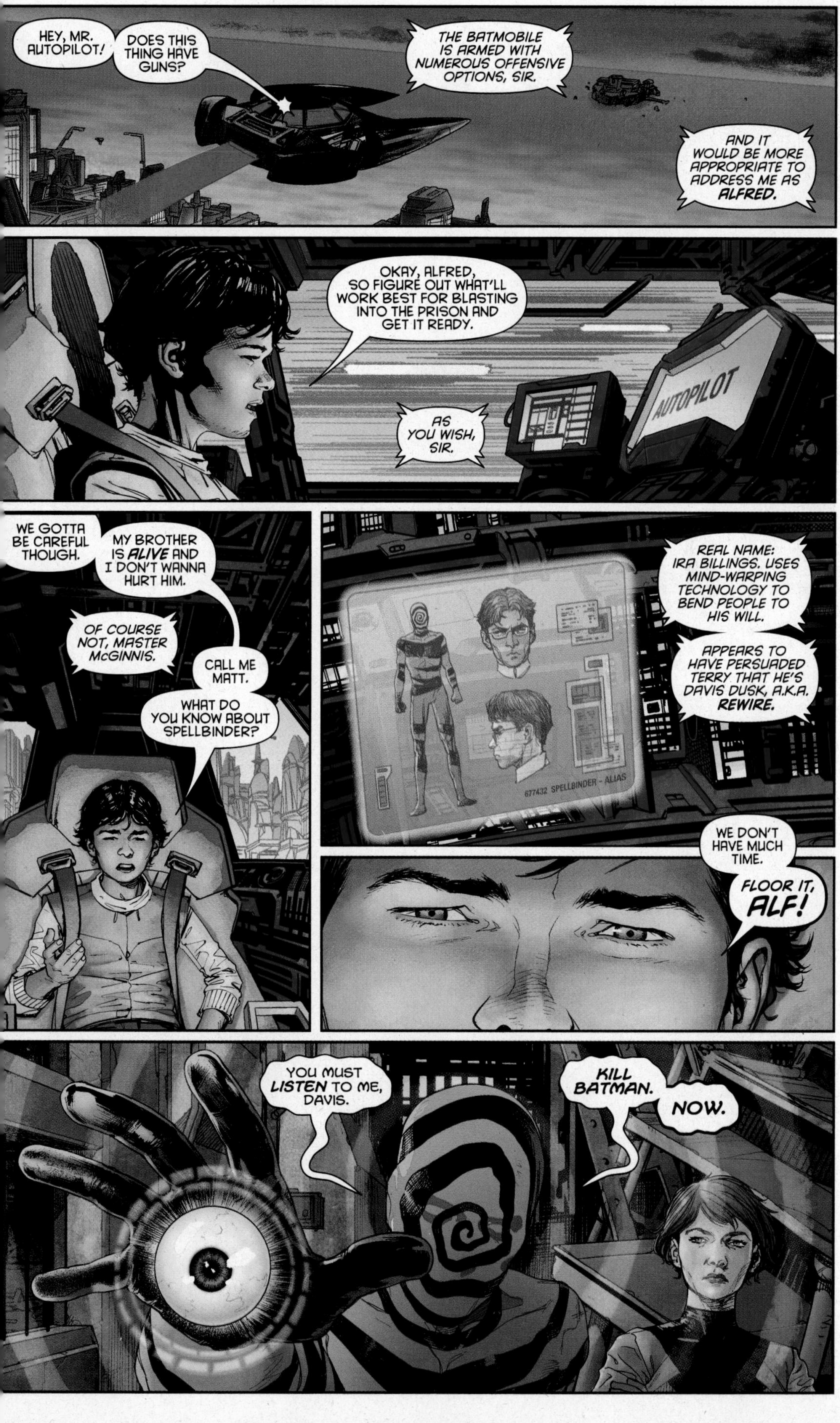
HEY, MR. AUTOPILOT!
DOES THIS THING HAVE GUNS?
THE BATMOBILE IS ARMED WITH NUMEROUS OFFENSIVE OPTIONS, SIR.
AND IT WOULD BE MORE APPROPRIATE TO ADDRESS ME AS ALFRED.
OKAY, ALFRED, SO FIGURE OUT WHAT'LL WORK BEST FOR BLASTING INTO THE PRISON AND GET IT READY.
AUTOPILOT
AS YOU WISH, SIR.
WE GOTTA BE CAREFUL THOUGH.
MY BROTHER IS ALIVE AND I DON'T WANNA HURT HIM.
OF COURSE NOT, MASTER McGINNIS.
CALL ME MATT.
WHAT DO YOU KNOW ABOUT SPELLBINDER?
677432 SPELLBINDER - ALIAS
REAL NAME: IRA BILLINGS. USES MIND-WARPING TECHNOLOGY TO BEND PEOPLE TO HIS WILL.
APPEARS TO HAVE PERSUADED TERRY THAT HE'S DAVIS DUSK, A.K.A. REWIRE.
WE DON'T HAVE MUCH TIME.
FLOOR IT, ALF!
YOU MUST LISTEN TO ME, DAVIS.
KILL BATMAN.
NOW.

I...MUST LISTEN.

KILL HIM.

NOW.

CRRACKLE KRRAK KRRAK

BRAKKA KRRAKKA CHAK!

WHA--?

CAREFUL NOT TO HIT MY BROTHER!

I AM ENDEAVORING NOT TO, SIR.

BWHDOOOM

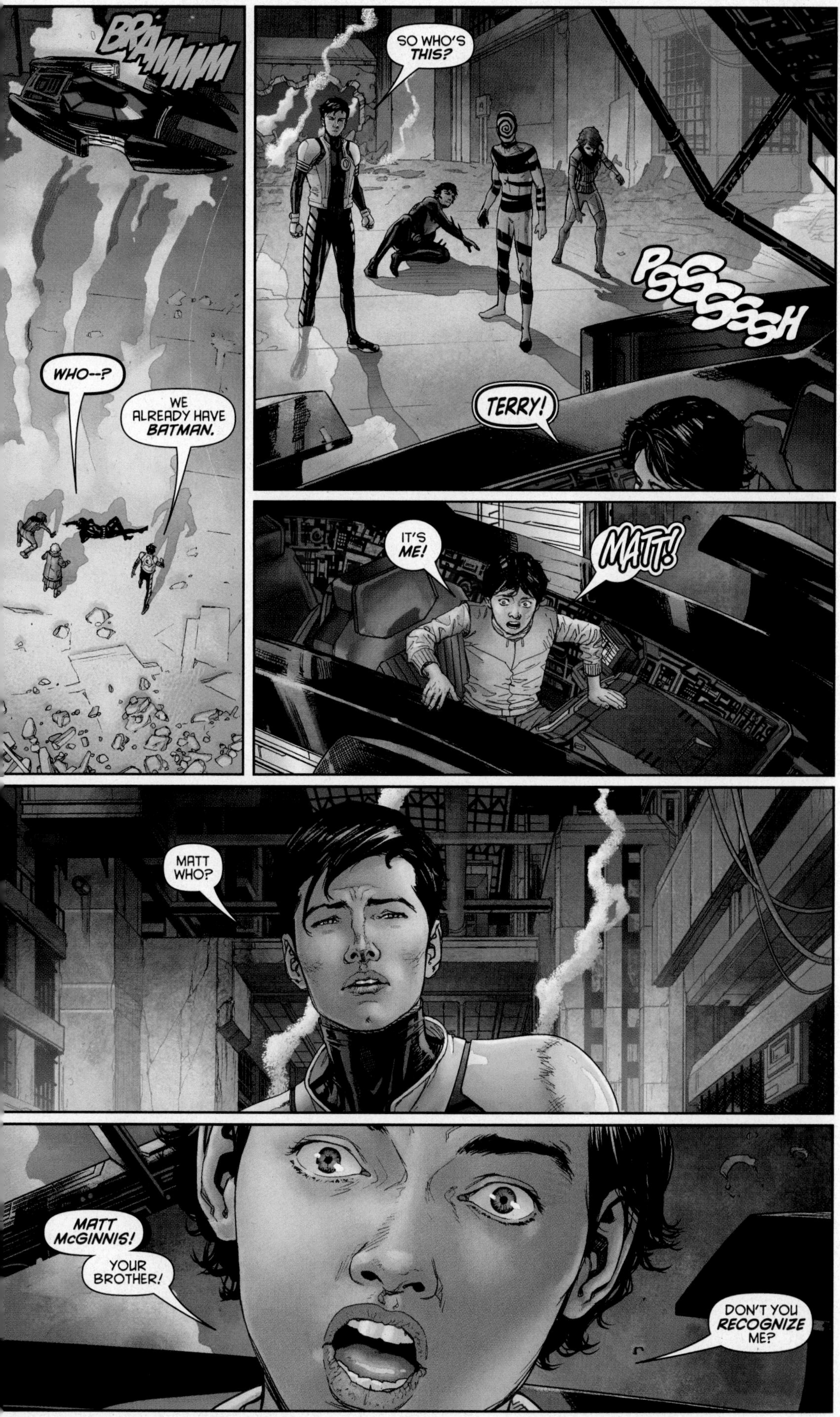
BRAMMMM
WHO--?
WE ALREADY HAVE BATMAN.
SO WHO'S THIS?
PSSSSSSH
TERRY!
IT'S ME!
MATT!
MATT WHO?
MATT McGINNIS!
YOUR BROTHER!
DON'T YOU RECOGNIZE ME?

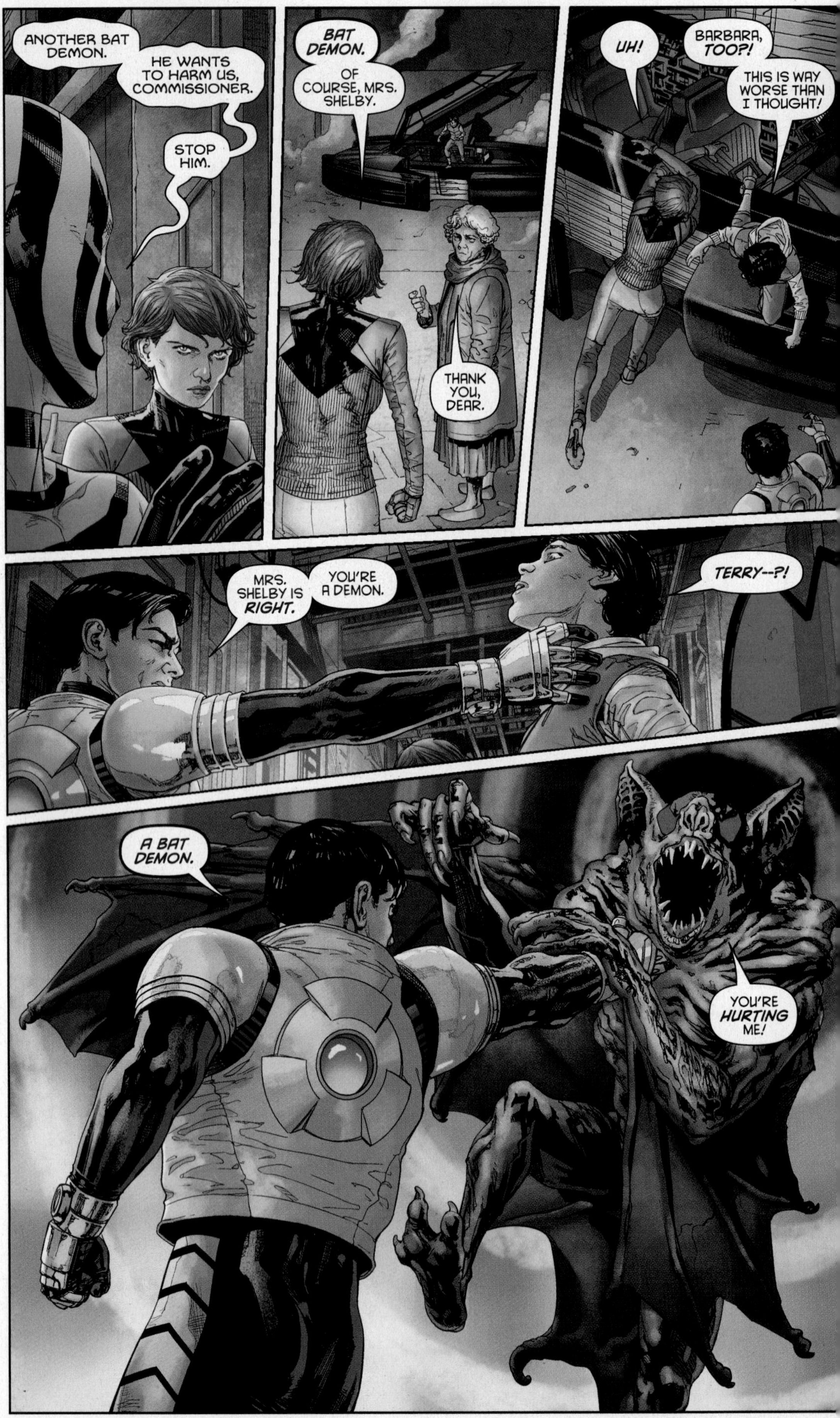
ANOTHER BAT DEMON.
HE WANTS TO HARM US, COMMISSIONER.
STOP HIM.
BAT DEMON.
OF COURSE, MRS. SHELBY.
THANK YOU, DEAR.
UH!
BARBARA, TOO?!
THIS IS WAY WORSE THAN I THOUGHT!
MRS. SHELBY IS RIGHT.
YOU'RE A DEMON.
TERRY--?!
A BAT DEMON.
YOU'RE HURTING ME!

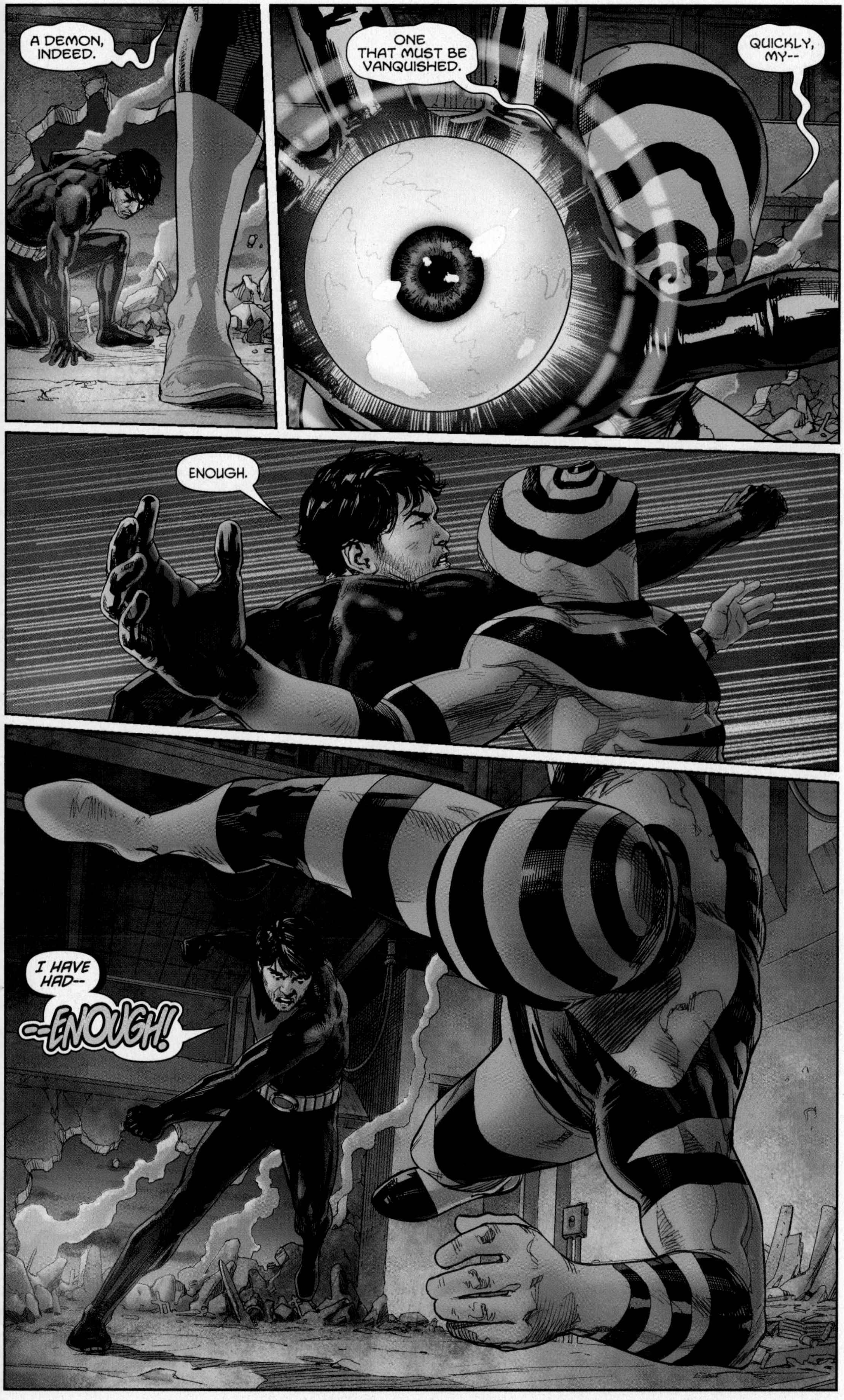
A DEMON, INDEED.
ONE THAT MUST BE VANQUISHED.
QUICKLY, MY--
ENOUGH.
I HAVE HAD--
--ENOUGH!

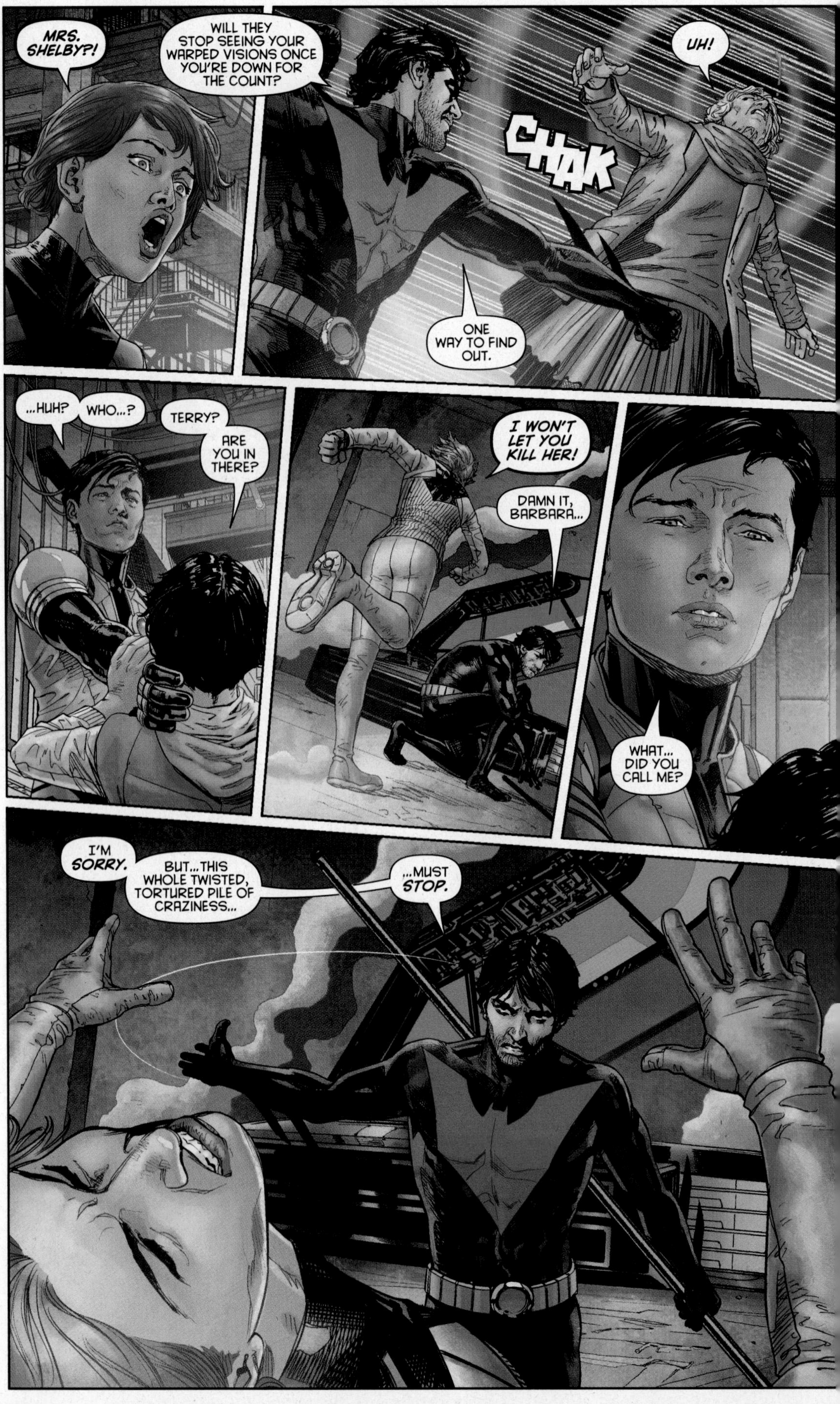
MRS. SHELBY?!
WILL THEY STOP SEEING YOUR WARPED VISIONS ONCE YOU'RE DOWN FOR THE COUNT?
UH!
CHAK
ONE WAY TO FIND OUT.
...HUH?
WHO...?
TERRY?
ARE YOU IN THERE?
I WON'T LET YOU KILL HER!
DAMN IT, BARBARA...
WHAT... DID YOU CALL ME?
I'M SORRY.
BUT... THIS WHOLE TWISTED, TORTURED PILE OF CRAZINESS...
...MUST STOP.

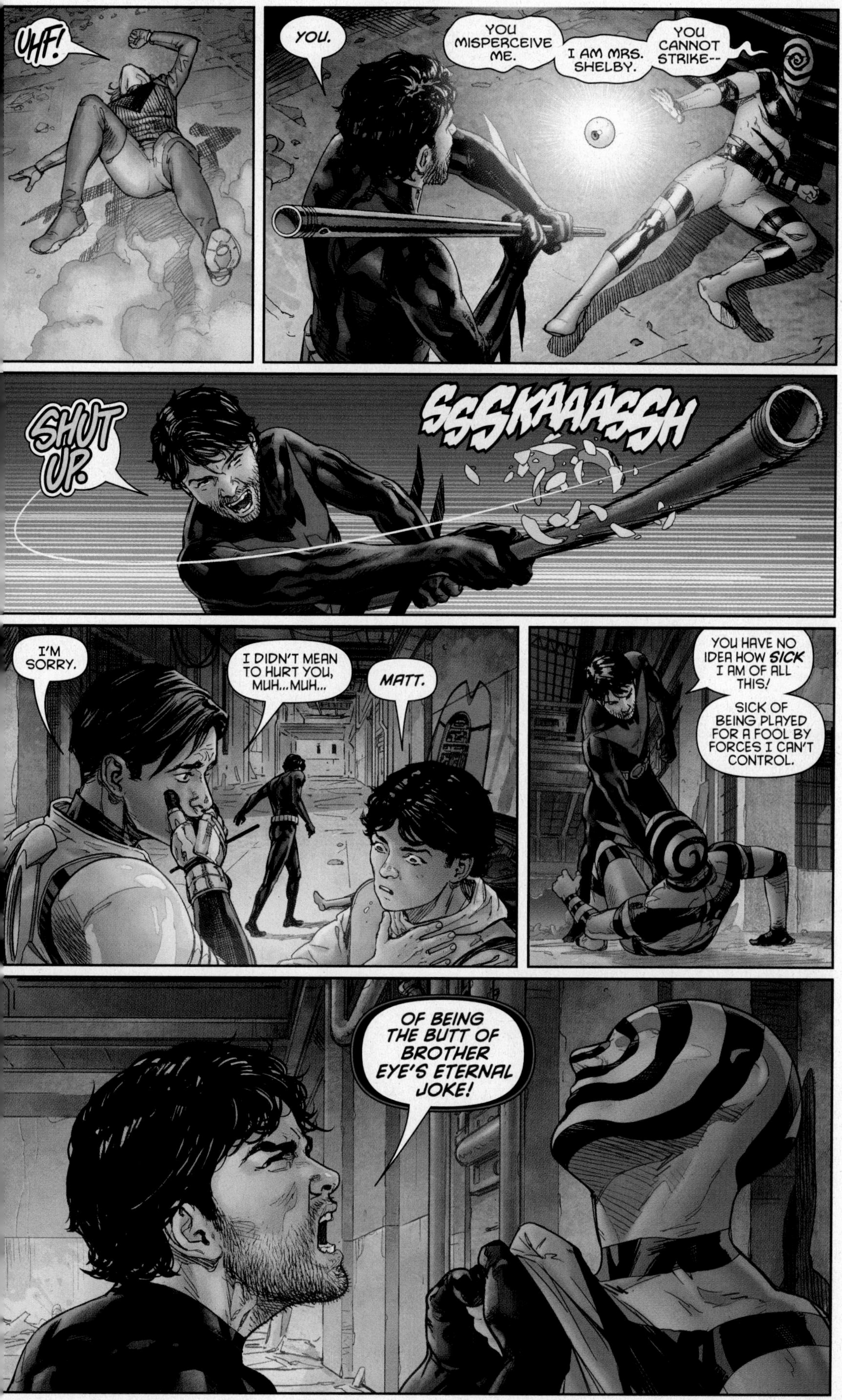
UHF!
YOU.
YOU MISPERCEIVE ME.
I AM MRS. SHELBY.
YOU CANNOT STRIKE--
SHUT UP.
SSSKAAASSH
I'M SORRY.
I DIDN'T MEAN TO HURT YOU, MUH...MUH...
MATT.
YOU HAVE NO IDEA HOW SICK I AM OF ALL THIS!
SICK OF BEING PLAYED FOR A FOOL BY FORCES I CAN'T CONTROL.
OF BEING THE BUTT OF BROTHER EYE'S ETERNAL JOKE!

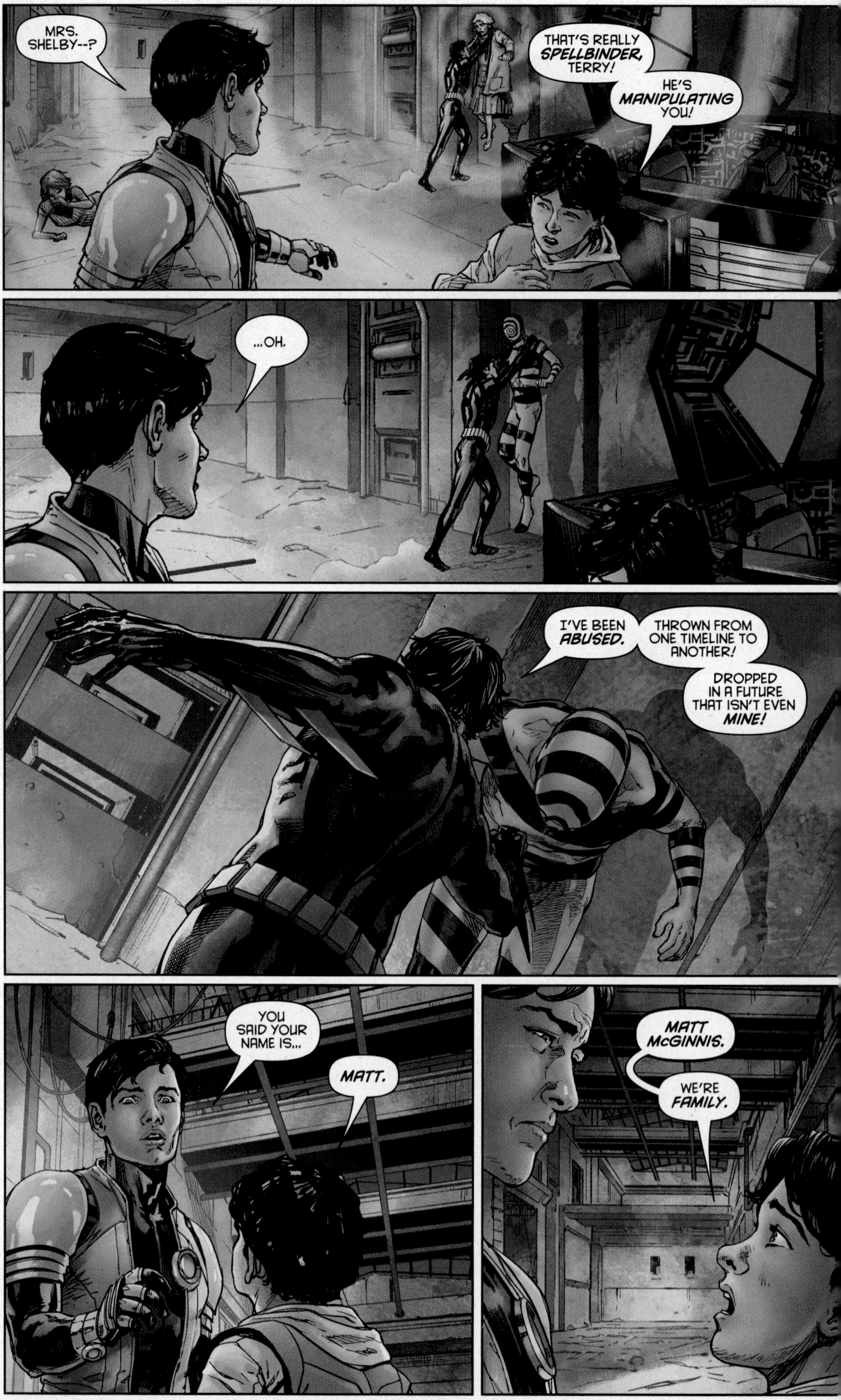

MRS. SHELBY--?
THAT'S REALLY SPELLBINDER, TERRY!
HE'S MANIPULATING YOU!
...OH.
I'VE BEEN ABUSED.
THROWN FROM ONE TIMELINE TO ANOTHER!
DROPPED IN A FUTURE THAT ISN'T EVEN MINE!
YOU SAID YOUR NAME IS...
MATT.
MATT McGINNIS.
WE'RE FAMILY.

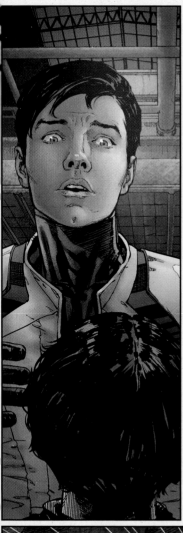

MATTY?

YEAH.

MATTY!

BROTHER EYE MIGHT NOT BE HERE, BUT *YOU ARE!*

YOU STEPPED INTO THE VOID HE LEFT...

...USED HIS MESS FOR PERSONAL GAIN...

...YOU'RE EVERY BIT AS BAD AS *HIM!*

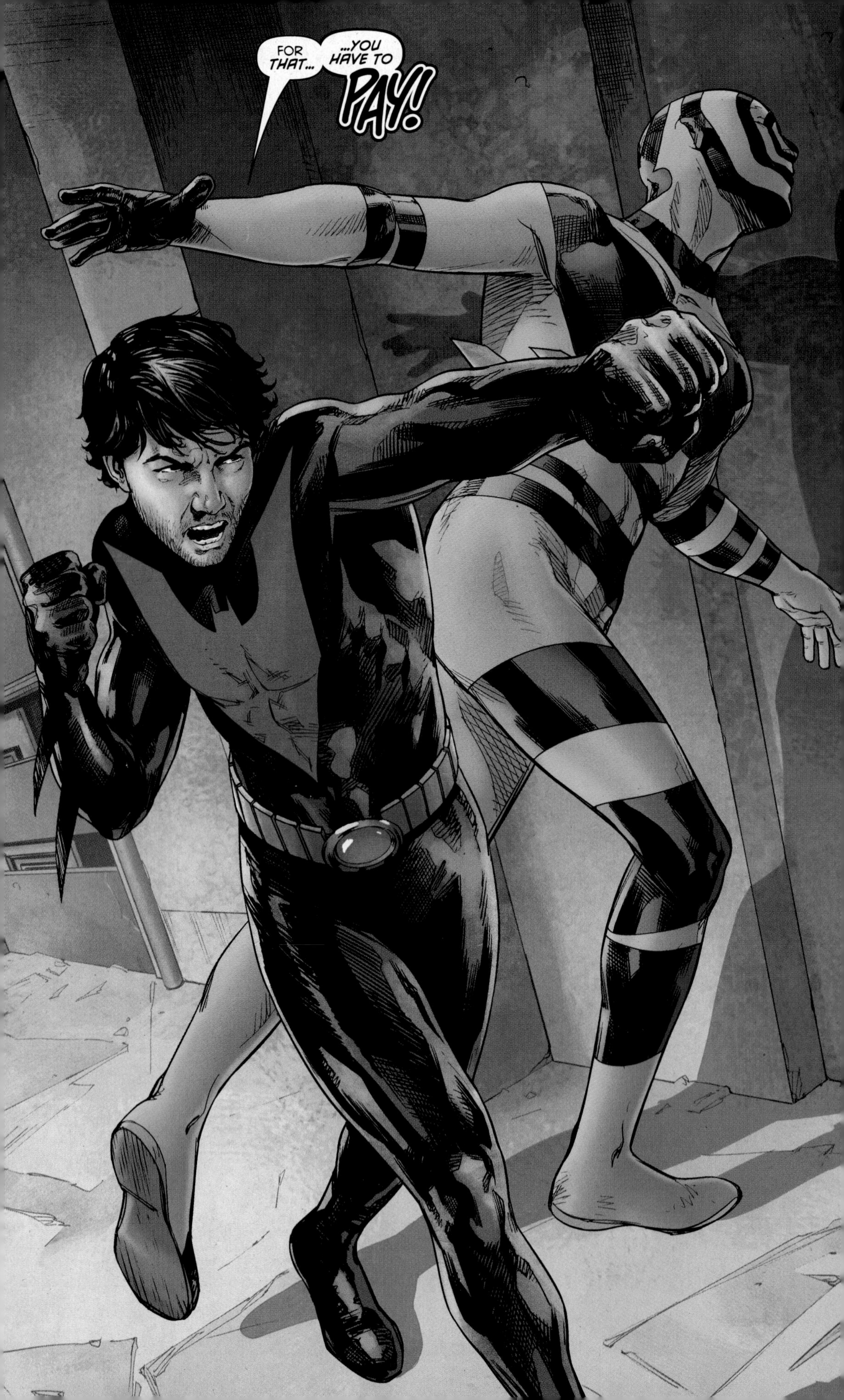
FOR THAT...
...YOU HAVE TO PAY!

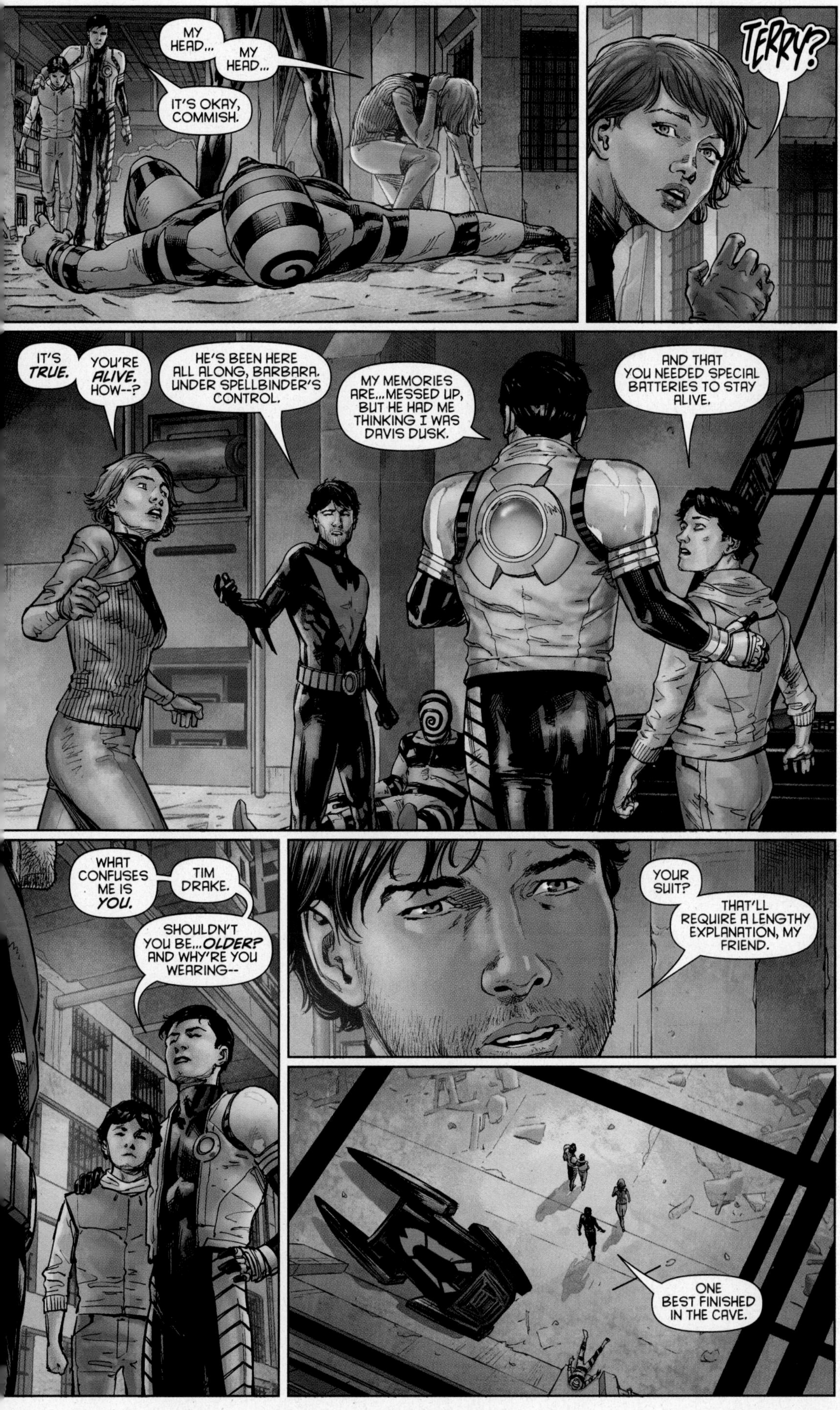
MY HEAD...
MY HEAD...
IT'S OKAY, COMMISH.
TERRY?
IT'S TRUE.
YOU'RE ALIVE. HOW--?
HE'S BEEN HERE ALL ALONG, BARBARA. UNDER SPELLBINDER'S CONTROL.
MY MEMORIES ARE...MESSED UP, BUT HE HAD ME THINKING I WAS DAVIS DUSK.
AND THAT YOU NEEDED SPECIAL BATTERIES TO STAY ALIVE.
WHAT CONFUSES ME IS YOU.
TIM DRAKE.
SHOULDN'T YOU BE...OLDER? AND WHY'RE YOU WEARING--
YOUR SUIT?
THAT'LL REQUIRE A LENGTHY EXPLANATION, MY FRIEND.
ONE BEST FINISHED IN THE CAVE.

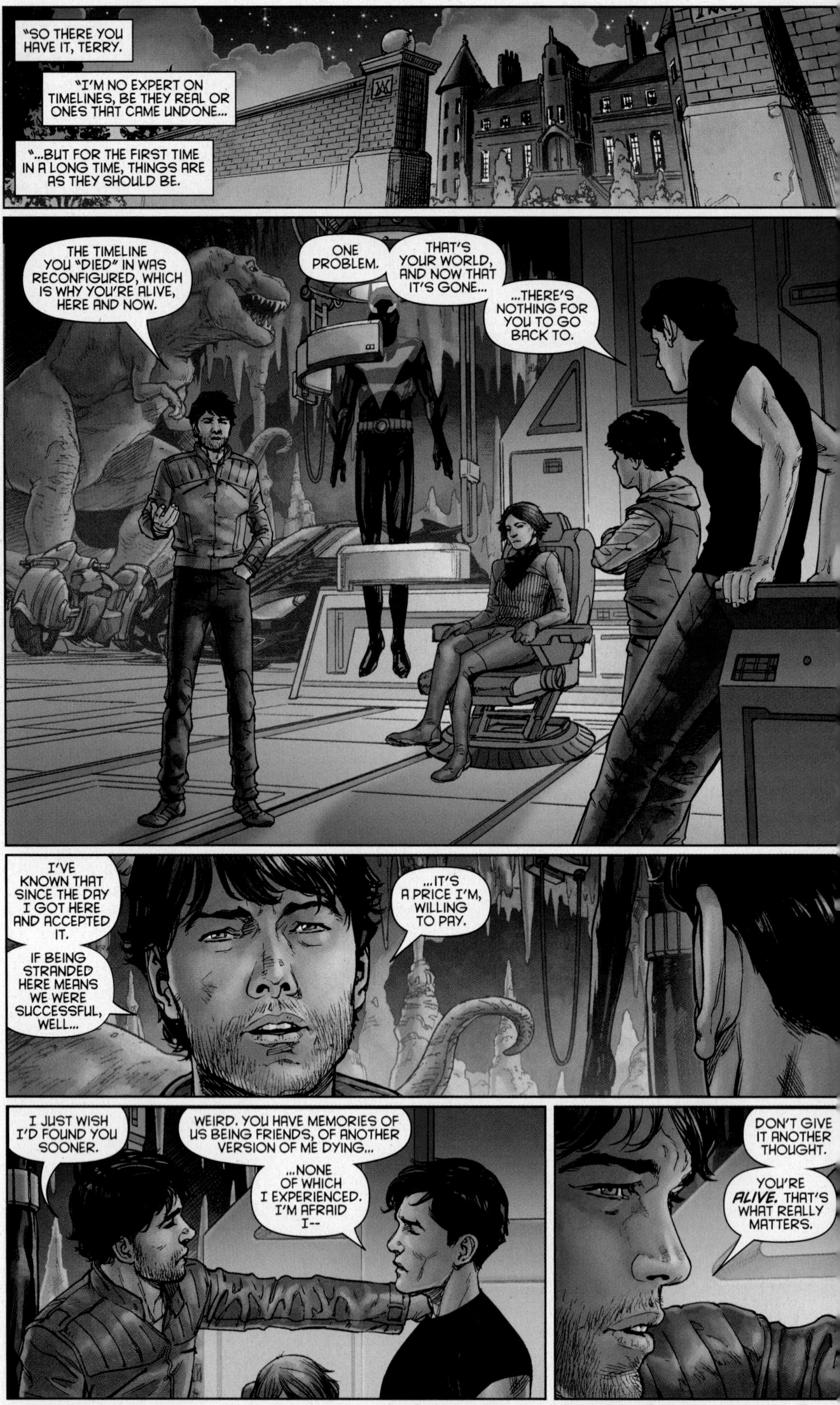
"SO THERE YOU HAVE IT, TERRY.
"I'M NO EXPERT ON TIMELINES, BE THEY REAL OR ONES THAT CAME UNDONE...
"...BUT FOR THE FIRST TIME IN A LONG TIME, THINGS ARE AS THEY SHOULD BE.
THE TIMELINE YOU "DIED" IN WAS RECONFIGURED, WHICH IS WHY YOU'RE ALIVE, HERE AND NOW.
ONE PROBLEM.
THAT'S YOUR WORLD, AND NOW THAT IT'S GONE...
...THERE'S NOTHING FOR YOU TO GO BACK TO.
I'VE KNOWN THAT SINCE THE DAY I GOT HERE AND ACCEPTED IT.
IF BEING STRANDED HERE MEANS WE WERE SUCCESSFUL, WELL...
...IT'S A PRICE I'M, WILLING TO PAY.
I JUST WISH I'D FOUND YOU SOONER.
WEIRD. YOU HAVE MEMORIES OF US BEING FRIENDS, OF ANOTHER VERSION OF ME DYING...
...NONE OF WHICH I EXPERIENCED. I'M AFRAID I--
DON'T GIVE IT ANOTHER THOUGHT.
YOU'RE ALIVE. THAT'S WHAT REALLY MATTERS.

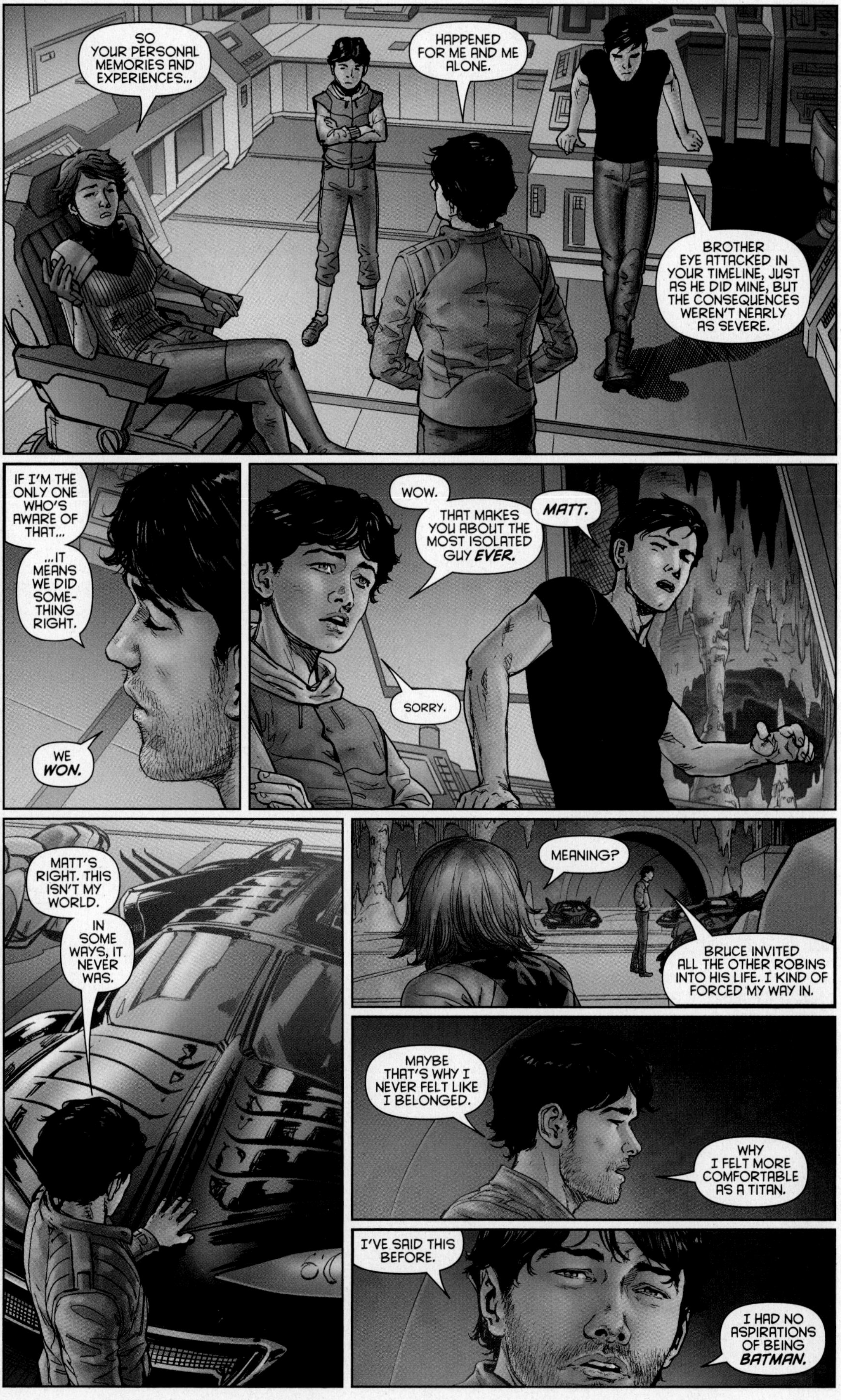
SO YOUR PERSONAL MEMORIES AND EXPERIENCES...
HAPPENED FOR ME AND ME ALONE.
BROTHER EYE ATTACKED IN YOUR TIMELINE, JUST AS HE DID MINE, BUT THE CONSEQUENCES WEREN'T NEARLY AS SEVERE.
IF I'M THE ONLY ONE WHO'S AWARE OF THAT...
...IT MEANS WE DID SOME-THING RIGHT.
WE *WON.*
WOW.
THAT MAKES YOU ABOUT THE MOST ISOLATED GUY *EVER.*
MATT.
SORRY.
MATT'S RIGHT. THIS ISN'T MY WORLD.
IN SOME WAYS, IT NEVER WAS.
MEANING?
BRUCE INVITED ALL THE OTHER ROBINS INTO HIS LIFE. I KIND OF FORCED MY WAY IN.
MAYBE THAT'S WHY I NEVER FELT LIKE I BELONGED.
WHY I FELT MORE COMFORTABLE AS A TITAN.
I'VE SAID THIS BEFORE.
I HAD NO ASPIRATIONS OF BEING *BATMAN.*

THAT HASN'T CHANGED.

THIS BELONGS TO *YOU.*

BUT--!

I'M DONE WITH IT, TERRY.

AND IT DOESN'T BOTHER ME ONE BIT.

BE WHAT BRUCE WANTED YOU TO BE.

BE BATMAN.

YOU'RE TALKING LIKE A MAN WHO'S GOING TO LEAVE, TIM.

WHA-- NO!

EVEN IF YOU DON'T WANNA BE BATMAN, YOU CAN BE *RED ROBIN!*

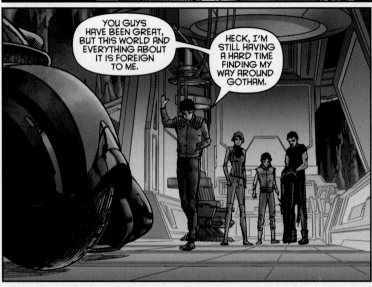

YOU GUYS HAVE BEEN GREAT, BUT THIS WORLD AND EVERYTHING ABOUT IT IS FOREIGN TO ME.

HECK, I'M STILL HAVING A HARD TIME FINDING MY WAY AROUND GOTHAM.

THERE'S A VERY DIFFERENT, VERY BIG WORLD OUT THERE. ONE THAT'S GONE THROUGH INCREDIBLE CHANGES.

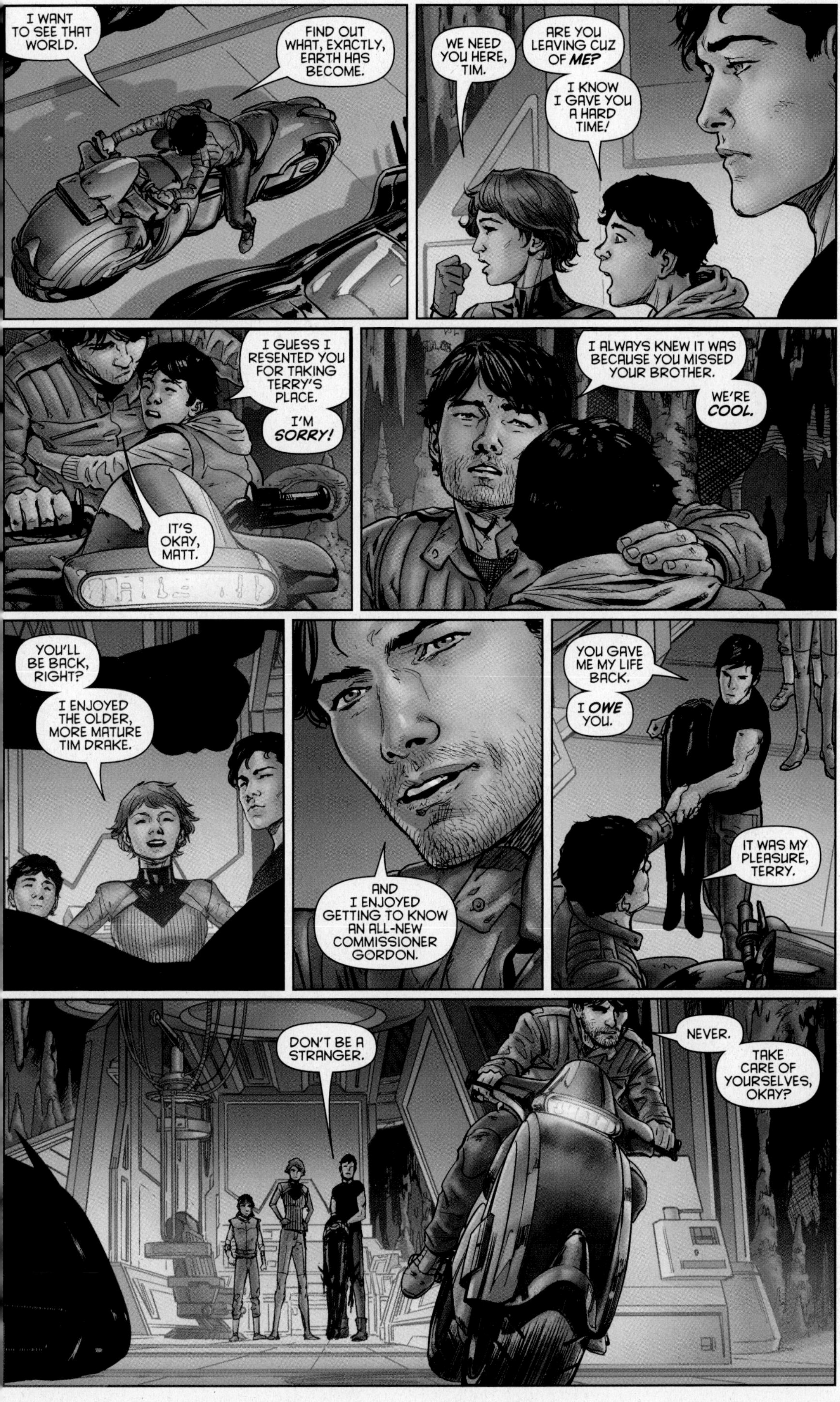
I WANT TO SEE THAT WORLD.
FIND OUT WHAT, EXACTLY, EARTH HAS BECOME.
WE NEED YOU HERE, TIM.
ARE YOU LEAVING CUZ OF ME?
I KNOW I GAVE YOU A HARD TIME!
I GUESS I RESENTED YOU FOR TAKING TERRY'S PLACE.
I'M SORRY!
IT'S OKAY, MATT.
I ALWAYS KNEW IT WAS BECAUSE YOU MISSED YOUR BROTHER.
WE'RE COOL.
YOU'LL BE BACK, RIGHT?
I ENJOYED THE OLDER, MORE MATURE TIM DRAKE.
AND I ENJOYED GETTING TO KNOW AN ALL-NEW COMMISSIONER GORDON.
YOU GAVE ME MY LIFE BACK.
I OWE YOU.
IT WAS MY PLEASURE, TERRY.
DON'T BE A STRANGER.
NEVER.
TAKE CARE OF YOURSELVES, OKAY?

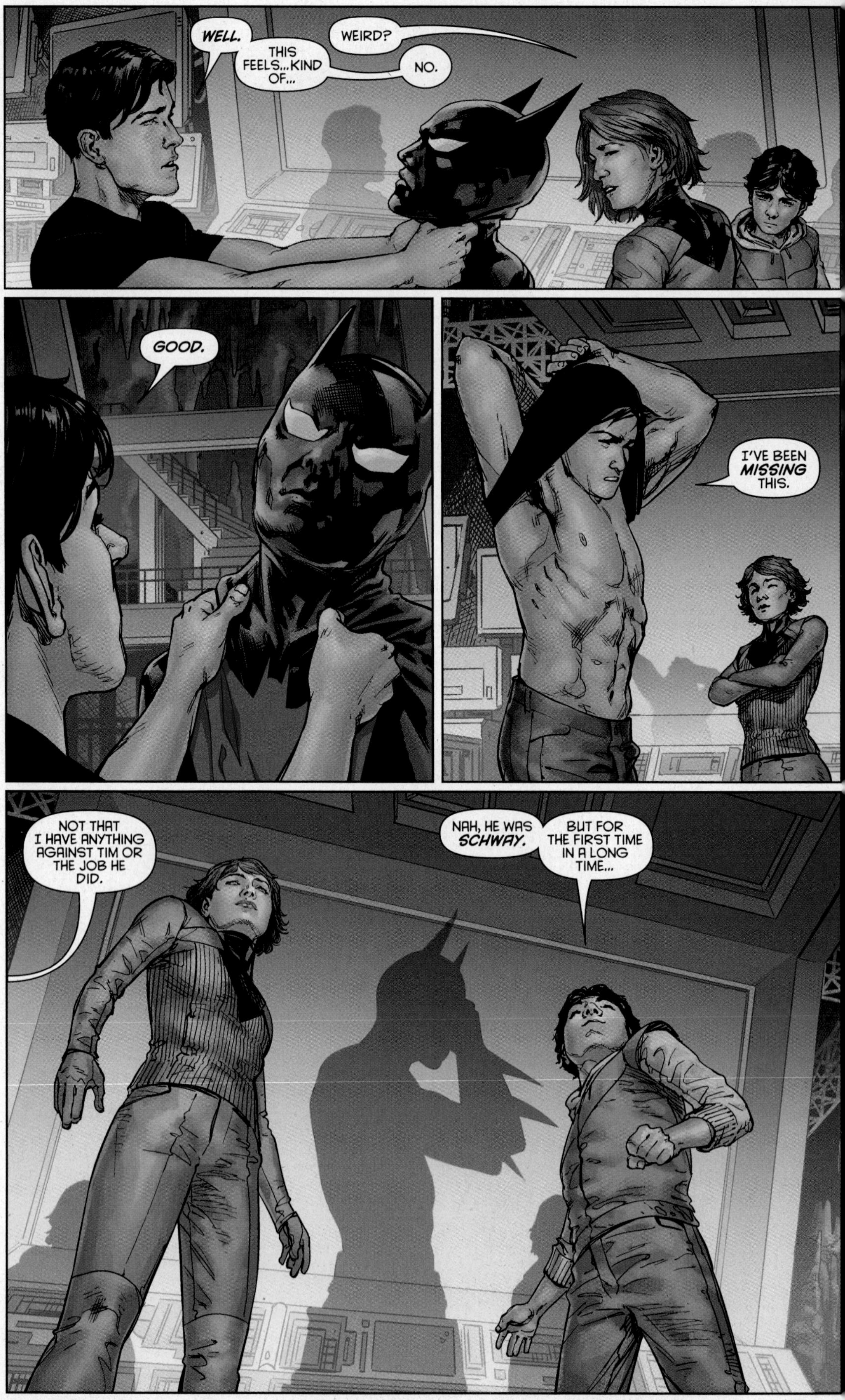
WELL.
THIS FEELS...KIND OF...
WEIRD?
NO.
GOOD.
I'VE BEEN MISSING THIS.
NOT THAT I HAVE ANYTHING AGAINST TIM OR THE JOB HE DID.
NAH, HE WAS SCHWAY.
BUT FOR THE FIRST TIME IN A LONG TIME...

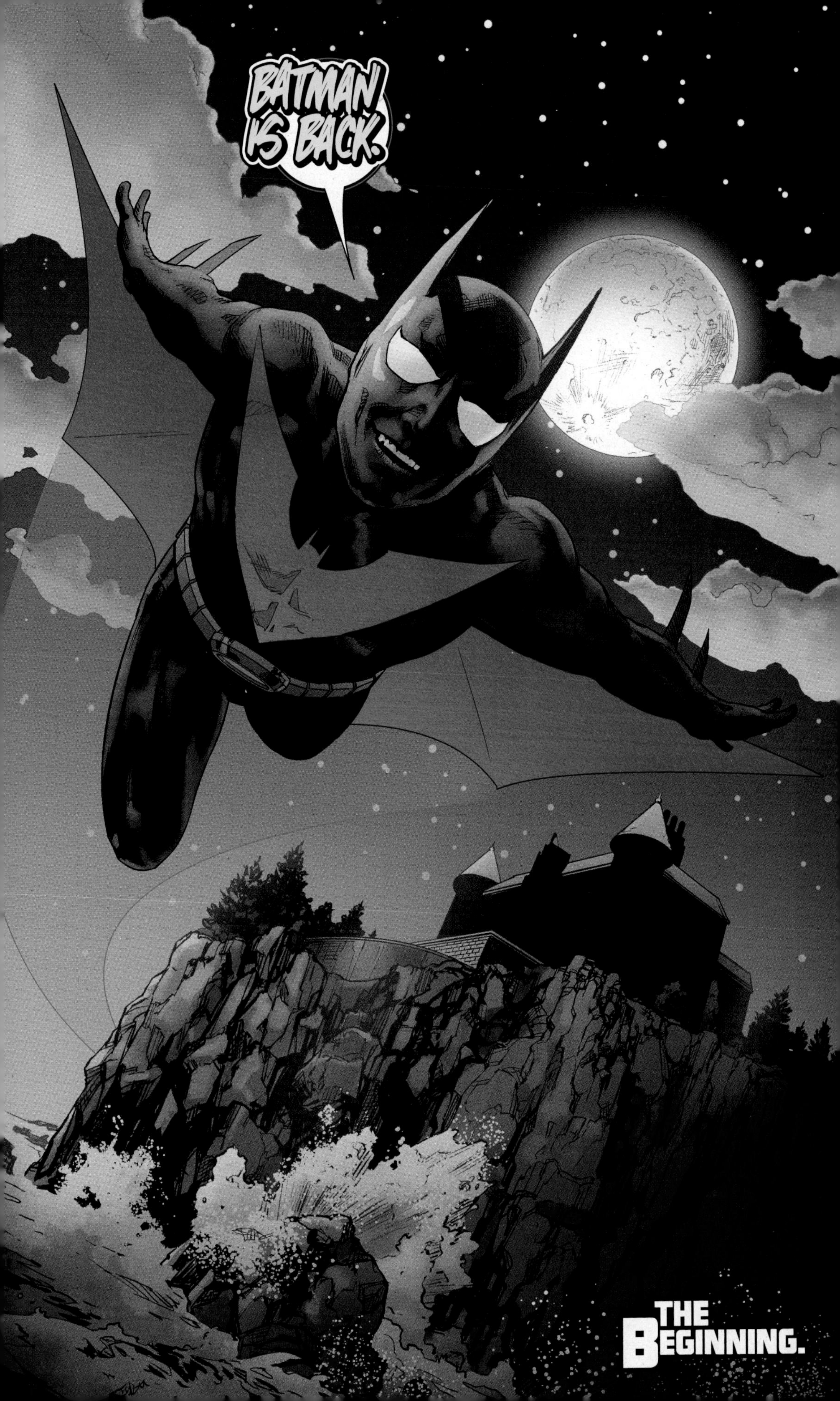
BATMAN IS BACK.
THE BEGINNING.

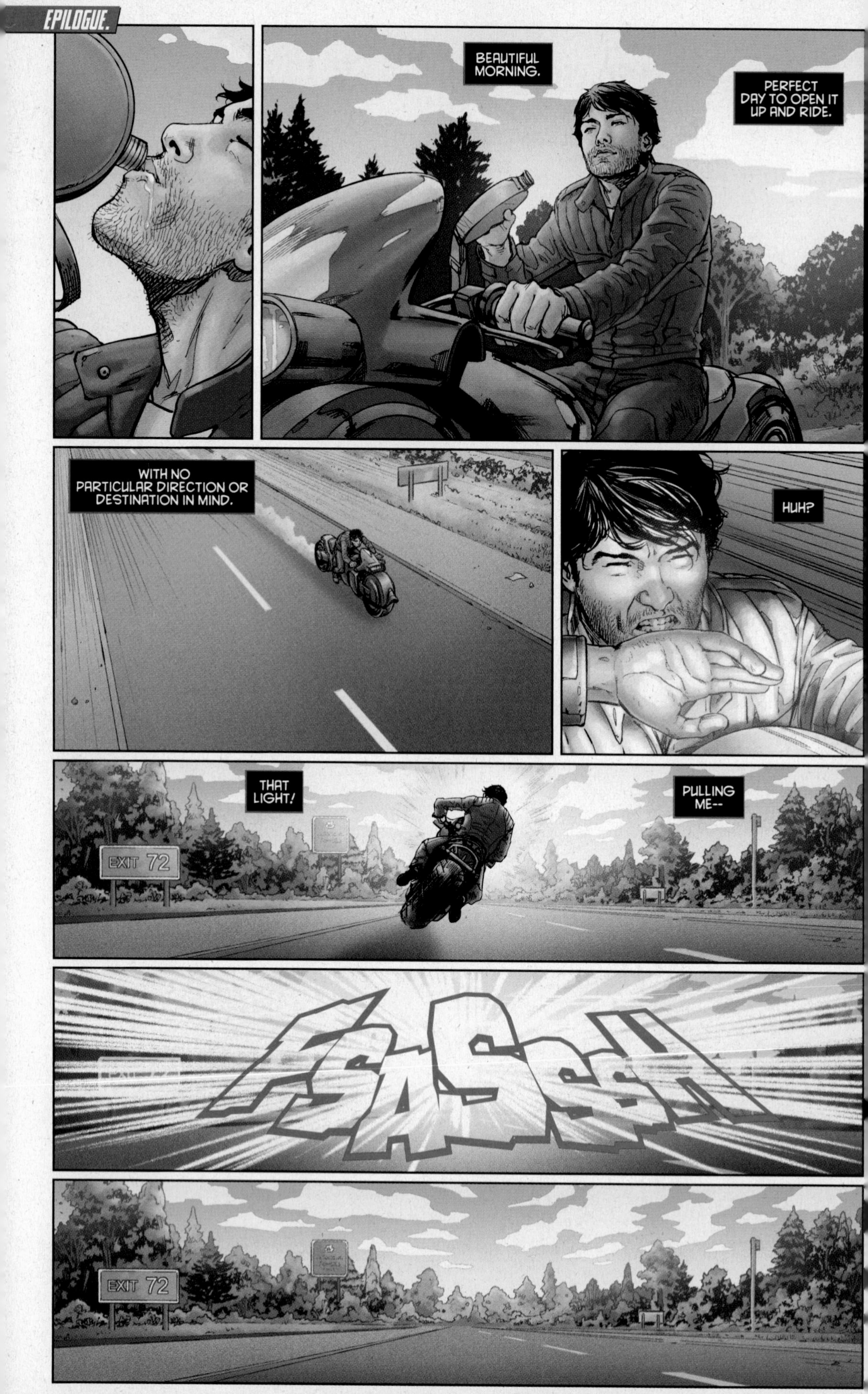
EPILOGUE.
BEAUTIFUL MORNING.
PERFECT DAY TO OPEN IT UP AND RIDE.
WITH NO PARTICULAR DIRECTION OR DESTINATION IN MIND.
HUH?
THAT LIGHT!
PULLING ME--
EXIT 72
FSASSH
EXIT 72

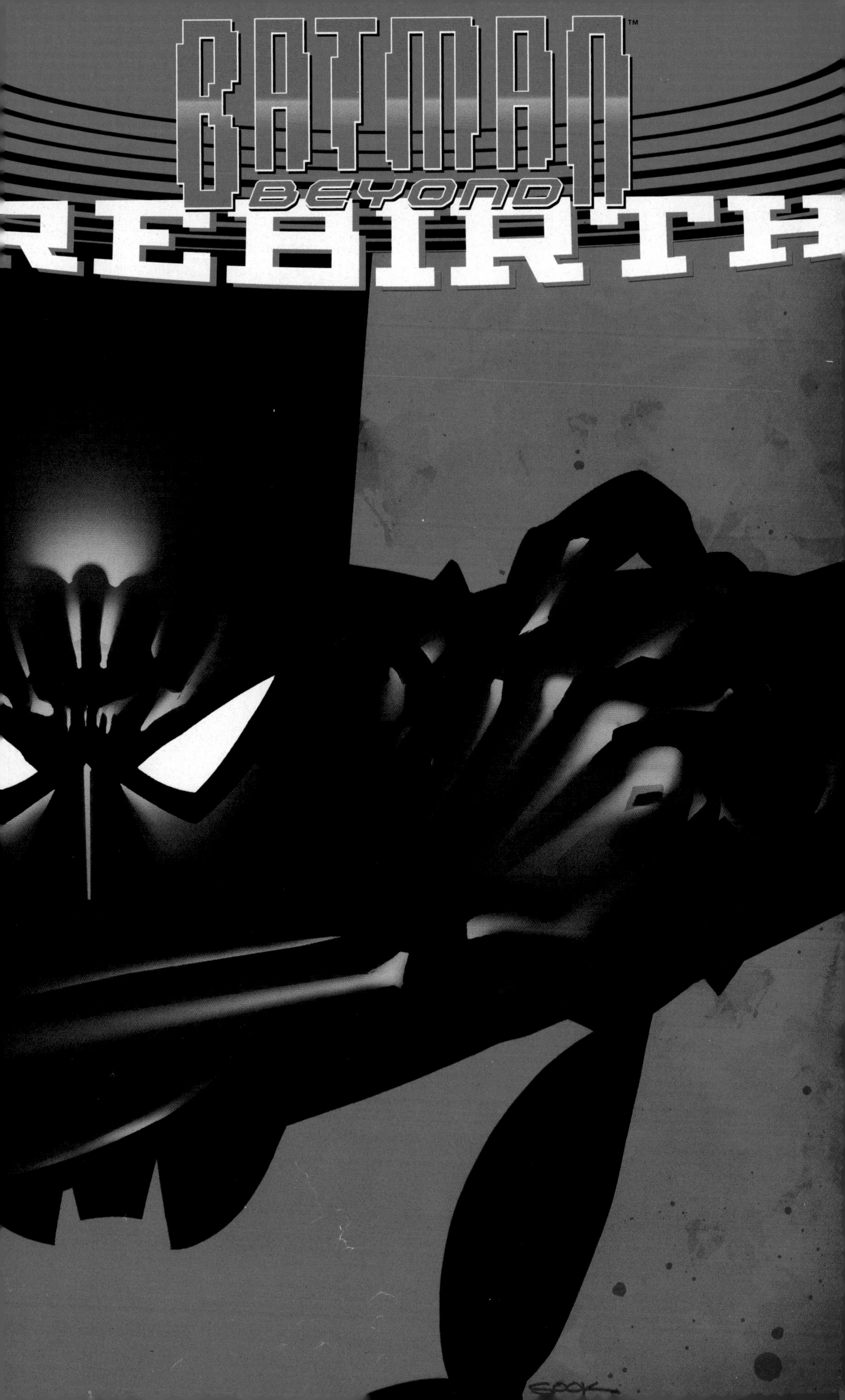
BATMAN™
BEYOND
REBIRTH

The future (and past) of the DC Universe starts with DC UNIVERSE: REBIRTH!

Explore the changing world of BATMAN BEYOND in this special bonus preview of **BATMAN BEYOND: REBIRTH #1!**

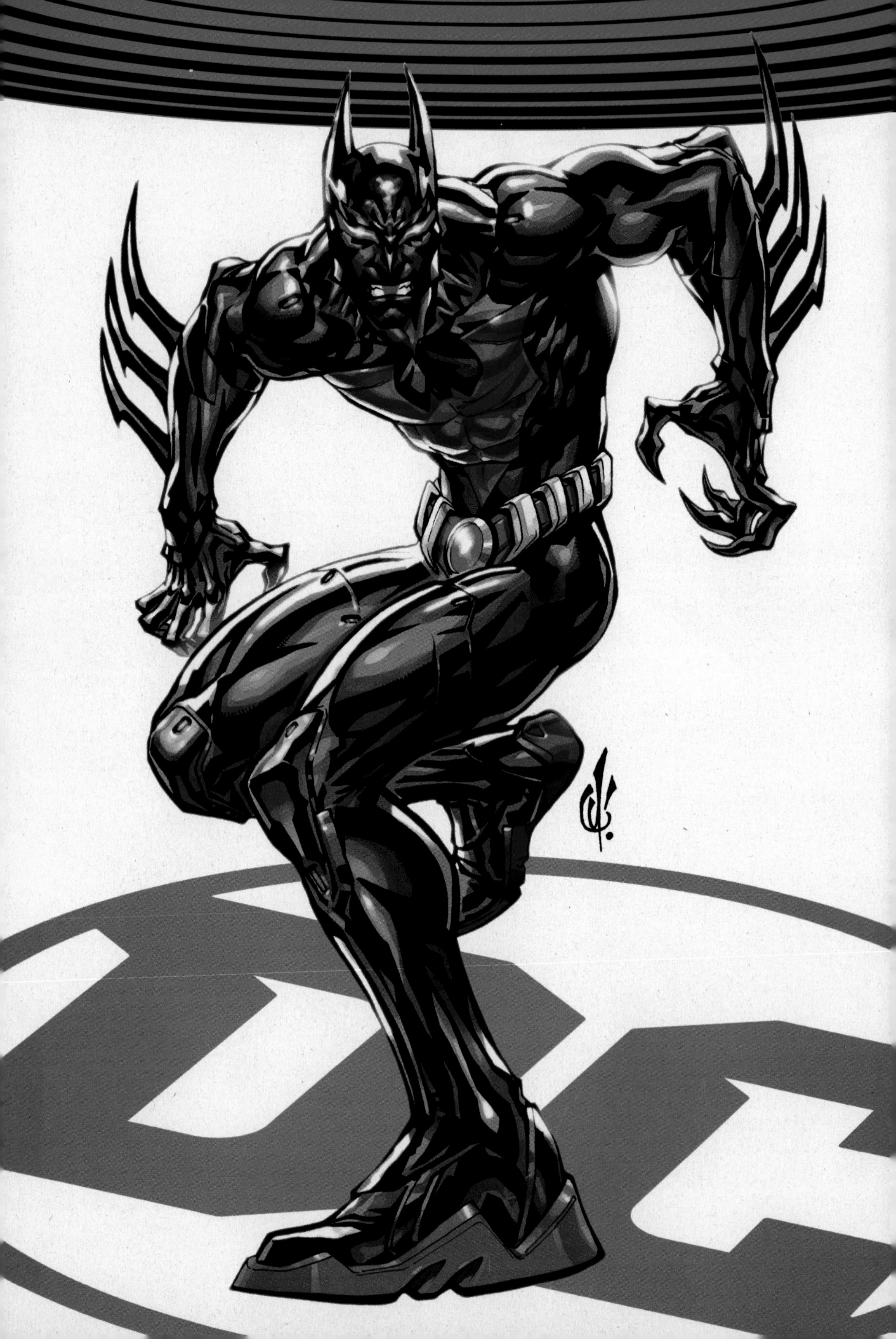

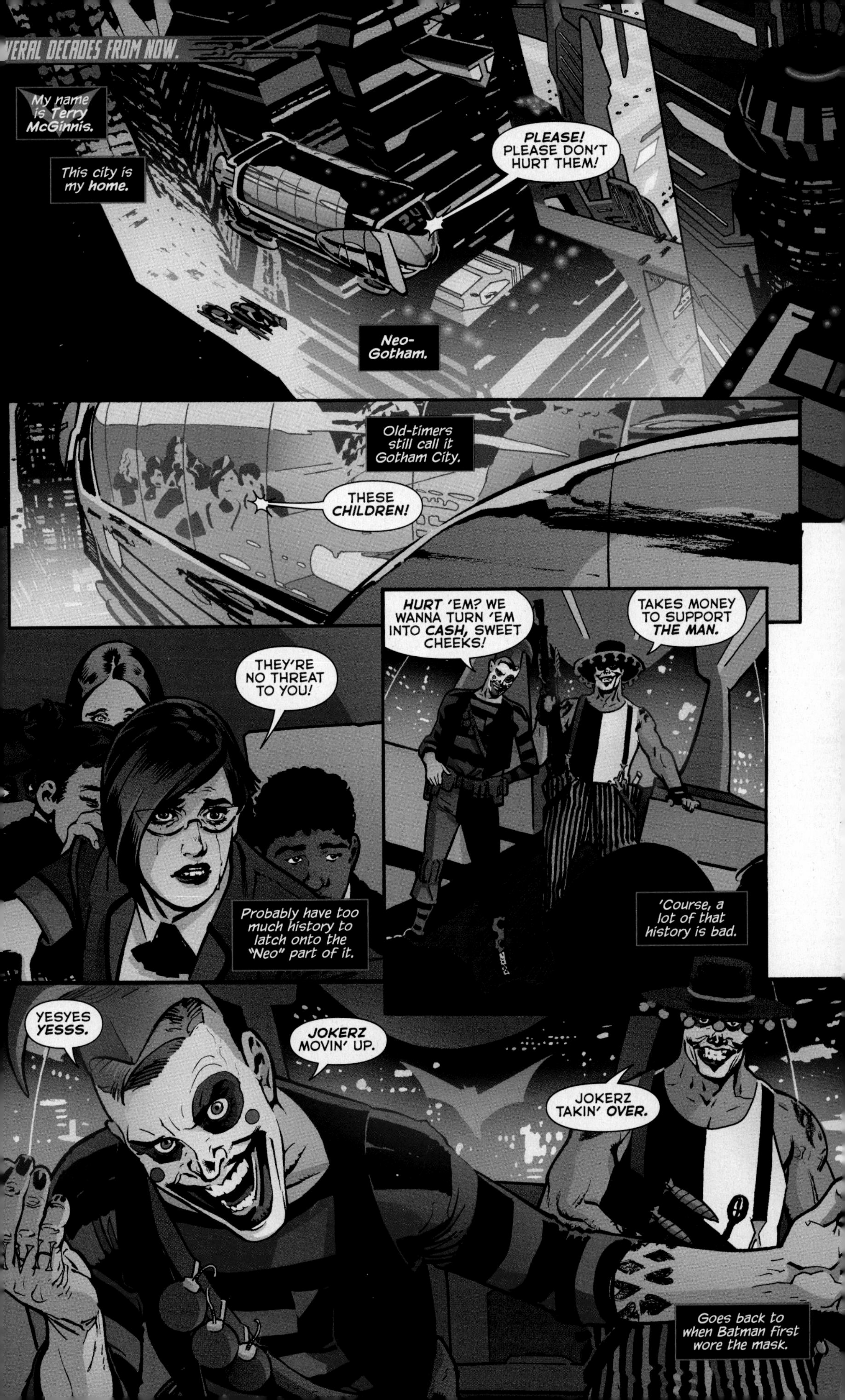

VERAL DECADES FROM NOW.
My name is Terry McGinnis.
This city is my home.
PLEASE! PLEASE DON'T HURT THEM!
Neo-Gotham.
Old-timers still call it Gotham City.
THESE CHILDREN!
THEY'RE NO THREAT TO YOU!
Probably have too much history to latch onto the "Neo" part of it.
HURT 'EM? WE WANNA TURN 'EM INTO CASH, SWEET CHEEKS!
TAKES MONEY TO SUPPORT THE MAN.
'Course, a lot of that history is bad.
YESYES YESSS.
JOKERZ MOVIN' UP.
JOKERZ TAKIN' OVER.
Goes back to when Batman first wore the mask.

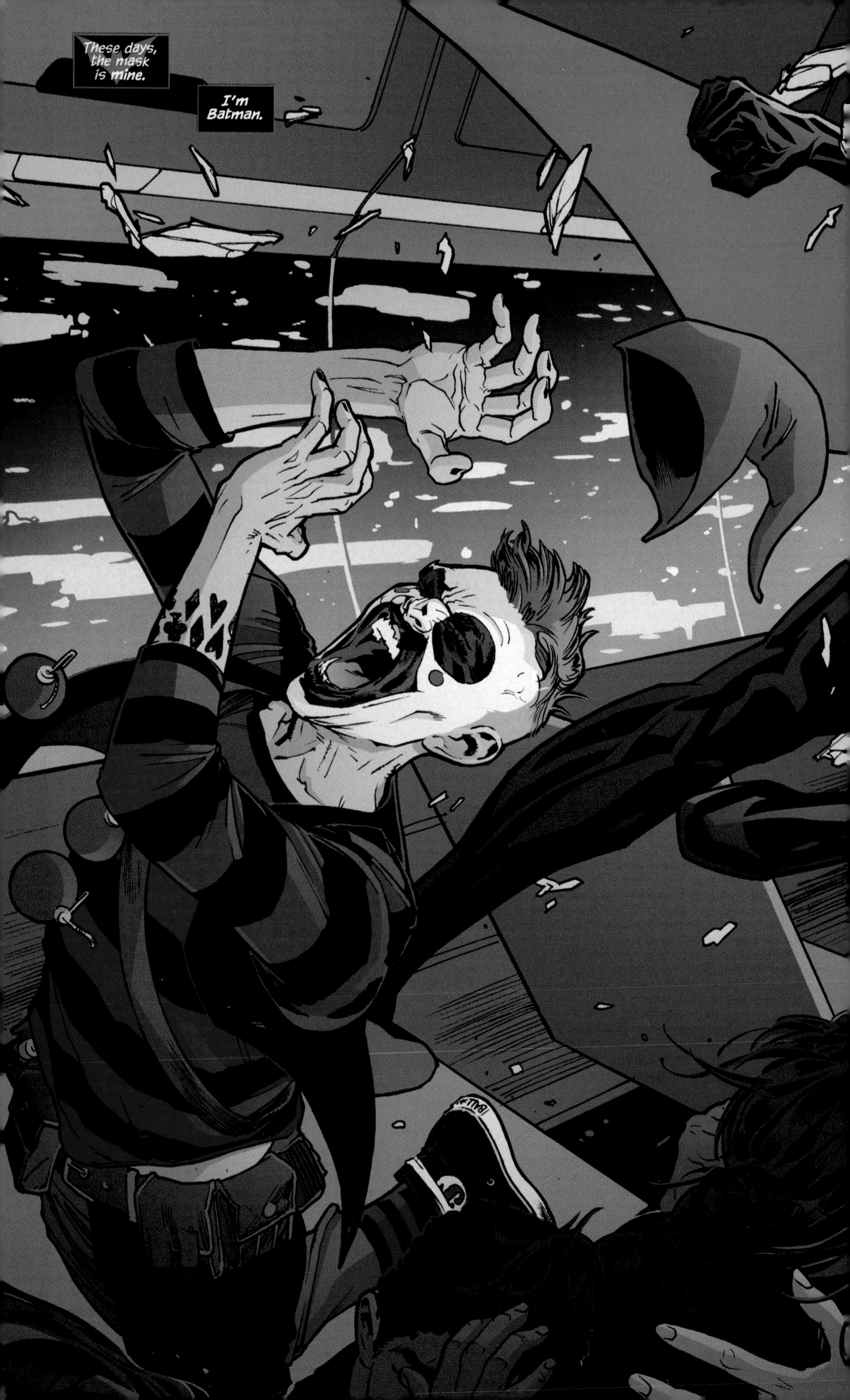
These days, the mask is mine.
I'm Batman.

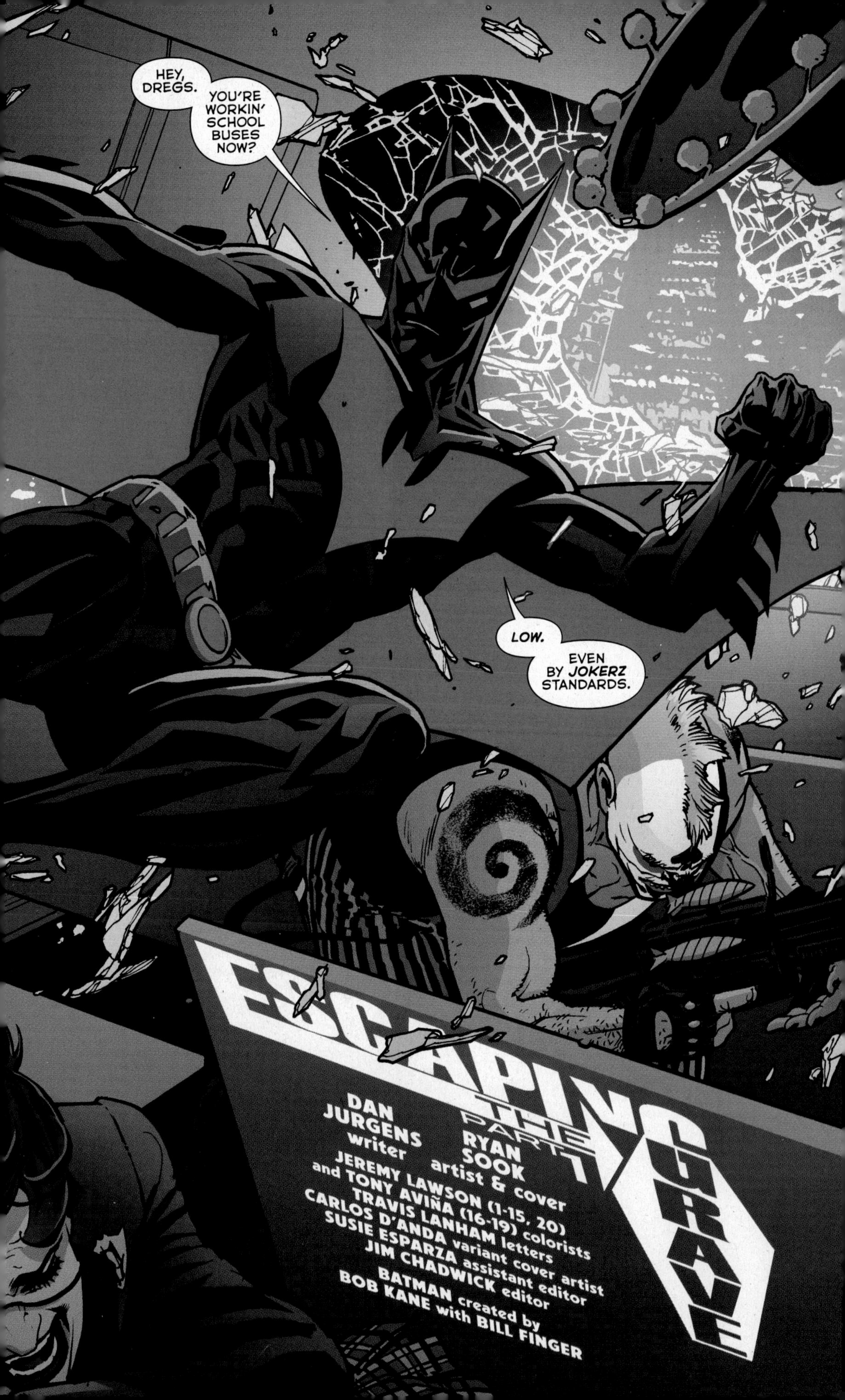

HEY, DREGS.
YOU'RE WORKIN' SCHOOL BUSES NOW?
LOW.
EVEN BY JOKERZ STANDARDS.
ESCAPING THE GRAVE PART 1
DAN JURGENS writer
RYAN SOOK artist & cover
JEREMY LAWSON (1-15, 20) and TONY AVIÑA (16-19) colorists
TRAVIS LANHAM letters
CARLOS D'ANDA variant cover artist
SUSIE ESPARZA assistant editor
JIM CHADWICK editor
BATMAN created by BOB KANE with BILL FINGER

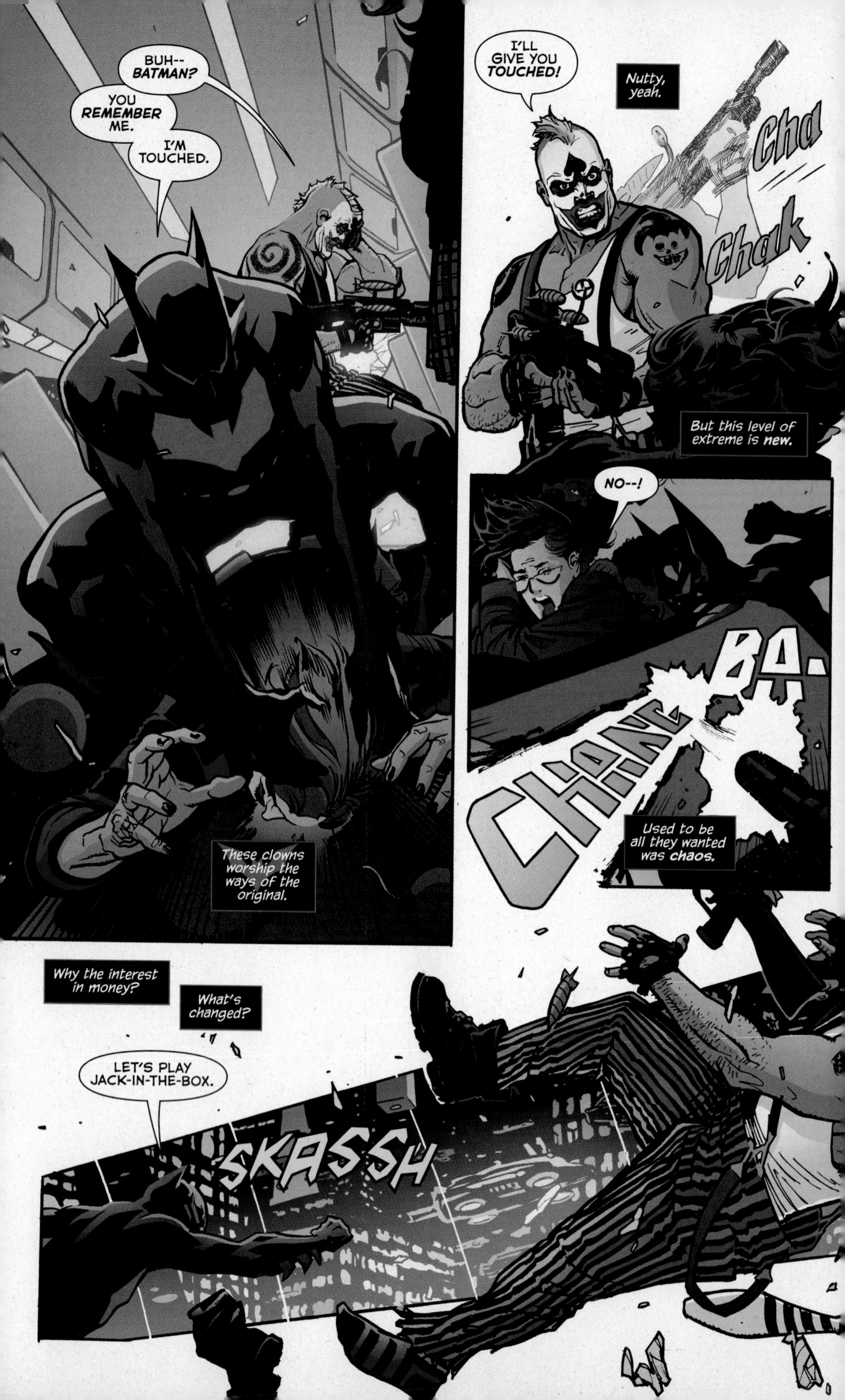
BUH-- BATMAN?
YOU REMEMBER ME.
I'M TOUCHED.
These clowns worship the ways of the original.
I'LL GIVE YOU TOUCHED!
Nutty, yeah.
Cha
Chak
But this level of extreme is new.
NO--!
BA.
CHOINC
Used to be all they wanted was chaos.
Why the interest in money?
What's changed?
LET'S PLAY JACK-IN-THE-BOX.
SKASSH

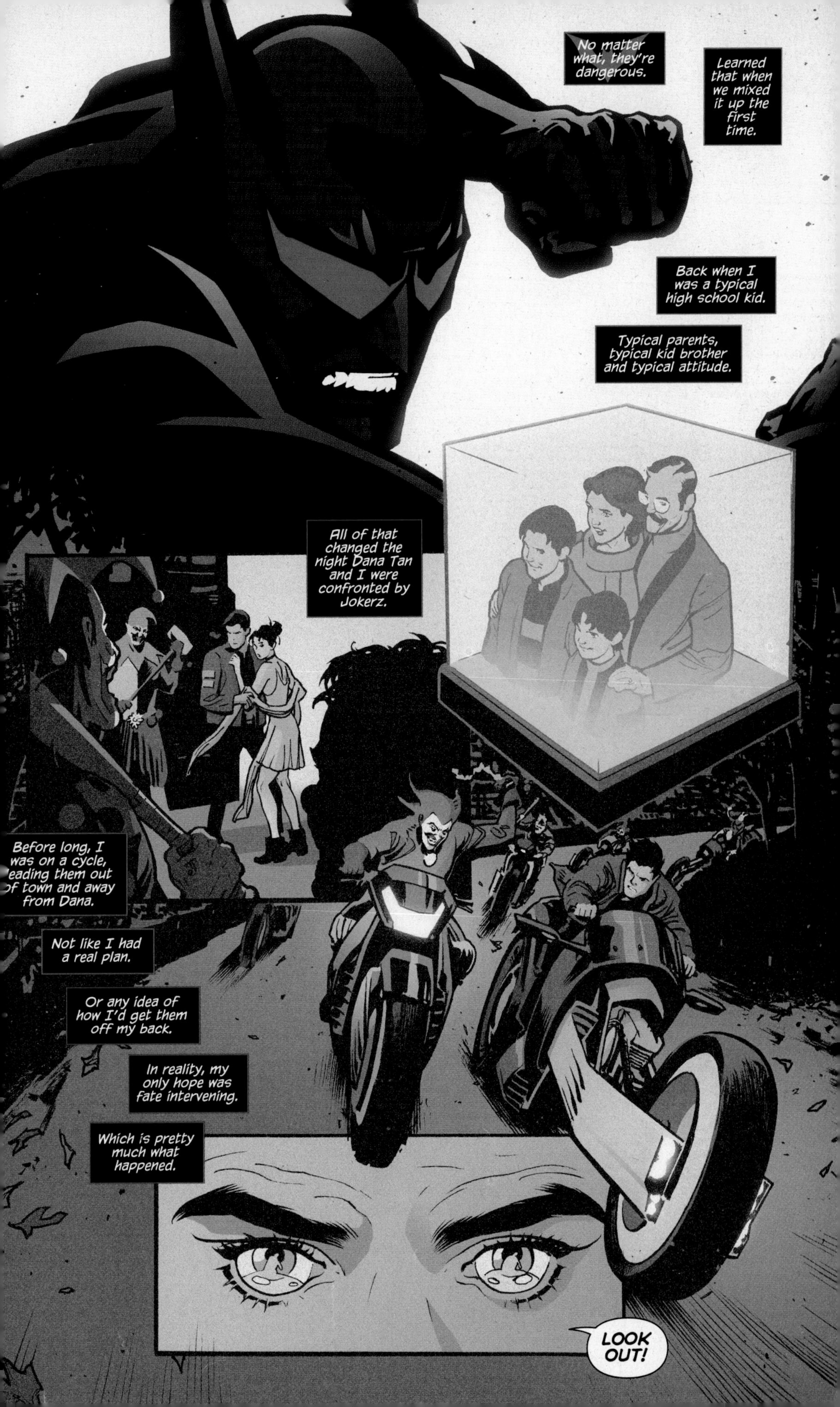

No matter what, they're dangerous.
Learned that when we mixed it up the first time.
Back when I was a typical high school kid.
Typical parents, typical kid brother and typical attitude.
All of that changed the night Dana Tan and I were confronted by Jokerz.
Before long, I was on a cycle, leading them out of town and away from Dana.
Not like I had a real plan.
Or any idea of how I'd get them off my back.
In reality, my only hope was fate intervening.
Which is pretty much what happened.
LOOK OUT!

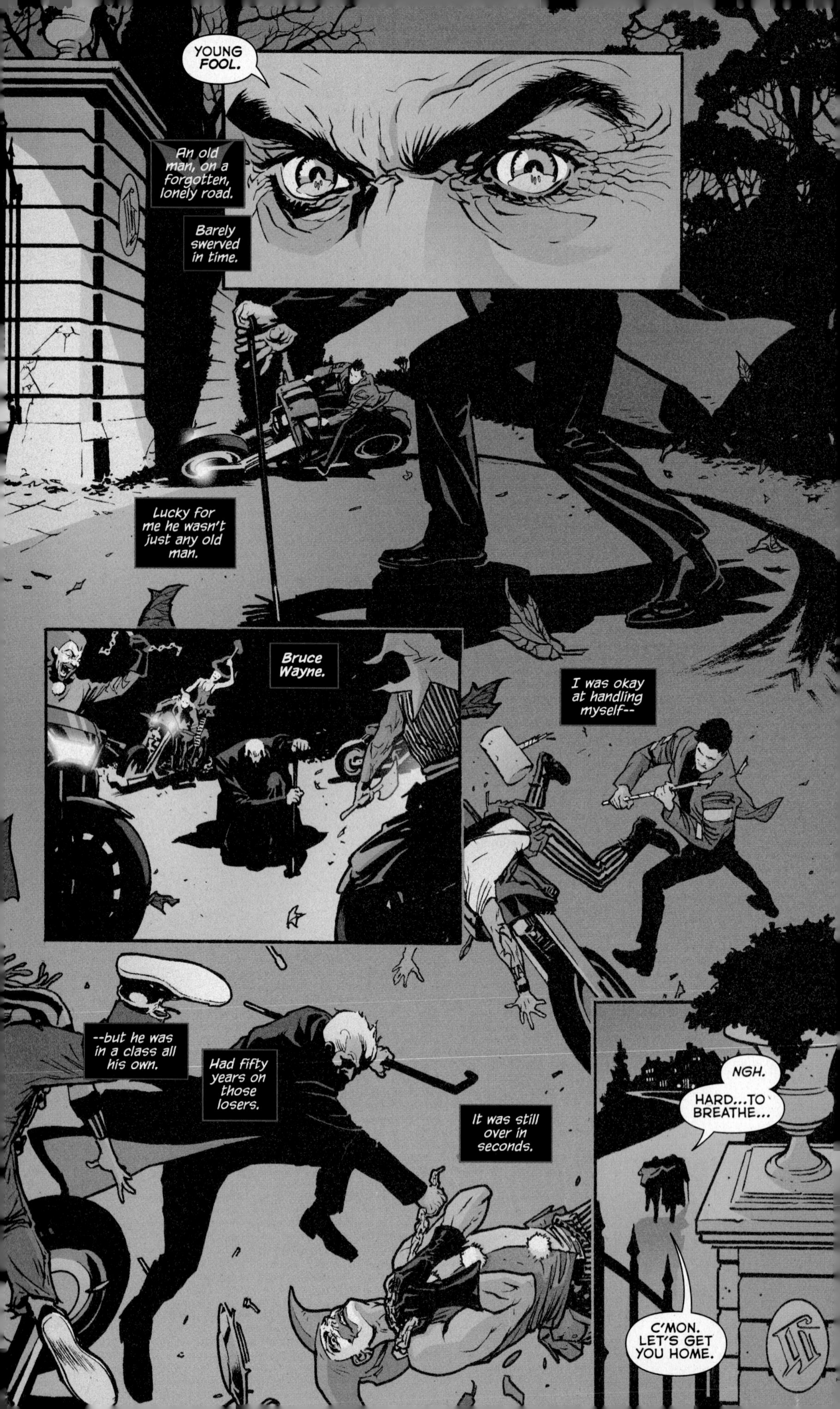
YOUNG FOOL.
An old man, on a forgotten, lonely road.
Barely swerved in time.
Lucky for me he wasn't just any old man.
Bruce Wayne.
I was okay at handling myself--
--but he was in a class all his own.
Had fifty years on those losers.
It was still over in seconds.
NGH.
HARD...TO BREATHE...
C'MON. LET'S GET YOU HOME.

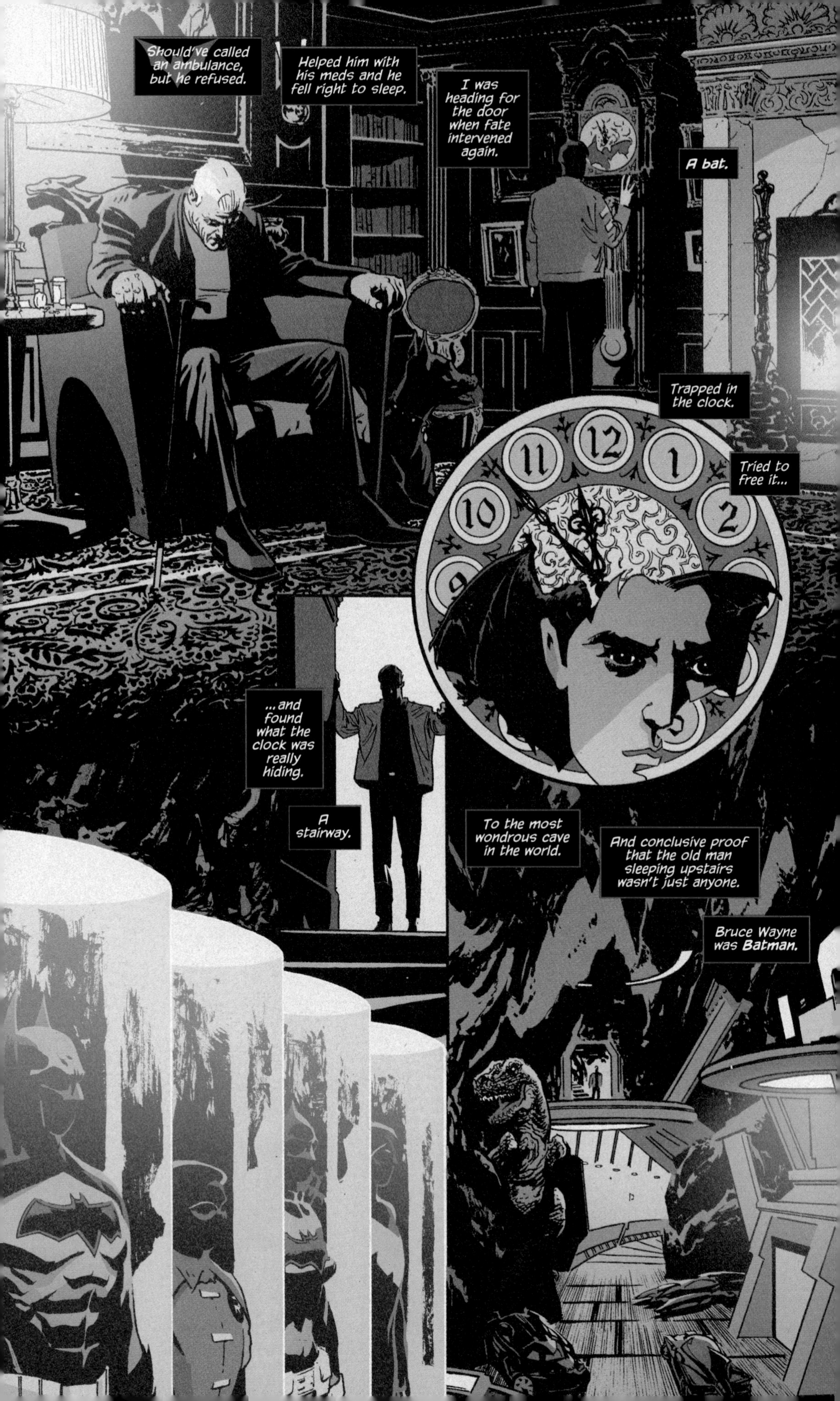
Should've called an ambulance, but he refused.
Helped him with his meds and he fell right to sleep.
I was heading for the door when fate intervened again.
A bat.
Trapped in the clock.
Tried to free it...
...and found what the clock was really hiding.
A stairway.
To the most wondrous cave in the world.
And conclusive proof that the old man sleeping upstairs wasn't just anyone.
Bruce Wayne was **Batman.**

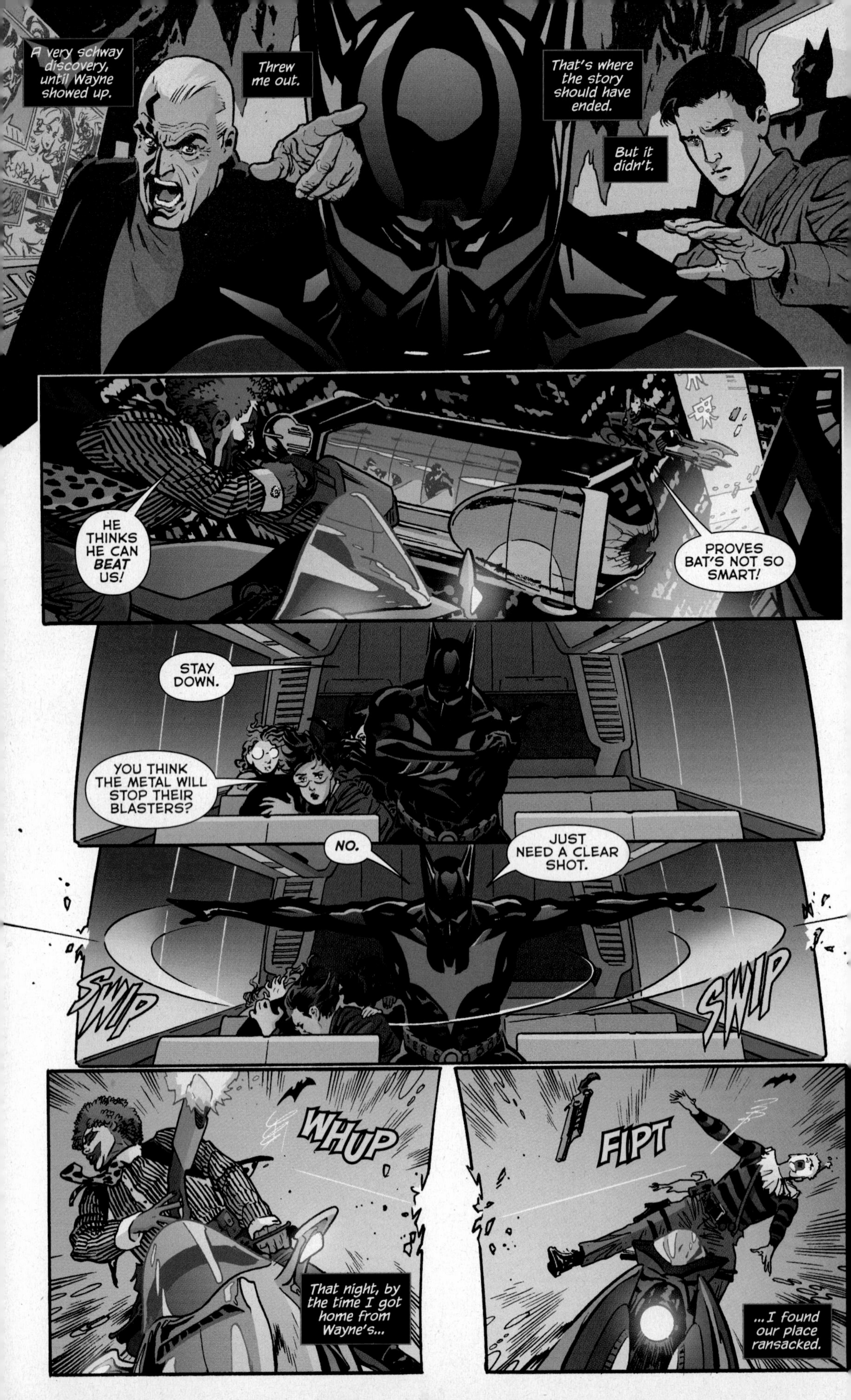
A very schway discovery, until Wayne showed up.
Threw me out.
That's where the story should have ended.
But it didn't.
HE THINKS HE CAN BEAT US!
PROVES BAT'S NOT SO SMART!
STAY DOWN.
YOU THINK THE METAL WILL STOP THEIR BLASTERS?
NO.
JUST NEED A CLEAR SHOT.
SWIP
SWIP
WHUP
That night, by the time I got home from Wayne's...
FIPT
...I found our place ransacked.

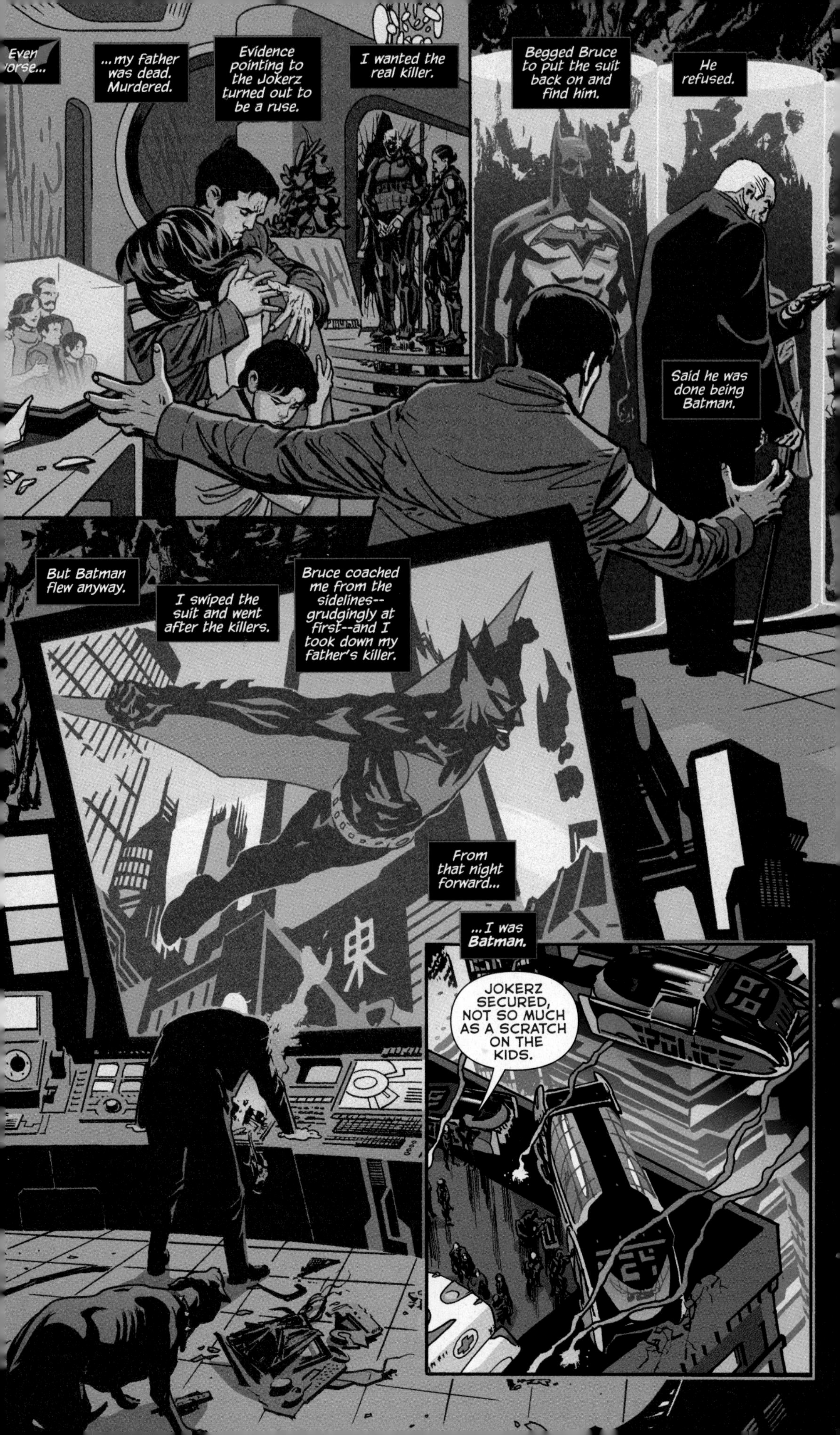
Even worse...
...my father was dead. Murdered.
Evidence pointing to the Jokerz turned out to be a ruse.
I wanted the real killer.
Begged Bruce to put the suit back on and find him.
He refused.
Said he was done being Batman.
But Batman flew anyway.
I swiped the suit and went after the killers.
Bruce coached me from the sidelines--grudgingly at first--and I took down my father's killer.
From that night forward...
...I was Batman.
JOKERZ SECURED, NOT SO MUCH AS A SCRATCH ON THE KIDS.

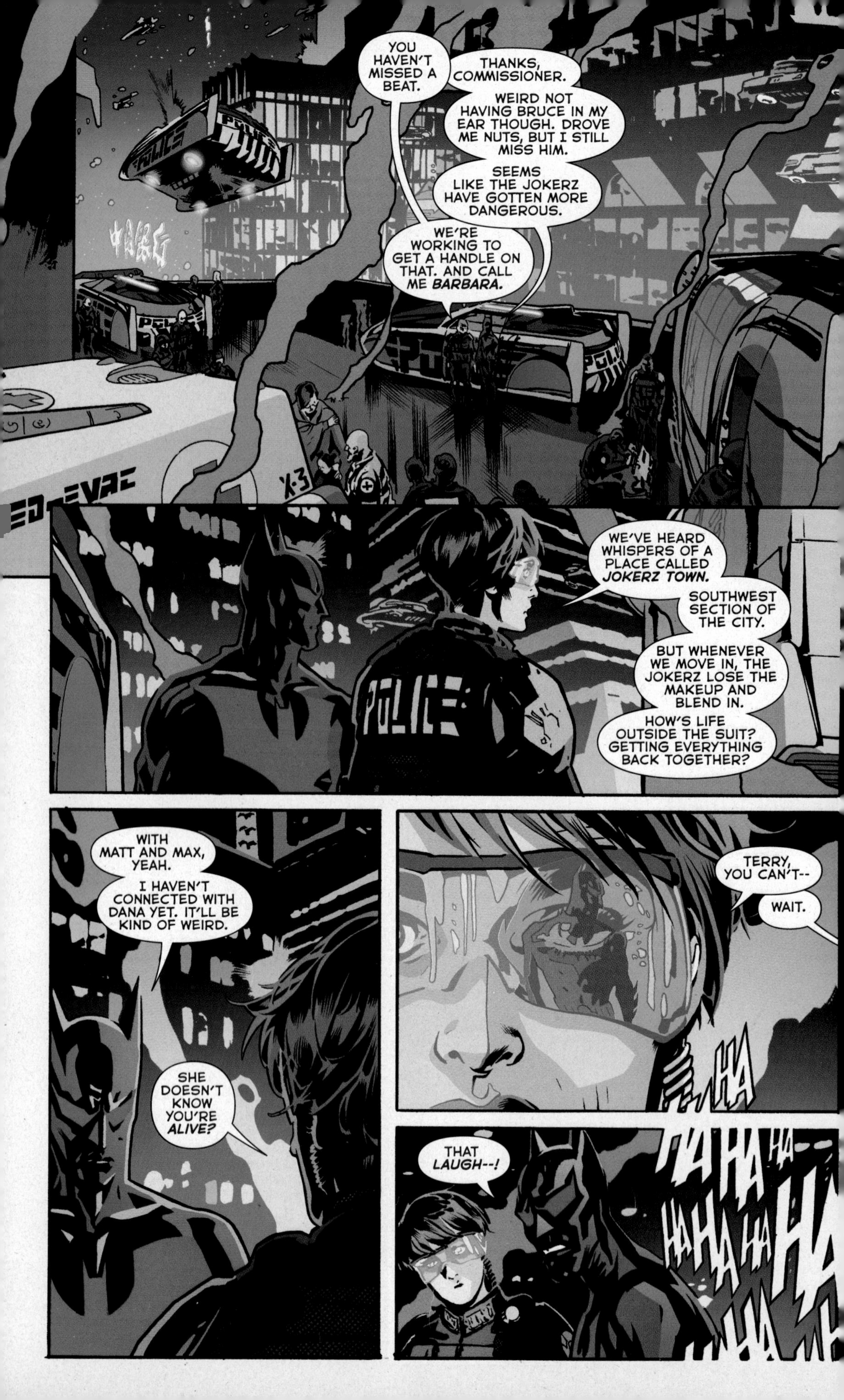

YOU HAVEN'T MISSED A BEAT.
THANKS, COMMISSIONER.
WEIRD NOT HAVING BRUCE IN MY EAR THOUGH. DROVE ME NUTS, BUT I STILL MISS HIM.
SEEMS LIKE THE JOKERZ HAVE GOTTEN MORE DANGEROUS.
WE'RE WORKING TO GET A HANDLE ON THAT. AND CALL ME *BARBARA.*
WE'VE HEARD WHISPERS OF A PLACE CALLED ***JOKERZ TOWN.***
SOUTHWEST SECTION OF THE CITY.
BUT WHENEVER WE MOVE IN, THE JOKERZ LOSE THE MAKEUP AND BLEND IN.
HOW'S LIFE OUTSIDE THE SUIT? GETTING EVERYTHING BACK TOGETHER?
WITH MATT AND MAX, YEAH.
I HAVEN'T CONNECTED WITH DANA YET. IT'LL BE KIND OF WEIRD.
SHE DOESN'T KNOW YOU'RE *ALIVE?*
TERRY, YOU CAN'T--
WAIT.
HA HA
THAT *LAUGH--!*
HA HA HA HA HA HA HA HA HA HA HA

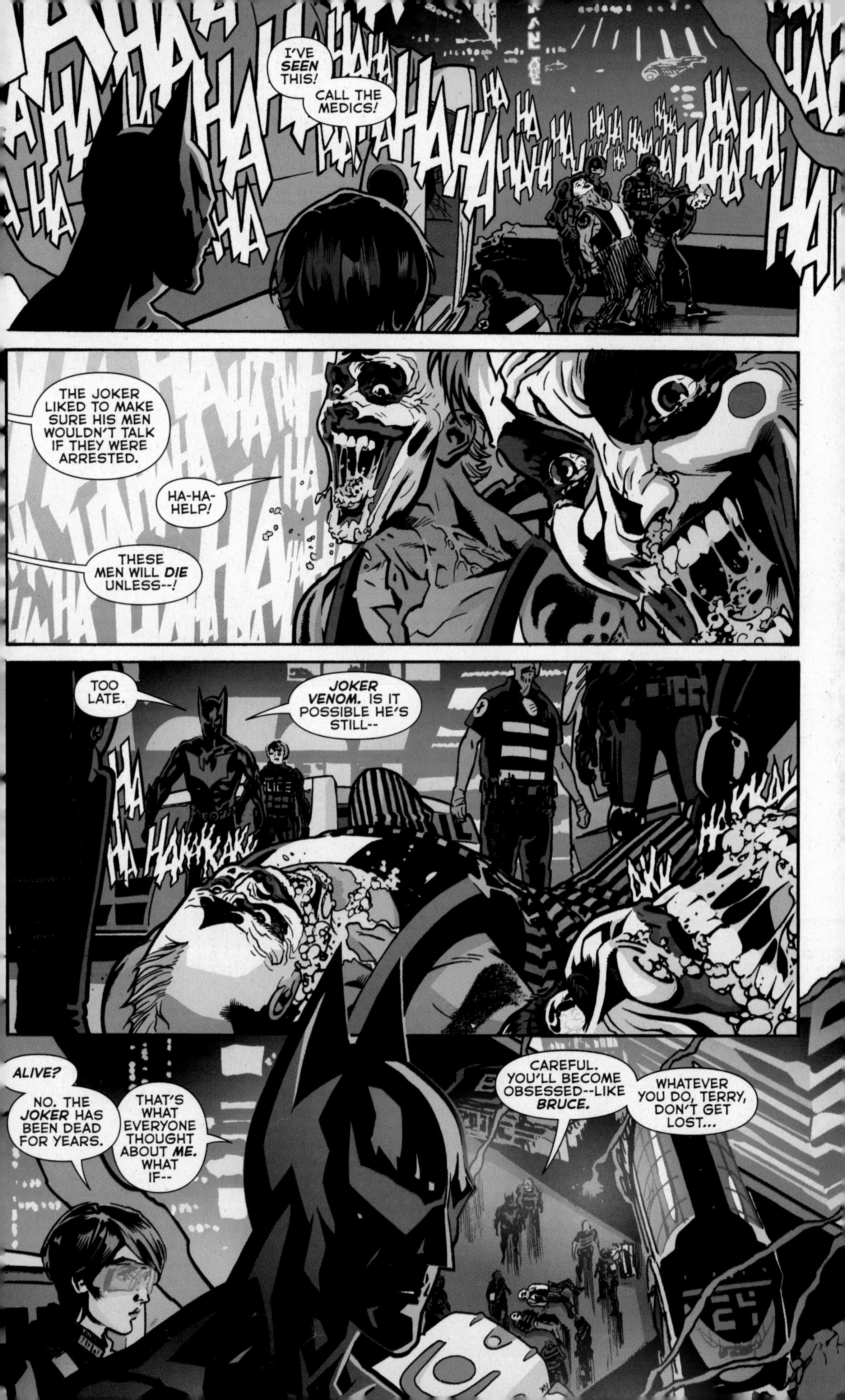
I'VE SEEN THIS!
CALL THE MEDICS!
THE JOKER LIKED TO MAKE SURE HIS MEN WOULDN'T TALK IF THEY WERE ARRESTED.
HA-HA-HELP!
THESE MEN WILL DIE UNLESS--!
TOO LATE.
JOKER VENOM. IS IT POSSIBLE HE'S STILL--
ALIVE?
NO. THE JOKER HAS BEEN DEAD FOR YEARS.
THAT'S WHAT EVERYONE THOUGHT ABOUT ME. WHAT IF--
CAREFUL. YOU'LL BECOME OBSESSED--LIKE BRUCE.
WHATEVER YOU DO, TERRY, DON'T GET LOST...

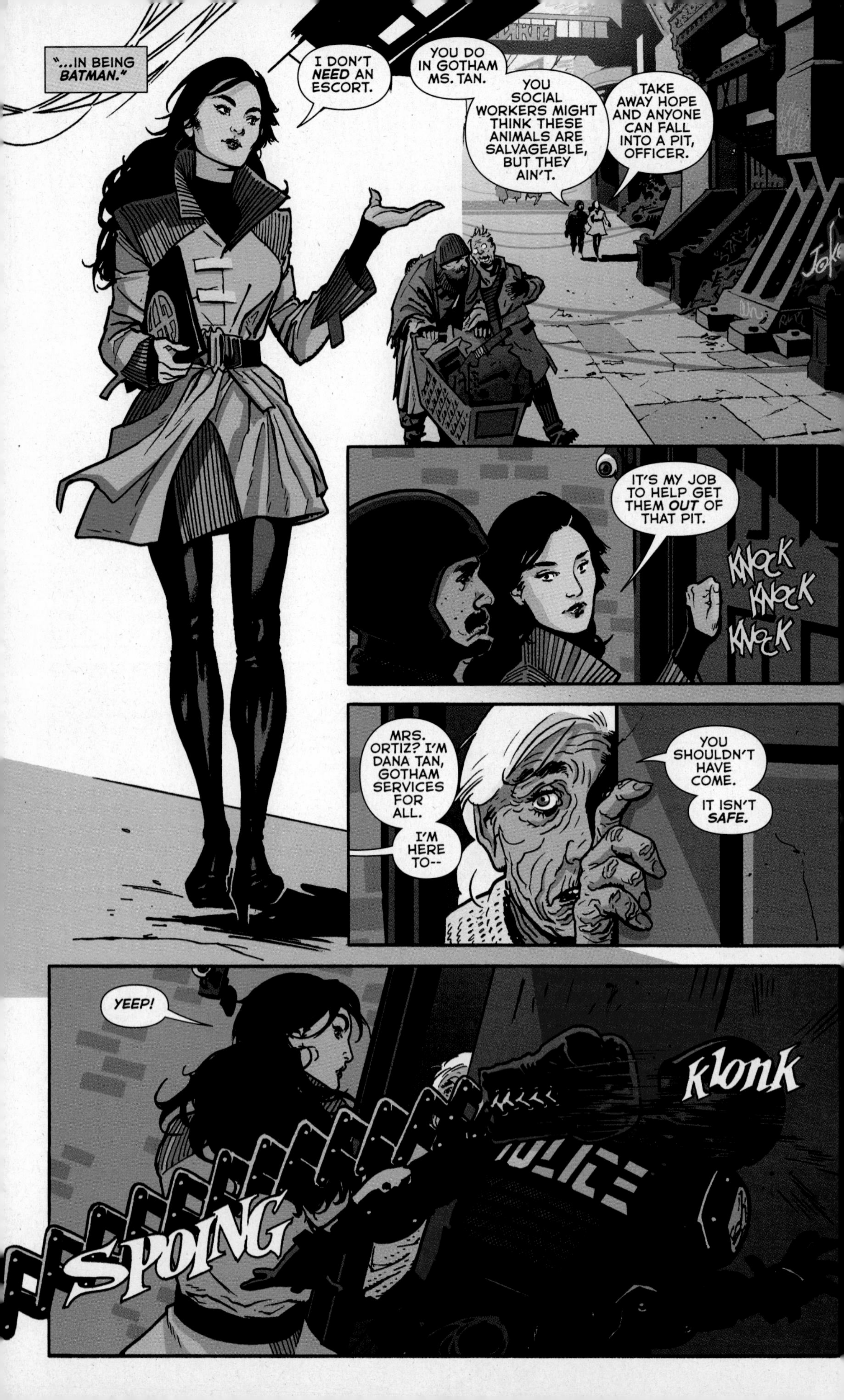
"...IN BEING BATMAN."
I DON'T NEED AN ESCORT.
YOU DO IN GOTHAM MS. TAN.
YOU SOCIAL WORKERS MIGHT THINK THESE ANIMALS ARE SALVAGEABLE, BUT THEY AIN'T.
TAKE AWAY HOPE AND ANYONE CAN FALL INTO A PIT, OFFICER.
IT'S MY JOB TO HELP GET THEM OUT OF THAT PIT.
KNOCK KNOCK KNOCK
MRS. ORTIZ? I'M DANA TAN, GOTHAM SERVICES FOR ALL.
I'M HERE TO--
YOU SHOULDN'T HAVE COME.
IT ISN'T SAFE.
YEEP!
KLONK
SPOING

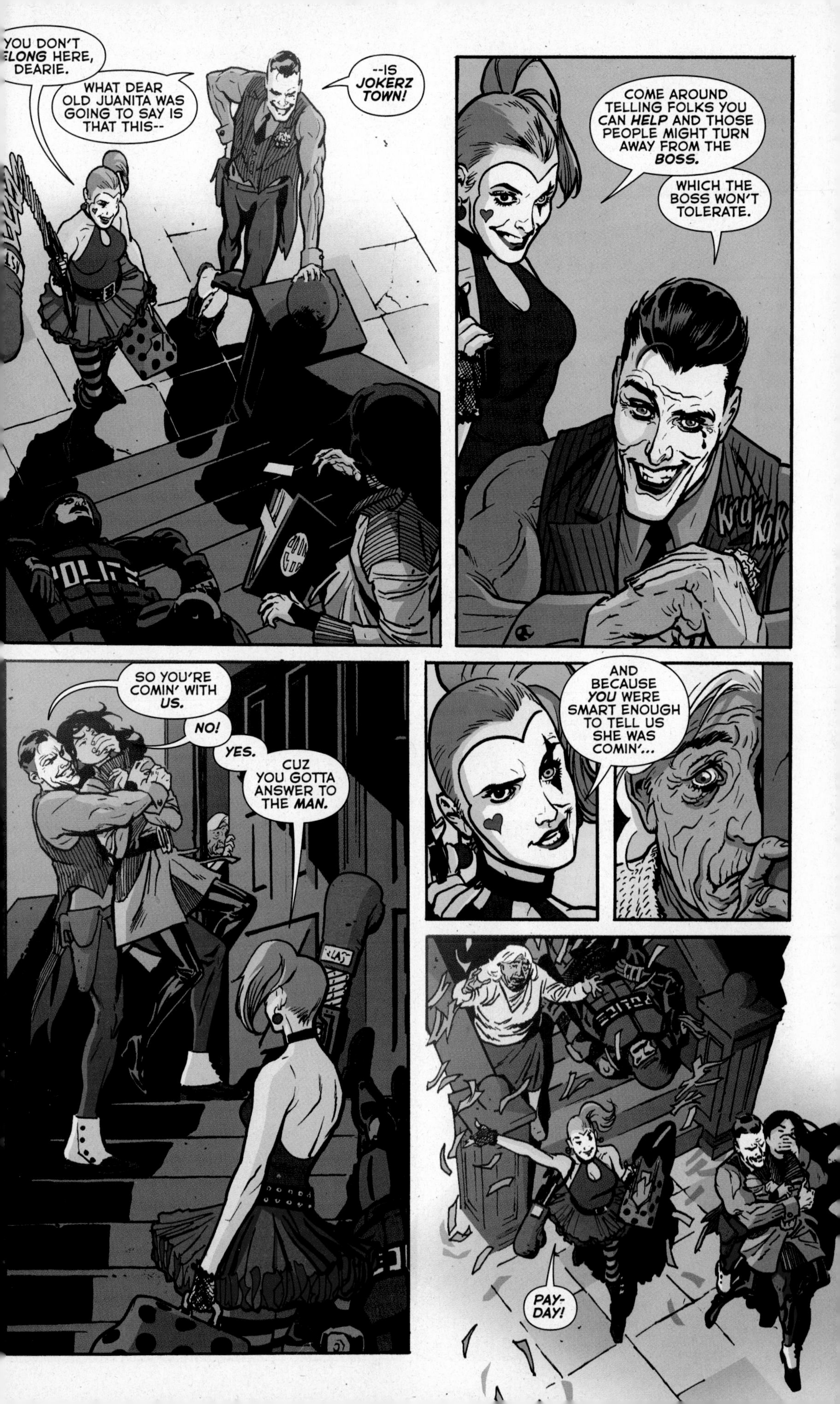
YOU DON'T BELONG HERE, DEARIE.
WHAT DEAR OLD JUANITA WAS GOING TO SAY IS THAT THIS--
--IS JOKERZ TOWN!
COME AROUND TELLING FOLKS YOU CAN HELP AND THOSE PEOPLE MIGHT TURN AWAY FROM THE BOSS.
WHICH THE BOSS WON'T TOLERATE.
SO YOU'RE COMIN' WITH US.
NO!
YES.
CUZ YOU GOTTA ANSWER TO THE MAN.
AND BECAUSE YOU WERE SMART ENOUGH TO TELL US SHE WAS COMIN'...
PAY-DAY!

YOU SAVED A SCHOOL BUS FULL OF KIDS?

ULTIMATE *SCHWAY*!

WHAT'S *SCHWAY* IS THAT THE KIDS ARE SAFE, MATT.

THAT'S ALWAYS MY PRIORITY.

YOU ACED IT, TERRY.

THAT'S WHAT REALLY KICKS.

WHAT KICKS IS BEING BACK.

NICE HAVING A KID BROTHER TO HANG WITH AGAIN.

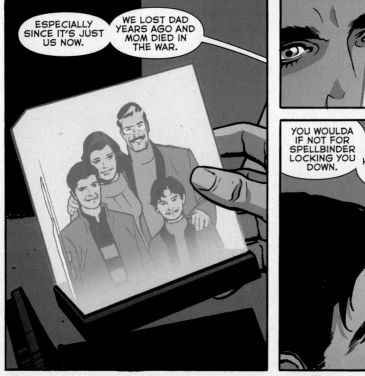

ESPECIALLY SINCE IT'S JUST US NOW.

WE LOST DAD YEARS AGO AND MOM DIED IN THE WAR.

IF NOT FOR MAX GIBSON TAKING YOU IN WHILE I WAS GONE...

YOU WOULDA IF NOT FOR SPELLBINDER LOCKING YOU DOWN.

YOU'RE HERE NOW AND THAT'S WHAT COUNTS.

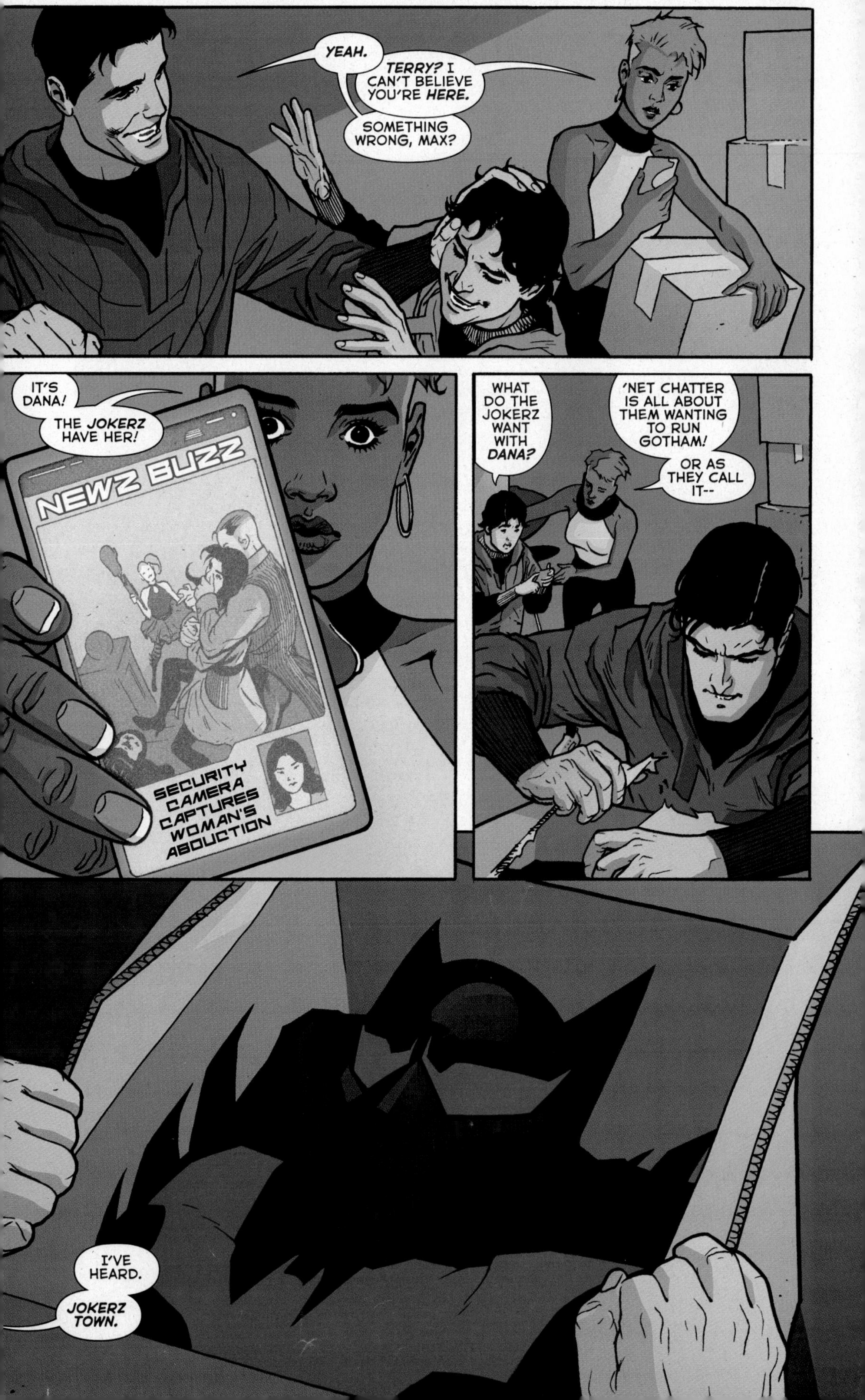
YEAH.
TERRY? I CAN'T BELIEVE YOU'RE HERE.
SOMETHING WRONG, MAX?
IT'S DANA!
THE JOKERZ HAVE HER!
NEWZ BUZZ
SECURITY CAMERA CAPTURES WOMAN'S ABDUCTION
WHAT DO THE JOKERZ WANT WITH DANA?
'NET CHATTER IS ALL ABOUT THEM WANTING TO RUN GOTHAM!
OR AS THEY CALL IT--
I'VE HEARD.
JOKERZ TOWN.

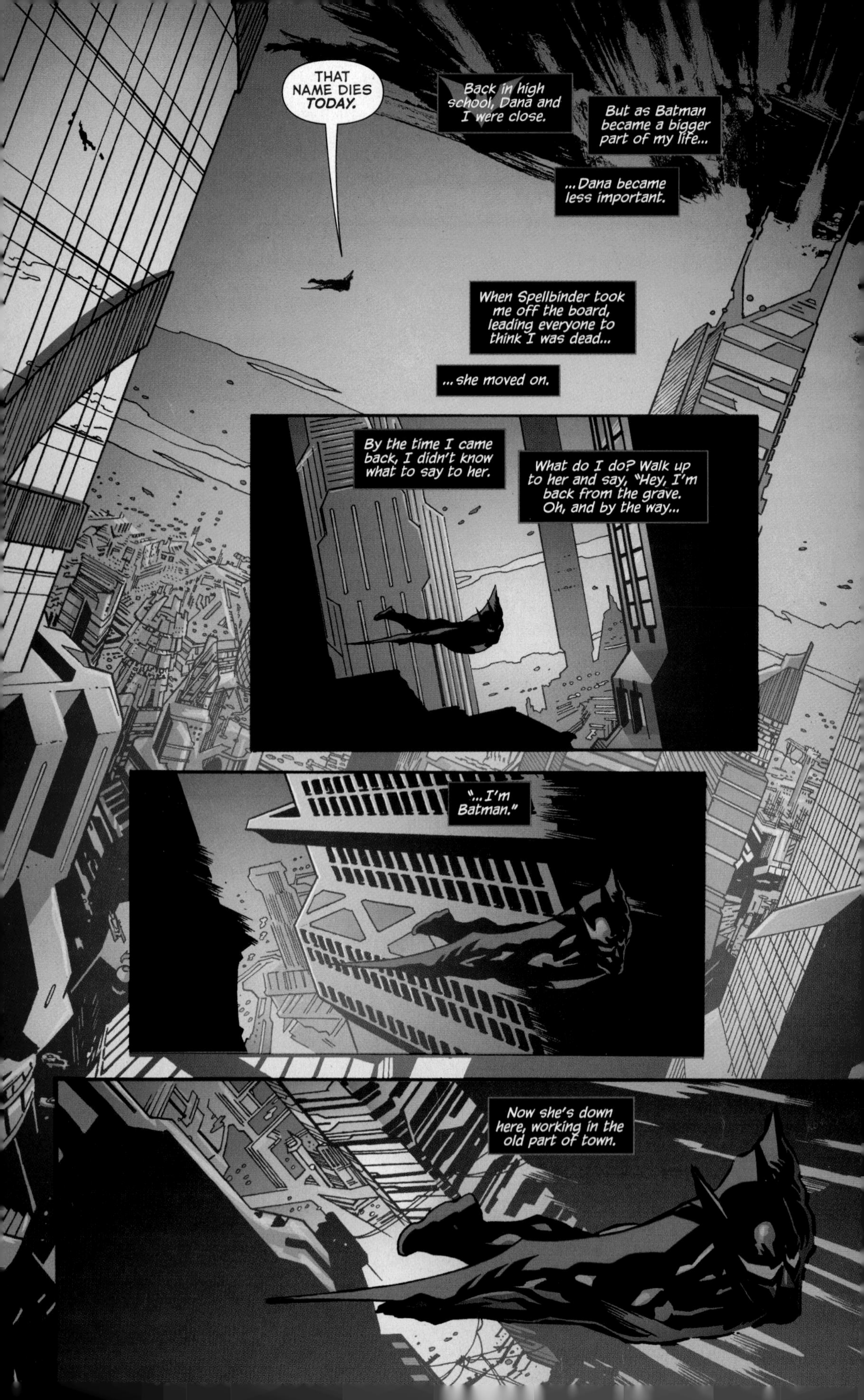
THAT NAME DIES *TODAY.*
Back in high school, Dana and I were close.
But as Batman became a bigger part of my life...
...Dana became less important.
When Spellbinder took me off the board, leading everyone to think I was dead...
...she moved on.
By the time I came back, I didn't know what to say to her.
What do I do? Walk up to her and say, "Hey, I'm back from the grave. Oh, and by the way...
"...I'm Batman."
Now she's down here, working in the old part of town.

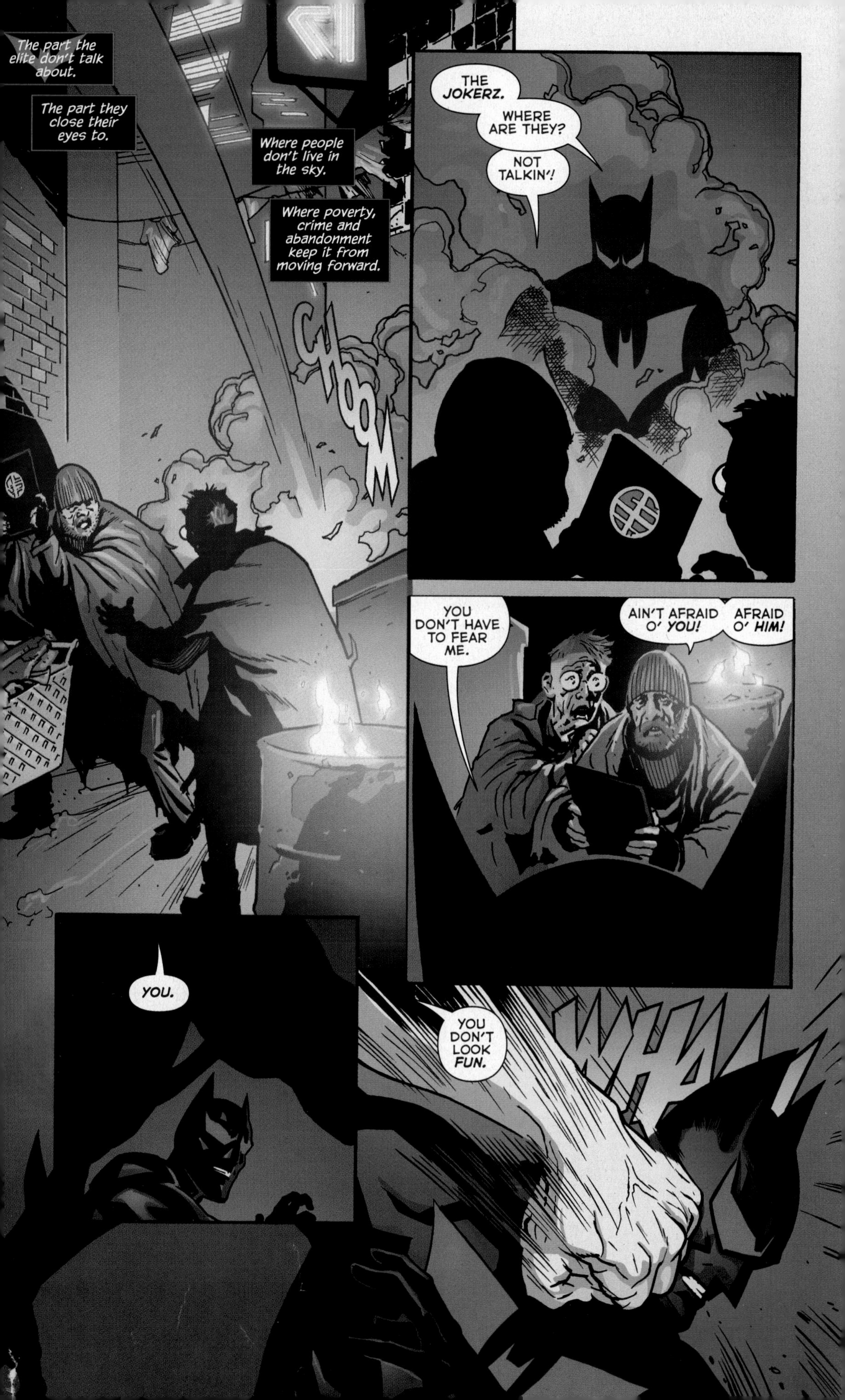

The part the elite don't talk about.
The part they close their eyes to.
Where people don't live in the sky.
Where poverty, crime and abandonment keep it from moving forward.
CHOOM
THE JOKERZ.
WHERE ARE THEY?
NOT TALKIN'!
YOU DON'T HAVE TO FEAR ME.
AIN'T AFRAID O' YOU!
AFRAID O' HIM!
YOU.
YOU DON'T LOOK FUN.

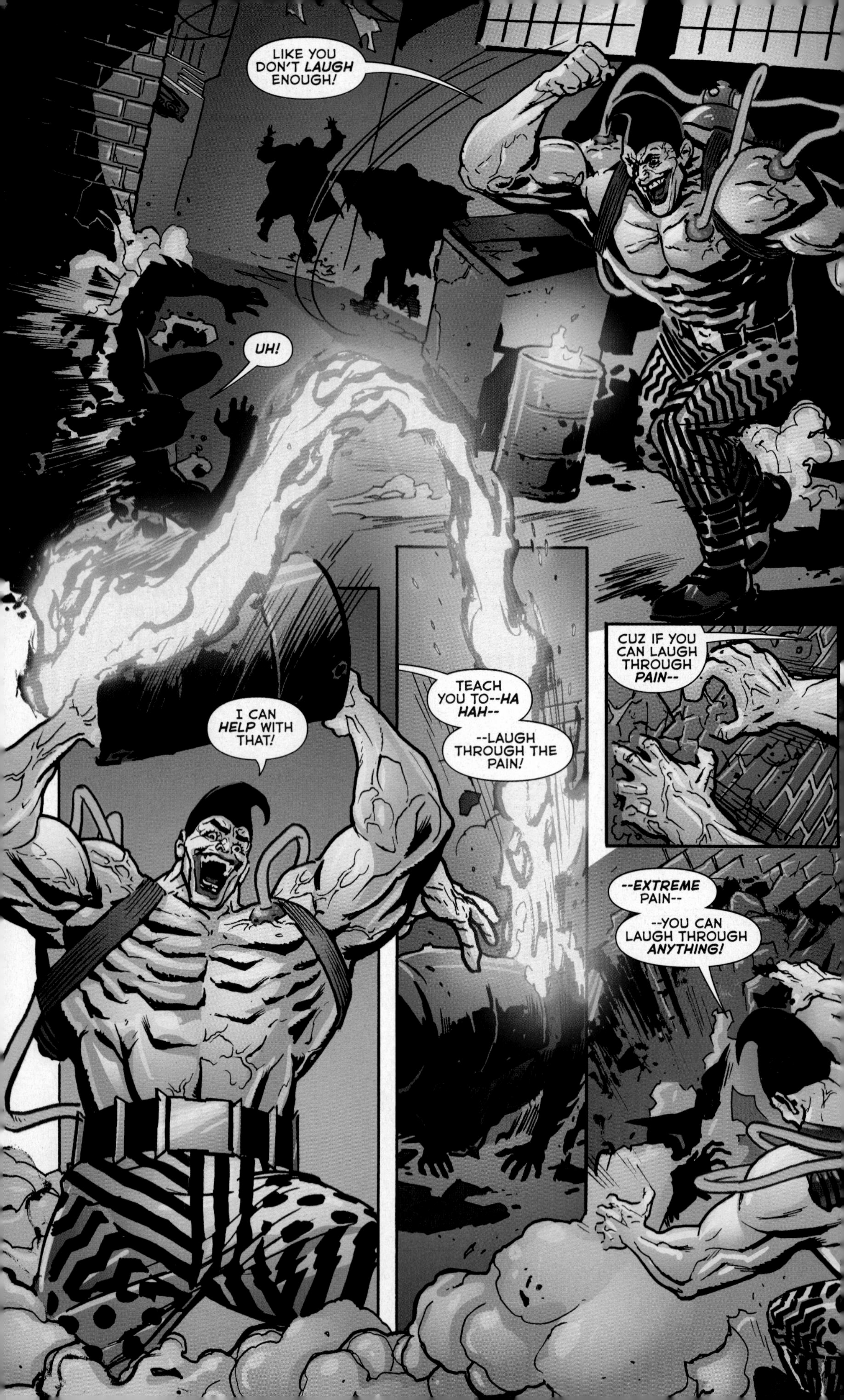
LIKE YOU DON'T *LAUGH* ENOUGH!
UH!
I CAN *HELP* WITH THAT!
TEACH YOU TO--*HA HAH*--
--LAUGH THROUGH THE PAIN!
CUZ IF YOU CAN LAUGH THROUGH *PAIN*--
--*EXTREME* PAIN--
--YOU CAN LAUGH THROUGH *ANYTHING!*

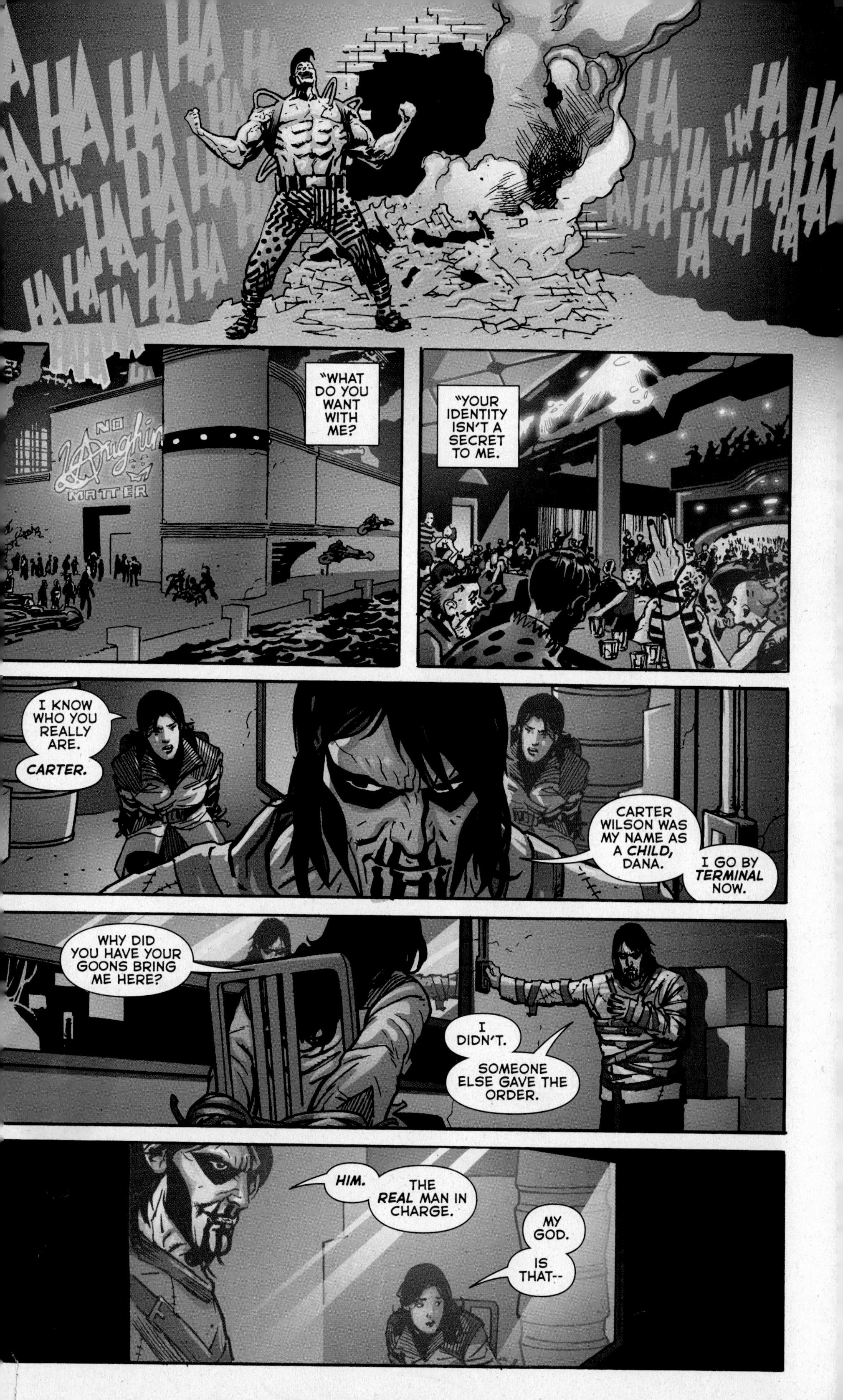
HA HA HA HA HA HA HA HA HA HA HA HA HA HA HA HA HA HA
HA HA HA HA HA HA HA HA HA HA HA HA HA
NO Laughing MATTER
"WHAT DO YOU WANT WITH ME?
"YOUR IDENTITY ISN'T A SECRET TO ME.
I KNOW WHO YOU REALLY ARE.
CARTER.
CARTER WILSON WAS MY NAME AS A CHILD, DANA.
I GO BY TERMINAL NOW.
WHY DID YOU HAVE YOUR GOONS BRING ME HERE?
I DIDN'T.
SOMEONE ELSE GAVE THE ORDER.
HIM.
THE REAL MAN IN CHARGE.
MY GOD.
IS THAT--

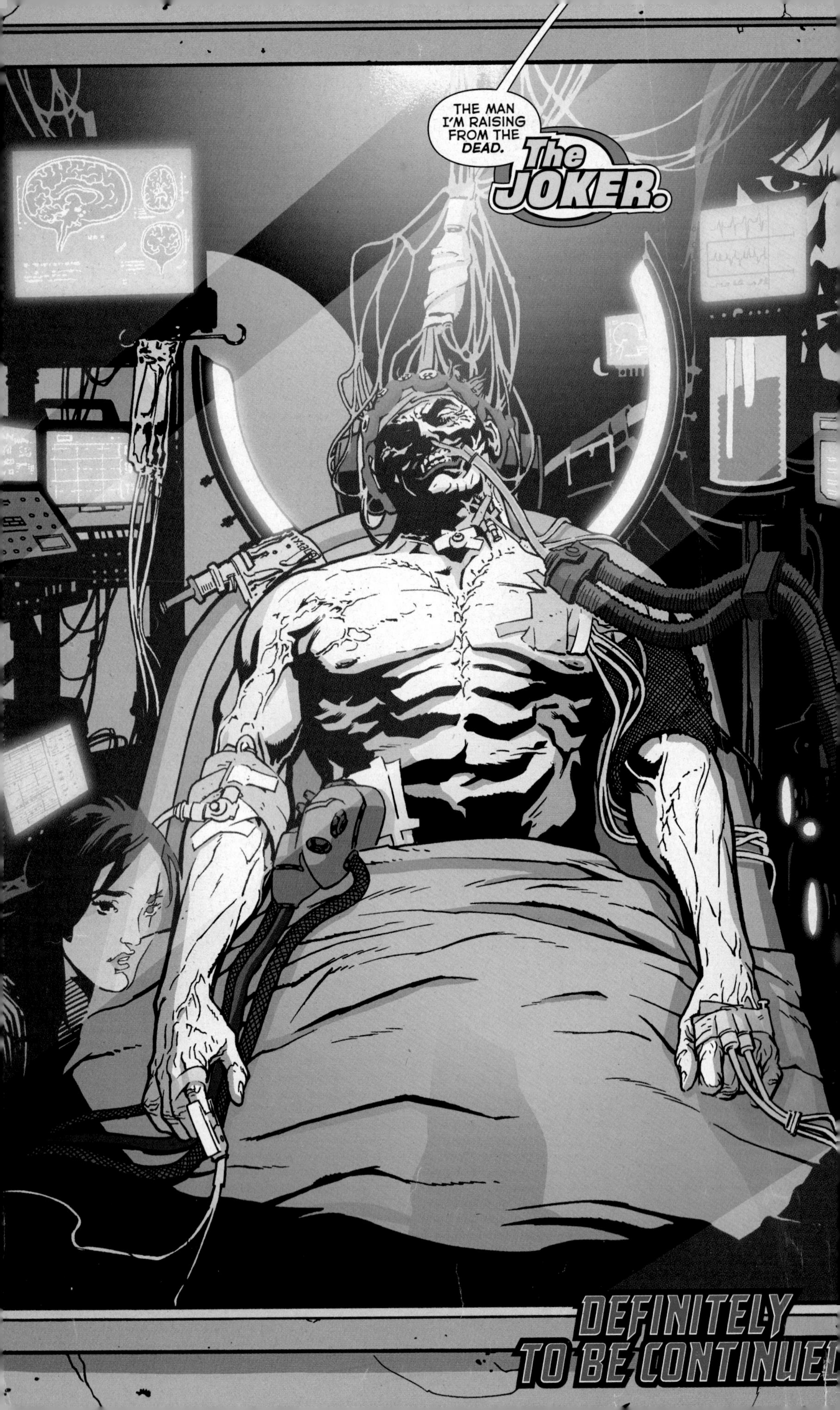

THE MAN I'M RAISING FROM THE DEAD.
The JOKER.
DEFINITELY TO BE CONTINUED